First Stop
in the
New World

ALSO BY DAVID LIDA

Travel Advisory

Las llaves de la ciudad
(a collection of journalism, written in Spanish)

First Stop
in the
New World

Mexico City, the Capital
of the 21st Century

DAVID LIDA

RIVERHEAD BOOKS

a member of Penguin Group (USA) Inc.

New York   2008

RIVERHEAD BOOKS
Published by the Penguin Group
Penguin Group (USA) Inc., 375 Hudson Street, New York, New York 10014, USA • Penguin
Group (Canada), 90 Eglinton Avenue East, Suite 700, Toronto, Ontario M4P 2Y3, Canada
(a division of Pearson Canada Inc.) • Penguin Books Ltd, 80 Strand, London WC2R 0RL,
England • Penguin Ireland, 25 St Stephen's Green, Dublin 2, Ireland (a division of Penguin
Books Ltd) • Penguin Group (Australia), 250 Camberwell Road, Camberwell, Victoria 3124,
Australia (a division of Pearson Australia Group Pty Ltd) • Penguin Books India Pvt Ltd,
11 Community Centre, Panchsheel Park, New Delhi–110 017, India • Penguin Group (NZ),
67 Apollo Drive, Rosedale, North Shore 0632, New Zealand (a division of Pearson
New Zealand Ltd) • Penguin Books (South Africa) (Pty) Ltd, 24 Sturdee Avenue,
Rosebank, Johannesburg 2196, South Africa

Penguin Books Ltd, Registered Offices:
80 Strand, London WC2R 0RL, England

Library of Congress Cataloging-in-Publication Data
Lida, David.
First stop in the New World : Mexico City, the capital of the 21st century / David Lida.
p.   cm.
ISBN-13: 978-1-59448-989-1
1. Mexico City (Mexico)—Description and travel.   2. Mexico City (Mexico)—Social life
and customs—21st century.   I. Title.
F1386.L48   2008   2008012610
972'.53084—dc22

Printed in the United States of America
1   3   5   7   9   10   8   6   4   2

BOOK DESIGN BY MEIGHAN CAVANAUGH

PHOTOGRAPHS BY FEDERICO GAMA

While the author has made every effort to provide accurate telephone numbers and Internet
addresses at the time of publication, neither the publisher nor the author assumes any
responsibility for errors, or for changes that occur after publication. Further, the
publisher does not have any control over and does not assume any responsibility
for author or third-party websites or their content.

For Francisco Goldman,
and in memory of Aura Estrada

CONTENTS

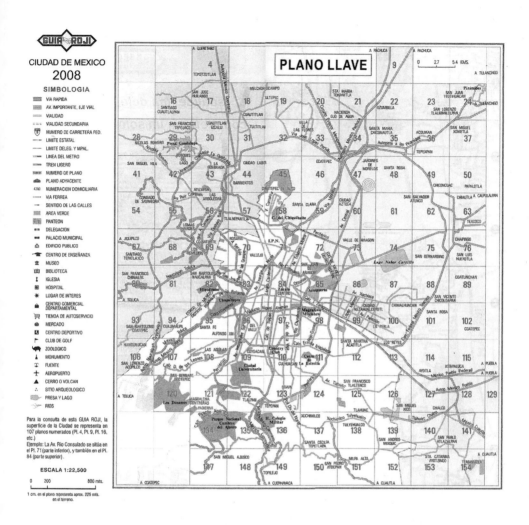

Citizens of Mexico City rarely use maps to get around their constantly expanding metropolis. But if they do, they use the *Guía Roji,* a book that divides the urban sprawl into 154 separate sections. The image above is *Guía Roji*'s back page, an attempt to give an overview of the city. Each numbered box indicates a more detailed map with actual streets and monuments. On the following pages is Map 84, which covers downtown and the *centro histórico*. Apart from its multiple maps, *Guía Roji*, which is updated each year, also includes a 250-page index of street names, *colonias* (neighborhoods), and landmarks, and its own magnifying glass so you can read the tiny print.

Introduction:
The Hypermetropolis

From my first visit as a tourist, Mexico enchanted me. I kept returning, but for four years didn't dare set foot in Mexico City. I was afraid of the capital, influenced by the propaganda dismissing it as a teeming, overpopulated, polluted bedlam, full of horrific testimonies of insuperable poverty. I imagined the armless beggars of Calcutta brandishing their stumps in tourists' faces, hoping the display would result in a handout.

Then, during one holiday in 1987, I had a layover in Mexico City. In the hour-long taxi ride from the airport to the hotel, I fell in love. I was astonished by the streets of the *centro histórico,* lined with massive stone buildings constructed by the Spanish conquerors in the sixteenth and seventeenth centuries. I was captivated by the contrast between the grandiosity of those structures and the humility of the office workers wending their way through the sidewalks—the smiling shoeshine man at his electric-orange post, the doughy matron in the blue skirt and white apron beseeching me to buy *tacos sudados*— "sweaty tacos," so called because they are steamed in a basket.

That afternoon I sipped coffee on a hotel balcony overlooking the *zócalo,* the city's enormous central square. A crowd began to gather in support of a teachers' strike. By twilight they would be one hundred thousand strong, yet an hour later everyone was gone, the plaza empty, as if it had been a hallucination.

At night I wandered along those streets dense with history, lit so dimly they appeared to be in black-and-white. In a crowded cafeteria, I ate tamales wrapped in banana leaves and stuffed with spicy pork. I drank tequila in a dark bar, where a round man with slick hair and a pencil mustache sang romantic songs, backed by three guitar players dexterously crowding notes into each phrase.

I stumbled upon Plaza Garibaldi, the rowdy nocturnal soul of the city. Squadrons of musicians, mostly mariachis in skintight, tin-studded black suits, trawled for customers willing to pay a few pesos for a melody. When they found temporary patrons, throngs gathered, and the most boisterous revelers sang along. It was a crowded Friday night, and the result was the most singular cacophony I'd ever heard.

In Garibaldi's most humble cantina, La Hermosa Hortensia—which dispenses *pulque,* a fermented cactus beverage created by the Aztecs—a staggeringly drunken man offered me his wife. She demonstrated her eagerness to consummate the proposition with a squeeze of my thigh and a smile, the seductiveness of which was undercut by the absence of several crucial teeth. I refused with as much courtesy as possible, after which the man removed from his neck, and gave me, a string that held an emblem of Mexico's patron saint, the Virgin of Guadalupe.

Before I went to bed, half-drunk in the wee hours, I watched a lonely group of soldiers in ill-fitting uniforms on drill in the otherwise empty *zócalo.* Unfortunately, I had to leave the next day. I had been utterly seduced by the constant sensations of contrast, surprise, even tumult. Within three years I would be living there.

———

That Mexico City was such a beguiling place came as a complete surprise. The 1980s were surely the worst moment in its history. Three million autos, the thin air of its 7,300-foot altitude, and the thirteen thousand factories that ringed the valley in which it is situated created an ecological nightmare with toxic levels of pollution.

The pumping of a billion gallons of water per day from as far away as fifty miles caused the city to sink 3.5 inches a year, and the lack of adequate plumbing and drainage made it a nightmare for many of its residents.

Said to be the biggest city in the world, by the early 1980s Mexico City had a population of seventeen million, and the government predicted that there would be thirty-six million by the year 2000. Most of the new inhabitants were squatters, streaming in from the impoverished countryside at a rate of a couple of thousand per day, creating slapdash shantytowns on the ever-expanding outskirts.

In the immediate aftermath of a devastating earthquake in 1985 the government seemed to disappear into thin air, and it was up to the citizens to rescue one another from under the rubble. Not only was there a lack of viable leadership, but politicians and police chiefs were noted more for how much they stole from the public trough than for any constructive projects they carried out.

If Mexico City today is still a challenging and sometimes exhausting place to live, with permanent service problems (principally in drainage, water pumping, and distribution) and a continued resistance to urban planning, it is worth pointing out that the worst predictions from the 1980s did not come to pass.

While pollution levels may still be unacceptably high, the situation is no longer a noxious horror. Since 1991, all new cars here have come with catalytic converters, and although four million or so make traffic a nightmare, they are not causing as much lethal damage as they did twenty years ago. Most of the factories in the valley have closed down, making way for a greater service economy and cleaner air. Plumbing has reached virtually 100 percent of the city, even in the most impoverished outskirts.

Mexico's is the second most dynamic economy in Latin America, after Brazil's, but its wealth is scandalously distributed. While Mexico City's gross domestic product is over seventeen thousand dollars U.S. per capita, half of the capital's residents live at or near the poverty level, and about 15 percent beneath it. At the same time, virtually everyone has a roof over his or her head, electricity, running water, and a TV set. More than half have cell phones. If someone starves to death in the capital, it is an anomaly. (This is in contrast to other parts of Mexico, mainly rural, that the United Nations has compared to Africa for their destitution.)

That effectively everyone in Mexico City eats goes a long way in explaining why the population has held fairly steady since the early 1990s, increasing by only a few million souls. Word finally reached those rural Mexicans who flooded the city for decades that the capital was no longer providing survival or sustenance as it had before. Those same Mexicans began to stream across the border into the United States, and continue to do so, despite mounting political pressure from the U.S. government to stop their flow.

It is no longer "the biggest city on earth," if it ever could have been accurately counted as such. Others such as Los Angeles have a far greater land mass, and several years ago the Tokyo-Yokohama corridor replaced Mexico City as the world's most populous metropolis. Numerous other cities, although with fewer residents, have far greater population density. Mexico City has eighty-four hundred people per square kilometer, while Mumbai, Lagos, Karachi, and

Seoul have more than double that figure. Bogotá, Shanghai, Lima, and Taipei also are significantly more jam-packed.

If Mexico City is a demanding place to live, it is also an extremely rewarding one. The hypercity, the ur-urb of the American continent, it is improving all the time as a cultural capital, with offerings more along the lines of First World cities than any other in Latin America. Its scores of museums and galleries have produced artists who exhibit around the world. On any given night there is an extensive selection of theater (classical, contemporary, experimental), film (mostly from Hollywood, but also from France, Japan, Romania, or Argentina), music (from the local symphony orchestra, to an avant-garde jazz combo from New York, to touring rappers from Beirut), and public presentations of just-published books.

There are limitless choices of food and drink. Mexican cuisine is unique; its play of colors, textures, temperatures, and flavors makes it the culinary jewel of the continent. One can sit in the cocoon of an elegant restaurant (choices include not only Mexican food, but the cookery of Poland, Lebanon, Japan, France, or Catalonia) or else be tempted by the open air; in Mexico City there is a complex street theater to the food stalls, enticing passersby with assorted aromas and hues.

Paradoxically, given its population of twenty million, there are many tree-lined neighborhoods with the quiet sociability of small towns, while others have the generic international-hip vibe one finds around the Bastille in Paris, Williamsburg in New York, or Soho in Hong Kong.

Its citizens may be savages when behind the wheels of their cars, but on the street there is a level of courtesy today found in few cities in prosperous countries. In the capital, waiters in cantinas shake hands with their familiar customers, and after your food has been served at a restaurant, people at the next table are likely to say *buen provecho* (the local equivalent to *bon appétit*). People hold doors open for each other, say good morning when they walk into an elevator, kiss each other's cheeks when they are introduced. If you sneeze in public, a chorus of voices says *salud*. It sometimes takes five minutes to get out of a taxi until all of the ritual phrases of "At your service" and "Have a good day" and "Take care of yourself" have been exchanged.

Mexico City was founded by the Aztecs in 1325 as Tenochtitlán. Built on an island in Lake Texcoco, within the next two centuries, through an inspired system of man-made islands, canals, and causeways, it grew into the seat of the Aztec empire. By the time the Spaniards arrived in 1519, Tenochtitlán was one of the world's largest cities, with a population of about two hundred thousand.

It was a city of pyramids and palaces, the majesty of which stunned the conquerors. Nonetheless, the Spanish promptly destroyed that city and built their own stone citadels atop the ruins. Mexico City became New Spain's headquarters. Much of the colony's Central American and Caribbean assets were administered from the capital. The colony lasted nearly three hundred years.

The capital's history in the nineteenth century was marked by violence. After the War of Independence liberated the country from Spain in 1810, the battles were internal, but in 1847 the United States invaded Mexico City, and the upshot of the resultant occupation was the sale of half of its territory at bargain-basement prices to its northern neighbor. From 1864 to 1867, Mexico was occupied by Maximilian of Hapsburg, who built the splendid Chapultepec Castle in the heart of the capital. The last decades of the century were marked by the dictatorship of Porfirio Díaz, whose governing style was known as *pan o palo* (bread or the stick): those who marched in line for him received sustenance, while those who disobeyed were met with brutality. Mexico's entrance into the modern era was also turbulent, with carnage rocking the capital not only during the Revolution of 1910, but continuing well into the subsequent decade.

After peace was restored, by the middle of the twentieth century Mexico City was known for its fresh air, clear skies, and for being Latin America's most cosmopolitan capital. At this point, while the city's growth was under control, each new neighborhood basically imitated the historic center of the city, usually spreading outward from a tree-lined square with the area's most important church and local government buildings. Yet in the second half of the twentieth century, Mexico City became the poster child of contemporary urban chaos and overdevelopment. Between 1950 and 2000, its population grew from roughly three million to about twenty million.

The city expanded horizontally in all four directions, swallowing and engulfing other towns, villages, and municipalities in a willy-nilly, ad hoc manner. During those fifty years, what passed for urban planning allowed for no more than catch-up, reactive measures. For example, the inner-city throughways, such as the Viaducto and the Periférico, became obsolete almost as soon as they were completed, given how quickly the population and its fleet of cars grew during the years they were built.

Apart from the obvious problems of traffic and transportation, the growth created other confusing complications. Today, out of the city's eighty-five thousand streets, there are about eight hundred fifty called Juárez, seven hundred fifty named Hidalgo, and seven hundred known as Morelos. Two hundred are called 16 de Septiembre, while a hundred more are called 16 de Septiembre Avenue, Alley, Mews, or Extension. Nine separate neighborhoods are called La Palma, four are called Las Palmas, and there are numerous mutations: La Palmita, Las Palmitas, Palmas Inn, La Palma Condominio, Palmas Axotitla, La Palma I y Palma I-II Unidad Habitacional.

Today, greater Mexico City is composed of the Federal District, home to approximately eight million residents. The other twelve million live in nearly sixty municipalities in Mexico State, which make up the rest of the urban sprawl to the east, west, and north. The Federal District is divided into sixteen delegations (the equivalent of boroughs in New York, subregions in London, or arrondissements in Paris), each with its own somewhat autonomous government. Only four of the delegations are considered the center of the city. Like most big metropoli, Mexico City is divided into smaller, sharply contrasting, and mostly self-contained neighborhoods that are called *colonias*. There are about five thousand in greater Mexico City.

Compounding the city's complications is the fact that the Federal District exists in a political and judicial limbo. It is neither a state nor a territory that belongs to another state. It is not sovereign. For most of its budget, it is dependent on the largesse of the federal government, to which it has had an increasingly antagonistic relationship in the last decade or so. Although it generates about half of the country's federal taxes and close to 25 percent of Mexico's gross domestic product, the Federal District receives only about seven centavos for every peso it delivers to the national treasury, as opposed to the states, which receive about double that amount.

It is an architectural eyesore. In any given neighborhood, sometimes within a block or two, there can be an elegant nineteenth-century mansion next to a squat and brightly painted Art Deco apartment house. Close by will be a pink Swiss chalet adjacent to a modernist nightmare that rises from the ground in the form of a tube. Around the corner is a gray concrete bunker opposite the husk of a construction that crumbled in the 1985 earthquake.

Although it has a few distinctive monuments, such as the statues of the Angel of Independence and Diana the Huntress on the broad avenue Paseo de la Reforma (the city's answer to the Champs-Élysées), Mexico City defies physical description and lacks notable iconography. A few neighborhoods, such as the *centro,* San Ángel, and Coyoacán, have lovely colonial architecture, while quite a few more (Condesa, Juárez, Narvarte, Santa María la Ribera) have Art Deco or neo-colonial buildings. But the pretty areas are exceptions. Architects describe Mexico City as "short and fat," given the number of one-, two-, and three-story buildings in its seemingly infinite land mass. Many of those buildings are unfinished, with rebar sprouting from the top in anticipation of the day its residents can afford to build another story.

Much of public space has been raped. Enormous billboards are not only in your face on the inner-city highways, but also hover over the main boulevards, and even in residential neighborhoods are painted on the sides of buildings or hang like banners over balconies and terraces. Others are pasted on walls hastily constructed beside empty lots. In the subway tunnels between certain stations, hologram ads for cars are projected out the windows, as if mocking the very people who can't afford to buy one.

From time to time the city government makes a big noise about how it will soon be clamping down on this mostly illegal signage. Rarely does anything happen beyond pasting large signs over the offending ads that make clear in bold type that they are there unlawfully. So we are left with blemishes on the cityscape partially obstructing other blemishes.

Walter Benjamin called Paris the capital of the nineteenth century, and in *Delirious New York* Rem Koolhaas posited Manhattan as the urban Rosetta stone of the twentieth. Mexico City will play a similar role in the twenty-first. The orderly European model for cities, and even the bustling but carefully planned United States archetypes that followed it, have already given way to another version, in which much of the world's population lives—enormous improvised hypermetropoli which, with virtually no planning whatsoever, have expanded to accommodate monstrously multiplying populations. Mumbai, Shanghai, Istanbul, São Paulo, Lagos, Cairo, and Karachi each have more than ten million inhabitants struggling over inches of space.

Only a three-hour plane ride from L.A. and four and a half from New York, Mexico City is the closest and most accessible new-model city to the United States and can show Americans what the urban future looks like. Like those other cities mentioned, it has absorbed and swallowed all the centuries of its history, yet most of them are still in evidence in some regurgitated form on the streets.

Moreover, Mexico City makes the great capitals of the last century seem somewhat less relevant and certainly less spontaneous. Perhaps because of the stratospheric prices of real estate, it is increasingly harder to be surprised by anything in New York, Paris, or London, yet Mexico City is constantly improvising a new invention of itself. Further, as the divide between the rich and the poor becomes ever more abysmal, those First World cities are slowly becoming more like Mexico City, with their schisms between haves (natives and others from prosperous backgrounds) and have-nots (usually down-on-their-luck immigrants and their children).

Globalization is making prosperous cities more alike and less idiosyncratic. New York is the most emblematic example. Today in Manhattan there is a bank branch and a Duane Reade drugstore on nearly every block. Yet most of the distinctive places that defined New York as little as twenty years ago have disappeared—from the secondhand bookstores that lined Fourth Avenue to the dozen art cinemas that existed in various neighborhoods, to music venues like CBGB (where the punk movement exploded in the United States) and Folk City (where Bob Dylan and Simon & Garfunkel had their first New York gigs) and any number of jazz clubs (Bradley's, The Cookery, Gregory's). Most of the department stores—Gimbel's, Orbach's, Klein's, B. Altman, Bonwit Teller—have disappeared, because so many buy their clothes at the Gap, Banana Republic, and the same stores whose outlets exist in the rest of the country. Famously, the sleazy movie theaters, grind-house porno emporiums, and neon video game parlors of Times Square were turned into a Disneyland fit for family consumption, with flagship stores of Nike, Swatch, Toys "R" Us, Hello Kitty, and Disney itself.

Meanwhile, at least in the short term, globalization makes Mexico City a more appealing place to live. Given its enormity, it was quite homogeneous until the early 1990s, ripe for some international infusion. An increasing population from the United States, Europe, South America, Asia, and the Caribbean has added to the city's integral excitement, enhancing the city with added elements of their own cultures. On any given evening you can have dinner in Koreatown on the fringes of the Zona Rosa, then go on to see a film from Thailand or dance in a nightclub to a Cuban band.

For most of the foreigners who arrive, it's a pretty good place to live, undoubtedly better than for the majority of the Mexicans. Most Argentines, Colombians, and Cubans find better opportunities for employment than their crumbling economies can offer, and a few have come to escape political persecution. Some Europeans and Americans are wowed by the chance to live a lusher lifestyle than at home, complete with enormous apartments equipped with maids they can bully. To others of a more Bohemian bent, it's the best thing since Paris of the 1920s, complete with cantinas, dance halls, and unbearable *poètes maudits*.

While foreigners here, principally Europeans, complain about the proliferation of Starbucks and Wal-Marts, middle-class Mexicans revel in the First World status bestowed by these establishments. What's more, despite globalization, the city, so far, has largely maintained its idiosyncratic identity. Mexico City still remains an emphatically Mexican city, with sprawling open-air markets in many ways like those that astonished the Spaniards in the sixteenth century; salesmen who bicycle their way through residential neighborhoods each evening, peddling Oaxacan tamales; and literally millions who improvise their livings on one sidewalk or another.

Economically, Mexico City exists in a sort of limbo between the developed and underdeveloped worlds. While it can be instructive to compare Mexico City to New York, Paris, or London, the way that it grew in the second half of the twentieth century is emblematic of how big cities have enlarged in most countries in the same period. The way it is dealing with its problems, however haphazardly, might be instructive for other cities as they try to solve theirs.

Despite its improvements, Mexico City has still maintained a largely lurid reputation. Much of that status is the result of a series of events that set Mexico on its ear in 1994. Near the northern border, Luis Donaldo Colosio, a presidential candidate, was assassinated in front of the crowd while at a campaign stop, and at the southern pole of the country there was a guerrilla uprising among peasants in Chiapas. An economic crash devalued the peso by half.

The clearest manifestation of the center not holding in Mexico

City was a crime wave, during which the capital became notorious for street holdups, express kidnappings in taxicabs, and cops who used their uniforms to shake down the citizenry. Although statistical and anecdotal evidence suggest that the city is safer than it was a decade ago, it hasn't yet been able to live down that reputation. While there is no denying that on a daily basis in Mexico City there are too many robberies and traffic accidents (and sometimes kidnappings or grisly murders), in fact most of its population gets through its days and nights without either committing or being victims of crimes, and without being any more exploited than the residents of cities with similar economies. Given how much that could go wrong here, I am constantly amazed at how well it functions, largely due to Mexicans' talent for improvisation and ingenuity.

I am not suggesting that Mexico City is no longer a complicated, challenging, and often difficult place to live. But part of what makes a city dynamic is the way that its citizens deal with its problems, and people here are nothing if not imaginative at problem solving. Indeed, the Mexicans and their ingenuity are very much a part of what gives Mexico City its dynamic energy.

At the time of this writing, for more than a decade the Mexican peso has held steady at an exchange rate of between ten and eleven to the dollar, with fluctuations as high as twelve and as low as nine. In the context of the past forty years, this represents unprecedented economic stability. Since the early 1970s, the peso tended to crash at a rate of once every six years, sometimes even more frequently, resulting in devaluations of 50 percent or more. Inflation rates throughout the 1980s tended to oscillate between 60 percent and 100 percent per year.

However, there is no guarantee of the Mexican economy's everlasting solidity. Nor does the peso represent most of the world's reference mark for foreign-exchange rates. For these reasons, when I mention how much something costs, I have chosen to note its price in dollars, except where otherwise indicated.

I have lived in Mexico City off and on (mostly on) since 1990, and have never felt so much at home anywhere else in the world. Primarily, I have made my living as a freelance journalist. My curiosity has been scrupulously promiscuous. To give an idea, I've written articles about a president and a Nobel Prize winner, a woman bullfighter and a deaf-mute transvestite, a dog trainer, a private detective, and a pornographic movie actor. I've interviewed a tailor who custom makes suits for politicians, a dollar-a-dance hostess, five men who imitate the pop star Juan Gabriel, and a man who draws caricatures with pancake batter as his medium and a griddle as his canvas.

In this book, with the help of all those people, Mexico City will be reflected from the street level. They will provide the details of the cityscape; I'll complement with the backdrop.

Every writer is at least unconsciously trying to fashion a narrative with which he can live. While this book is about Mexico City, it is reflected through my idiosyncratic gaze and experience. If one fact stands out more than any other, it is that in the past eighteen years I have never been bored here. All those people have kept me alive and awake, have kept me in Mexico City, have helped me to make it my home. I hope the book reads as a love letter to them.

Mexican Lexicon, Part One

La ciudad de México (Mexico City), el Distrito Federal (the Federal District), el D.F. (the D.F.), México (Mexico).

When urbanists speak of Mexico City, they refer to the entire urban sprawl. This makes sense inasmuch as it is one continuous horizontal mass, with nothing but a discreet sign on the peripheral highways demarking your passage from city to state. The central part is only called el Distrito Federal by stuffy bureaucrats (like the District of Columbia for Washington). El D.F., like D.C., is much more commonly used.

People from the rest of the country tend to think of Mexico City residents as arrogant. A key offense is that they often refer to the city as just plain México, which minimizes, if not entirely negates, the existence of everywhere else. In Mexico City, the rest of the republic, even cities with five or six million inhabitants, is referred to as *la provincia*.

Chilango, defeño, capitalino. Different words, each meaning someone who lives in Mexico City. *Chilango,* especially from the mouth of someone who lives in *la provincia,* is usually an insult, connoting a loud, arrogant, ill-mannered, loutish person. However, the word has been appropriated by younger generations of city dwellers, who proudly identify themselves as *chilangos,* much in the way U.S. blacks co-opted the word "nigger" in the 1970s.

Defeño is an expansion of the initials D.F., themselves a contraction of Distrito Federal. People born in Mexico City like to call themselves *defeños* and espouse a theory that *chilangos* are people who were born in *la provincia* and moved to the city. (They are the only ones who make this distinction.) Perhaps because *capitalino* is the most polite, specific, and correct word, it is almost never utilized.

El Centro

Mexico City's borders spread out over nearly six hundred square miles, incessantly extending farther and wider. As such, it is a city with no beginning or end. But it has a middle, known as *el centro histórico,* the heart of the city not only geographically, but also historically, politically, economically, and symbolically. There are buildings from as far back as the sixteenth century in the *centro,* and it was named a UNESCO World Heritage site. It is probably the most vibrant and lively such site in the world.

The center of the center is the *zócalo,* an austere, thirteen-acre concrete plaza. The monuments that surround it are testaments to the city's history and conflicting cultures as well as the way they still live side by side, elbowing each other for space. The *zócalo* was where the Aztecs built their most important temple in the pre-Hispanic era. When the Spaniards conquered, they destroyed nearly all remnants of the indigenous city, but the ruins of the Templo Mayor refused to be buried. In 1978, linemen digging to lay cable found stone carvings, and the remains were excavated.

Next to the Aztec archaeological site is the Metropolitan Cathedral, built in the eighteenth century in the Spanish Baroque style. It is still the power center of the Catholic Church, and Cardinal Norberto Rivera holds mass here each Sunday (when he isn't being heckled by those in favor of abortion or others charging him with shielding priests accused of pederasty). At a right angle to the cathedral is the enormous, sand-colored Palacio Nacional, the seat of the federal government, where presidential ceremonies are sometimes held. Across from the cathedral is an edifice of heavy gray stone that is home to various bureaus of the city government.

In the *zócalo* and in surrounding streets, in myriad office buildings—some grandiose ex-convents from the colonial period, others ramshackle rectangles from the late twentieth century—thousands of bureaucrats toil (or at least claim to). In the middle of the square, the Mexican flag flaps in the breeze, with equal squares of red, green, and white, and an emblem of an eagle with a serpent in its beak.

But it is neither the monuments nor their symbols that give the *centro* its tangible energy. The palpitating buzz comes from the people packed into the neighborhood. A little more than two hundred thousand live in the *centro*, yet another 1,200,000 arrive each day to work, shop, eat, and drink, go to wrestling matches, museums, or concerts. In the street across from the Palacio Nacional, they examine ruby earrings and gold chains in jewelry store windows or the straw Panamas and felt cowboy numbers in the Hermanos Tardán hat shop. Up the block they sit at a McDonald's with sidewalk tables, hock their furniture and TV sets in the National Pawn Shop, and mostly ignore a strip of handymen who hunker down each morning beside signs that offer their services as plumbers, electricians, painters, and plasterers.

On the plaza, a troupe in Aztec drag—the men in loincloths and feathered headdresses, the women in *cueitl huipilli* skirt-and-blouse sets reminiscent of Wilma Flintstone's attire—performs ceremonial dances, and for spare change will offer passersby a *limpia,* in which the subject's body is imbued with smoke from burning incense, supposedly cleansing his spirit in the bargain. In November 2007, Mayor Marcelo Ebrard installed an ice-skating rink made of polyethylene for the Christmas season. The result was controlled chaos, with thousands of people per day who had never put on ice skates before, most of them inching along, many grabbing the railings for their lives.

Periodically there are free open-air concerts in the *zócalo,* and when they are performed by Mexican stars like the pop idol Juan Gabriel or the rock group Café Tacuba, the plaza is so crowded that you are pinioned by the surrounding bodies. However, on most days the *zócalo* is more likely to be occupied by protesters seeking jobs, housing, or trying to redress one or another injustice. The protesters have groups with names—el Frente Popular Francisco Villa, el Unión Popular Revolucionario Emiliano Zapata, el Movimiento Urbano Popular—but they are here so often that, to most city residents, they are interchangeable.

The buildings in the *centro* were built between the seventeenth and the twentieth centuries. As such, the architecture is something of a hodgepodge; within a block or two you might find façades with Corinthian columns, Moorish arches, Gothic spires, lion gargoyles, placid statues of Minerva and Pan, or Art Deco curves and angles. Some structures are in great shape, while others look like they would fall down if someone sneezed in their direction. Yet even in the decadent sections it is impossible to walk through the neighborhood without sensing its majesty.

No matter how often I wander the streets of the *centro,* I am always surprised by some fresh detail: an openmouthed, stark naked mannequin in a shop window; the troupe of break-dancers across from the youth hostel; a previously unnoticed cantina with its tempting swinging doors; a shop advertising *"0% descuento."*

For the supposedly bustling urban core, the action gets off to a late start. Few stores open before ten or ten-thirty in the morning, but they all seem to unbolt at once, with a phalanx of shopgirls cleansing the sidewalks with pails of soapy water and hard-brush brooms. Office workers don't tend to arrive any earlier, but when they finally show up, they come in droves.

By this time the organ grinders are out, cranking "The Skater's Waltz," "The Strawberry Blonde," or *"Ella"* on hurdy-gurdys more than a hundred years old. They wear beige uniforms, as do their assistants, who stand with their caps extended hoping for a handout. Supposedly there is one man in the entire city who tunes these instruments, but two reporters at a magazine where I worked could never find him. Given the out-of-sync sound quality, it would seem that most of the organ grinders can't find him, either.

Many who work in the neighborhood eat breakfast from stands on the sidewalk. The traditional morning meal for the financially strapped is a *torta de tamal:* a weighty steamed corn cake served in a roll, accompanied by a glass of hot *atole,* a thick and viscous pre-Hispanic corn porridge, usually sweetened with fruit or sugar. This combination, which costs about fifty cents, will keep an impoverished laborer full for most of the day. I had this breakfast once, and afterward felt as if I had consumed the wall of a building.

There are also tamales deep-fried in canola oil that look heavy as bricks; huge piles of frying meat to be fashioned into tacos; *sopes, gorditas,* and *tlacoyos*—variations of the fried corn cake, usually topped with beans and cheese; shrimp broth and fried fish sticks. Boiled hot dogs sold at three for a dollar are topped with mayonnaise, mustard, ketchup, and chopped green chiles; the combined colors and substances transform them into a lethal piñata party.

At the Plaza Santo Domingo, all but the indigent are approached by a small army of enterprising men who ask in furtive murmurs, *¿Qué buscas, amigo?*—What are you looking for, friend? Although everything about their manner suggests drug dealers, they are in fact shilling for the printing shops that line the square, hoping to drum up interest in business cards, wedding invitations, or the binding of a student's thesis.

Outside the doors of the printing shops are *escritores públicos:* men hunched over typewriters who fashion business letters, fill out forms, or occasionally construct a love letter, at the service of customers either illiterate or without access to a machine of their own. Around the corner on Calle Donceles there are more than a dozen secondhand bookstores, featuring the dusty, moldy detritus of the dead of the last century or so, often in two or three languages. There are streets where in shop after shop they only sell bridal gowns, or lamps, or bathroom fixtures.

Snapshots: A toothless lady sucking on a mango pit. A blind man with dark glasses and a cane, leading a single-file parade of three other blind men, each with a hand on the shoulder of the man in front of him. Swarms of yellow jackets surrounding the candied sweet potatoes, zucchini, and figs at the Mercado de Dulces. Hungover, crippled sixteenth-century churches, after multiple earthquakes tilting like so many towers of Pisa. Good morning, Vietmex: rickshaw taxi drivers pedaling their way through the trafficked streets. Inside the cathedral, an old man stealthily filling a plastic bottle from the fount of holy water.

In the first years of the new century, some sixty buildings in the nicest part of the *centro*—west of the *zócalo* toward the Palacio de Bellas Artes—were acquired for about $60 million by Carlos Slim Helú, the Mexican who in 2007 was declared the richest man in the world by *Fortune* magazine and the second richest by *Forbes*.

He spent nearly ten times as much renovating these buildings into swanky apartments and well-appointed office spaces.

Suddenly these structures, sandblasted and repainted, their picture windows sparkling and wrought-iron balconies ashine, looked as good as they did when they were built in the eighteenth and nineteenth centuries. In this gentrified corridor of about six by eight blocks, the rents, of course, rose correspondingly, and the character of the neighborhood began to change.

In 2005, a basement jazz club called Zinco (as hip as any in New York) and a cavernous hall called Pasagüero, devoted mostly to rock concerts and dance parties with deejays, opened in this area. So did Starbucks and Subway. The success of these enterprises encouraged the inauguration of more restaurants, bars, and shops on the surrounding streets. Ten years ago, Slim's section of the *centro* was dead at night, provoking fear and danger. These days, even in the wee hours, many night owls (principally the young and youngish) troll the sidewalks.

However, only a couple of blocks from Slim's part of the center, it's impossible not to notice the surrounding poverty, neglect, and desperation. Here the buildings are crumbling and filled with lurkers wearing sidewise scowls. Apart from delinquents, many streets are teeming with beggars and the disabled. Abandoned buildings are co-opted as squats by homeless children and the destitute elderly. The streets surrounding the Mercado Merced are lined with prostitutes who charge as little as ten dollars a throw. Many are underage, while others are ancient; some are almost naked and others covered in turtlenecks and long pants, their faces unadorned or covered in makeup laid on with a trowel.

For the past two decades, until a few months ago, the streets east of the *zócalo,* between the Palacio Nacional and the Anillo de Circunvalación, were Mexico City's *souk.* If your eyes were closed and you didn't understand Spanish, you might have thought there was a popular uprising in progress. But the cries came from vendors who for a few pesos tried to unload sunglasses, panties mounted in multi-colored heaps, battery-operated toy cars, rubber hoses, hair clips, pirated DVDs, flip-flops, baby socks, Barbies with green cornrows and homemade sequined gowns. The merchandise they carried was often bought for pennies in China and resold at a small profit; some of it was stolen goods. The only taxes the vendors paid were tributes to the mafias that control them.

In this part of the *centro,* vendors occupied the sidewalks and most of the streets; their merchandise was so dense that human traffic could only stir in slow motion. Official statistics have it that a neighborhood known as Santa Fe generates the greatest income per square foot in the city. But it was often speculated that the informal economy of the *centro* produced as much or even more money.

Since I arrived in 1990, street vendors have been a problem, and each successive mayor has announced plans to do away with them. However, the vendors' numbers and political power have grown exponentially in the last fifteen years. According to *Proceso,* a political weekly, in 2002, Marcelo Ebrard, then the chief of police, was able to clear four blocks' worth of them around the Palacio Nacional. But he had to negotiate with the political leaders who aligned with them. In exchange for their exit, he was obliged to find them fifteen hundred spots in low-rent shopping centers, fifteen hundred apartments, unspecified amounts of cash, medical benefits, and food stamps. In late 2006, the opening of the Victoria shopping mall was announced with great fanfare, providing space for 488 vendors. There are literally hundreds of thousands of street vendors in the whole of Mexico City; 488 is a teardrop in the Amazon.

Tacitly, they have been tolerated. In a city where there isn't enough work to go around, few politicians are willing to take measures that would separate people from their jobs. Yet suddenly, in the middle of October 2007, Mayor Ebrard cleared the streets of the *centro* of all of them. They disappeared in a heartbeat, as if they had never been there. Although eating on the street is a cornerstone of Mexico City culture, even the food vendors were gone. During the first weeks of their absence, it was a strange sensation, as if a friend you'd known all your life with wild, unruly hair had suddenly shaved his head. There was even an element that seemed embarrassing or unseemly, as if the streets were nude in public.

Within a few weeks, however, the boldest of the salespeople were back on Calle Moneda, beside the Palacio Nacional. It was a month before Christmas and people needed to do their shopping. They had also taken Calle Manzanares around the corner. If those two streets had become occupied again, most of the rest of the neighborhood remained free of the vendors' traffic. To give them someplace to work, Ebrard announced the construction of various small shopping centers in the *centro*. The mayor's plans included the furtive demolishing of fourteen buildings that had been part of the UNESCO cultural patrimony. Their destruction was not announced until after the fact.

During the next few years, at least some of the vendors, or new generations of them, will undoubtedly attempt to take the streets again. Ebrard will just as unquestionably do everything he can to prevent their progress. He is widely believed to have presidential aspirations, and if he becomes a candidate in 2011 he will have to renounce his job as mayor. At that point, the vendors might take to the streets again, all at once, like rats escaping from their warrens.

Where the Money Is and Isn't

In the square outside the county hall of Ciudad Nezahualcóyotl, an enormous tent has been erected under the tyrannical May sun. Hundreds of people have arrived for a job fair, and are either in the exhibition area inside the suffocating tent or waiting outside in a line that snakes around the plaza. The applicants, packed tightly as olives in an unopened jar, include men who are sweating under their best-foot-forward suits and ties, women who have carefully sprayed their hair and painted their faces, as well as the requisite clueless who have shown up unshaven and disheveled. The hopefuls range in age from the barely pubescent to about sixty years old.

Work that pays five thousand pesos a month—about four hundred fifty dollars U.S.—is advertised under enormous banners, as if such a salary represented untold riches (in a city where meat, fish, eggs, fruit, a roll of toilet paper, and a tube of toothpaste cost nearly as much as they do in the United States). One such offer is from a company that hires security guards. The poster depicts men in blue uniforms and dark glasses pointing semiautomatics and submachine guns, as if asking, *Would you kill for this job?*

A gray-haired, bespectacled man with a distracted manner, standing on a platform, drones available opportunities into a microphone: messengers, at wages of three hundred dollars a month; operators to make telephone calls to people who owe money (which comes with a salary plus commission—if the dunning is successful); beer-truck driver. Who wants to be an assistant accountant? Raise your hands! Now where was that guy offering the assistant accountant's job? He must be around here somewhere. . . .

Wal-Mart is hiring warehouse workers, cashiers, and maintenance personnel to clean and wax floors. Commission-only catalog sales jobs are offered by various outfits, including Avon, Mary Kay, and Frederick International (which sells underwear but has nothing to do with its Hollywood namesake).

Nextel is looking for a human resources assistant—but not just any human resources assistant. They want a woman, between twenty-two and twenty-six years old, with a minimum of six months' professional experience. (If one fills those requirements, she might even be grateful to earn the three hundred dollars a month they offer.) A liquor distributor wants to hire someone to work the counter—a woman, between seventeen and thirty-eight, at two hundred fifty dollars a month. They're also looking for a man from sixteen to forty-eight to be a handyman at one hundred ninety dollars a month, and a female messenger, between eighteen and twenty-eight, at two hundred seventy dollars a month.

The Mexican Constitution, a glorious document in theory, prohibits both age and gender discrimination and declares every citizen's right to work for a living wage. Employers believe that stating age and gender requirements in a job listing is a way of weeding out those who would be wasting their time should they apply. Applicants may feel this is unfair and unpleasant, but they need work so badly that they don't complain.

Another outfit is looking for hot dog salesmen. Apart from a base salary they offer commissions. For sales of between 242 and 264 pounds of wieners, the bonus comes to four pesos—some forty-three cents. It goes up to forty-eight cents if sales are between 266 and 286 pounds; for 308 pounds and over, the commission is a whopping fifty-four cents.

Spartacus, a legendary Ciudad Nezahualcóyotl gay bar, canvasses for go-go boys. (For those not sufficiently Adonis-like to make the cut, they offer free passes for the Tanga of the Year contest.)

Just across the county line from where the Federal District ends and Mexico State begins, Ciudad Nezahualcóyotl, known to its inhabitants simply as Neza (and sometimes Neza York) is a legendary part of the greater urban sprawl. Founded in 1963, the little community soon grew exponentially with undereducated, mainly rural Mexicans who, fleeing the poverty of their states, flooded into the city at a rate of two thousand a day until the early 1990s. Housing was built catch-as-catch-can, from brick, concrete, cardboard, and corrugated plastic. Electricity was siphoned from existing lines, and water supply and plumbing problems were endemic. Neza soon became synonymous for poverty and high crime. Today, with about a million and a half residents, it has become an established neighborhood, with its own government and police force, and the same services available in the rest of the city. Both safety and the economy have improved, but Neza has hardly lived down its reputation. The lines to enter the job fair attest to its continued hardship.

I have never met anyone in Mexico City who admits to being prosperous. People with money tend to refer to themselves as middle class, or in certain instances under extreme duress, upper middle class. Yet these terms have different meanings than in the United States or Europe.

A case in point is Rodrigo, a thirty-four-year-old public relations man, noted for the parties he plans for liquor companies, which invariably make their way into the society pages. Baby-faced, curly-headed, with ivory skin and the sparse beard of a teenager, he dresses with the studied casualness of someone who pores over fashion ads: an untucked striped shirt, jeans, a brown velvet jacket with the collar turned up. "I don't believe what the papers say," he said recently. "There are a lot of new middle-class people in Mexico City."

It surfaced that his conception of middle class meant those who earn close to two hundred thousand dollars a year, drive a Mercedes or an Audi, have mortgaged a lavish apartment, sport a Cartier or a Rolex watch, and wear designer clothing. "That kind of money won't buy you everything," he said ruefully. "I live in a small apartment and drive a six-year-old car, but I travel to New York or Paris once a month." He scoffed at a Mexican fashion designer whose shirts retail at three hundred fifty dollars. "I buy my clothes on sale in San Diego," he said. "I pay one hundred dollars for shirts. The most I've ever spent on a shirt is two hundred fifty dollars, and that was Comme des Garçons."

Earth to Rodrigo: The minimum wage in Mexico City is about five dollars a day. Only 12 percent of the working population earns more than twenty-three dollars per day. The largest sector, about 45 percent, earns between nine and twenty-three dollars per day. Another 24 percent earns between four and a half and nine dollars, and 8 percent earn less than the minimum. The remaining 11 percent don't specify.

Who are the unfortunates earning so little? Look around on the streets: dozens of functionaries of both sexes, squeezed into suits of synthetic fabric, streaming out of the metro every morning. The shoeshine man, the messenger, the woman in uniform standing guard outside the bank. The maids. The convenience store clerks, the gas station attendants, the security guards, the construction workers. The hordes of people selling things on the streets—food, flowers, newspapers, Chiclets.

Among the "middle class," there's a lot of lip service about what a scandal it is that the wealth is so poorly distributed. But in fact, the relationship between people with money in Mexico City—about 15 percent, most of whom are white—and those without, the great majority of whom are brown—is at best tenuous. On the street, browns and whites rarely look each other in the eye.

Indeed, in Mexico City, where social divisions can be as pointillistic as in England, and a caste system is as firmly in place as in India, people with money perceive the poor as abstractions, blurs who only come into focus when they wait on them. The woman who cleans your home, the man who hands you a towel after you've washed your hands in the restroom, the guy in the yellow jumpsuit who sells you a phone card at the traffic intersection—you are certain these people exist, because they have interacted with you. You've exchanged words, they've addressed you as *señor* or *jefe* and assured you that they are at your service.

Serving you, if not precisely their raison d'être, is the confirmation of their existence. Even though they dissolve and disappear after your encounter, the evidence of their being is in the blinding brilliance of your patent pumps, the folded headlines at your side, the citrus smell of your newly spic-and-span apartment.

In tony neighborhoods such as Las Lomas, a live-in maid is sometimes referred to as *la felicidad del hogar*—a home's source of happiness. More commonly she is called *la muchacha* (the girl). She tends to earn between five hundred and six hundred dollars per month. Additionally she sleeps rent free in a small room, which usually includes a television set, and is given meals (which she eats alone, in the kitchen or in her room) and one day off per week.

Her six working days rarely have a schedule of hours; she's usually on call from morning until night. Her set of duties also varies and, depending on the exigencies of the family that hires her, can include not only cleaning but babysitting, cooking, serving meals and doing the dishes afterward, washing and ironing clothes, and the retrieval of dry cleaning. Over the weekend in Acapulco, it is common to see young brown women watching over white children on the beach, while their parents are elsewhere.

Brown maids are such an integral part of the survival of Mexico City homes that, soon after Rigoberta Menchú, the indigenous Guatemalan activist, won the Nobel Peace Prize, the following joke circulated:

Q: *Why did they make a Rigoberta Menchú doll?*
A: So Barbie could have a maid.

Well-off *capitalinos,* by restricting themselves to specific zones of the city, do their damnedest to insulate themselves from the existence of the poor. Still, they can run but they can't hide. No matter how rich someone is, the poor are never far away. A few years ago, a couple I know bought two penthouse apartments in a brand-new building overlooking the Parque Hundido, one of the most beautiful parks in the city. They knocked down some walls to make it one enormous dwelling, with various bedrooms, home offices, and two ample terraces facing the greenery. Their next-door neighbor was a cabinet minister.

I slept in a guest room one night, and at three or four in the morning was awakened by the sound of roosters crowing at the top of their lungs. After sunrise I looked out the window at the street behind them, a cobblestoned affair with one-story houses that had brightly painted stone façades. Looking closely I saw that the colorful porticos were nothing more than freestanding stone walls. Behind them were tin-roofed shacks with dirt floors, upon which those roosters were pecking.

One of the consequences of blurring the great mass of the poor is that it is difficult to compare oneself to a faceless abstraction. Hence, no matter how much money someone in Mexico City has, he never thinks he is rich; there is always someone with far more—someone who has a face and a name. Meet Carlos Slim Helú, whose net worth has been reported at between $60 billion and $70 billion, and as such, along with Bill Gates, is in a photo finish in the race to be the richest man in the world. Slim exists far more concretely for the well-to-do than the child who bags groceries at the supermarket, the valet parking attendant, or the brown waitress in the white embroidered uniform who serves coffee at Sanborn's, one of Slim's enterprises.

Carlos Slim has a scowling bearded countenance and a corpulent form which are seen in newspapers and magazines day after day. Even to those who don't know him, the accrued details of his life make him a tangible individual, the rich uncle that most of us are unfortunate never to have had.

In a country where half the citizens live in poverty, how does one man become the richest on the planet? On the street it's often said that 40 percent of every peso spent by the Mexicans goes toward one of Slim's enterprises. While this is probably hyperbolic, about a third of the stocks traded on the Mexican exchange are among businesses owned by Slim.

Slim is the youngest son of a Lebanese immigrant who came to Mexico City in 1902. His father made a fortune in real estate he bought cheaply after the 1910 revolution sent the economy into a swan dive. Family lore has it that the enterprising Carlos, born in

1940, began to earn money from investments at age twelve, with
twenty dollars that his father gave him as a birthday gift.

In 1982, after plummeting oil prices and a devaluation trashed the
Mexican economy yet again, Slim saw his opportunity, buying some
of the companies that make up his empire at bargain-basement prices.
His businesses extend throughout the Americas. As of this writing,
Slim has a 20 percent share in Philip Morris Mexico, which manu-
factures the leading brands of cigarettes, including Marlboro. Other
elements of his empire include or have included banking, cement, copper, supermarkets, chain stores, bakeries, chickens, and eggs. In recent
years he has been expanding into retail and commercial real estate.

These endeavors can make a man wealthy, but what has made
Slim obscenely rich is telecommunications. Teléfonos de México,
known as Telmex, was a state-owned monopoly until 1990, when
Slim acquired control for the bargain price of $1.7 billion. He was
said to have been the highest bidder for the company, although at the
time many alleged that he was in fact the beard, or at the very least
the partner, of the president, Carlos Salinas de Gortari.

The privatization process was supposed to allow for competition.
Yet the company remains a near monopoly, with more than 90 percent
of Mexico's fixed lines and 80 percent of its cellular phone service.

Being the only game in town affords Slim many privileges. Telmex
charges some of the world's highest rates for service. According to an
article in the *New York Times,* a phone call in Mexico costs 50 percent more than the average among a group of countries that includes
the United States, the United Kingdom, Switzerland, Luxembourg,
Canada, Australia, and Sweden. A *Forbes* story said that a small
business in Mexico should expect to pay $132 per month in phone
service, while in the United States it would only cost sixty dollars.

Complaints against Telmex and its cellular phone counterpart,
Telcel, are virtually endless. According to the magazine *Proceso,* the

company earned $3 billion in 2005 due to "rounding off" telephone bills, a term that by any other name would be called overcharging. If you contract the company's Internet services, you cannot use Skype or Vonage for telephone calls. There are charges for roaming even to telephones within the same network. The Economist Intelligence Unit suggested that in any other country, Telmex would have been broken up years ago.

Slim has avoided competition by ingenious and endless litigation. *The Wall Street Journal* reported that it took eight years of lawsuits until other companies were allowed to provide broadband Internet in Mexico (and then only conditionally, without voice services). He has achieved his goals in part because he's had important politicians in his pocket during every presidential administration since he bought Telmex. During the term of Vicente Fox, from 2000 to 2006, the telecommunications minister, Pedro Cerisola—a former Telmex district manager—perversely insisted that in Mexico there is no dominant telecommunications operator.

Some in the business community defend Slim as merely doing his best to make his business as profitable as possible. And indeed, it isn't his fault if the government allows him to monopolize telecommunications. There is a Federal Competition Commission in Mexico, supposedly meant to foster fair trade, yet competition barely exists here. Two companies make and distribute nearly all the beer consumed in Mexico, while two others produce nearly all programs seen on network TV in the country. One company makes nearly all of the packaged bread, cakes, and cookies available in supermarkets and convenience stores, while another has a 70 percent market share of corn flour (no mean feat when the staple of the Mexican diet is the tortilla).

If Slim tends to be admired in the business and banking communities, most ordinary citizens think it is an outrage that the richest man in the world lives in a country with so many poor. The wealthier he gets, the harder it is to contain his public relations problems. He hardly talks to the press any longer. In an interview with Reuters, the magnate used the following metaphor to make clear his opposition to competition: "Wealth is like an orchard. You have to share the fruit, not the orchard. With the orchard, what you have to do is make it grow, reinvest it to make it bigger, or diversify into other areas."

Through a philanthropic organization, by early 2007 Slim had donated 95,000 bicycles, 70,000 pairs of eyeglasses, 150,000 study grants, and 200,000 operations for the ill. As *Proceso* pointed out, these figures are underwhelming, given that Slim's wealth has surpassed that of Bill Gates and Warren Buffett, world famous for their philanthropic efforts. (It is worth pointing out that the wealthy of Mexico City are not exactly noted for their charitable endeavors, with the exception of some wives of the well-to-do, who serve on the boards of museums and help in their fund-raising efforts.)

Slim's greatest expansion outside telecommunications in the past few years has been through a company called Ideal that invests in infrastructure projects: construction, highways, airports, oil rigs, ports, and bridges.

Felipe Calderón, current president of Mexico, has indicated that part of his platform will be to eradicate unfair trade practices and encourage competition. At the time of this writing, there have been no concrete actions. Still, Slim seems to be hedging his bets by expanding both his infrastructure and telecommunications empires in Central and South America, and is rumored to have his eyes on the United States.

I have never had either a professional or social opportunity to meet Carlos Slim, or any of the city's hyperrich. I would imagine that

they, at least among themselves, tacitly acknowledge that they are
wealthy.

But if they admit that they have money, they are the only ones.
Even people with extravagant lifestyles have taboos about such qualifications and seem to believe themselves little more than solvent. I
once wrote a magazine story about Viviana Corcuera who, under her
maiden name, Della Vedova, was crowned Miss Argentina in 1964.
Four years later she came to Mexico City and married Enrique Corcuera, the playboy black sheep of one of Mexico's most distinguished
families, who was thirty years her senior. The marriage instantly
transformed her into one of the city's most prominent socialites; her
husband died in 1999.

Gracious and generous, svelte and golden, Viviana opened the
doors of her houses in the most exclusive sections of Mexico City and
Acapulco to me. She is to entertaining what Fred Astaire was to
dance: you never see her sweat. In both of her homes, glasses and
plates are refilled at the precise moment by impeccably discreet, nearly
invisible waiters; it is almost as if the food and drink had a will of
its own.

While I was preparing the story she invited me to watch a World
Cup match at her home in Las Lomas, along with two of her girlfriends. We were in the library, dominated by portraits of her and
her late husband (as well as a 52-inch television set). Viviana served
fried empanadas, baked salmon, and New Zealand lamb with mint
sauce, lubricated with Chilean sparkling wine or French red. It was
far too much food for the four of us to consume; after we finished,
she told the waiter that he and the rest of the servants could have the
leftovers.

When the game was over, Viviana declared that, at sixty years old,
she was happier than she had ever been. When younger, she'd been
overly concerned with material things, but now she realized that the

spiritual realm was more important. Money was only useful inasmuch as it enabled one "to live."

"How do you mean, 'to live'?" asked one of her friends.

"To live," she said. "Like us."

Like us: a two-story house in a gated community in Mexico City, another with eight bedrooms in Acapulco, maids, a chauffeur, a butler, investment properties, a few million in the bank. Yet while I prepared the article, I heard Viviana mention several times that she is "not rich." When I asked her to clarify, she conceded that I didn't really have to worry about her, as long as "the Communists don't come to take everything away." All she would own up to was having "a resolved economic situation."

This sort of modesty is an idiosyncratic paradox, inversely proportional to what most would consider an ostentatious lifestyle. But after all, Viviana is not Carlos Slim.

When I told a friend that I'd accepted a job at a magazine in Mexico City, she smiled and said, *"Sólo los pendejos trabajan"*—only assholes work. A salaried job is seen as a mug's game. In Mexico City, upward mobility is virtually nonexistent. You are given a place and expected to stay in it until you die or are discarded. In the three and a half years I worked for the publisher, I never received a raise; this is par for the course for people who labor for much longer periods than that.

Consequently, hundreds of thousands of people in Mexico City find alternatives to compensated employment in the underground economy, where nearly anyone can earn more than he or she could at a regular job.

According to the most recent statistics from the UN Development Program—from the year 2000—35 percent of the working population of Mexico City makes its living in the informal economy. This includes anyone who works off the books, but their principal population is found selling things on the street. Both research and anecdotal evidence suggest that this number has increased since then, probably to about 50 percent. (At the time of this writing the UN was preparing another report from 2005 numbers.)

A good example of someone who takes advantage of the informal opportunities of Mexico City is Jerónimo, a slender, diminutive man in a yellow-and-green jumpsuit who, when traffic stops at the intersection of Avenida Insurgentes and Calle Ohio in the Colonia Nápoles, runs from car to car selling copies of two newspapers, *Reforma* and *Metro*. He is conspicuous for two things—the permanent smile on his face, and the astonishing speed at which he runs to make a sale (he can move four or five papers during one red light).

A native of Maxcanú, Yucatán, Jerónimo worked on construction sites in various parts of the country before arriving in Mexico City in 1994, when he was thirty-eight years old. He started out in the same work here, too, participating in important projects like the renovation of the Palacio de Bellas Artes and the assembly of a parking lot under the Plaza Garibaldi. But he didn't get along with his bosses, so decided to try his luck selling papers.

Reforma, a broadsheet fat with advertisements and divided into countless sections each day, is the rich man's paper. It costs ten pesos, while the compact tabloid *Metro* sells for only five. Jerónimo earns two pesos for each copy of *Reforma* he sells, and 1.20 for every *Metro*. His gross earnings are between thirty and thirty-five dollars a day. He spends close to four dollars on transportation, including a two-and-a-half-dollar cab ride to bring between 220 and 250 newspapers from the street where he picks them up to the corner where he sells them. Two sandwiches and a bottle of soda, which he consumes at midday, set him back another two dollars and twenty-five cents.

He pays one hundred fifty dollars a month to rent a room, complete with a hot plate and a TV, in the risky Colonia Guerrero. There is no refrigerator and the bathroom is in the hall.

The news agency supplies him with his uniform, although they tend to give him large ones, which he has to alter. (Like many natives of the Yucatán, Jerónimo is under five feet and only approaches one hundred pounds at the end of the day, when he is laden with all the loose change with which his customers have bought the papers.)

Jerónimo works seven days a week. He wakes up at four in the morning and fixes scrambled eggs, which he washes down with a glass of milk. He leaves home at five so he can be on his corner by six. On most days, he is back in the Colonia Guerrero by five in the afternoon. He will stop at the market on the way home to buy something for supper. He says that perhaps he'll watch a little TV or read before he sleeps, but he cannot remember the name of the last program he watched or the last book he read.

Apart from his expenses for food and transportation, he hardly spends any money. As a young man, Jerónimo was a heavy drinker, but when he got to Mexico City he noticed alcoholics sprawled on the ground in the Plaza Garibaldi. "Some of them were old," he said. "I began to wonder if I wouldn't end up like them." So he treated himself to one last spree in a cantina, accompanied by two prostitutes from the streets around the Mercado Merced, and has been completely dry for the last fourteen years.

His only luxuries are these two-hundred-peso ladies, whom he visits once or twice a month, and two vacations that he takes each year. In August he visits his family in Maxcanú for two or three weeks, and in December he goes for ten days to a beach near Tapachula, Chiapas. (Each of these trips requires bus rides of more than twelve hours each way.)

His father was a humble farmer of corn, beans, and zucchini, but family lore has it that his grandfather had money. If there was no cash, there was at least land, which Jerónimo's father has divided among his children. With the money he has saved selling newspapers, Jerónimo has already built a house, and is almost finished constructing another building, inside which he wants to open a mini-mart and a cafeteria. He calculates that it will take him another two or three years to accumulate enough money to finish the building and open the store, at which point he will leave Mexico City forever.

Jerónimo's story is indicative of many who work here in the informal economy. If he lives in circumstances that would be considered close to the margin by most people in Europe and the United States, compared to a billion or so others in the world, he's not doing that badly. People at the poverty level in Africa and Asia—and in some parts of rural Mexico—cannot afford two vacations a year, and they cannot even dream of getting ahead. Yet like Jerónimo and his mini-mart, everyone I talked to who works in the informal economy had either realized a dream or was on his or her way to do so through savings. Their dreams are based on personal accomplishment—building a home or saving enough to open a business—after years of backbreaking work and personal sacrifice. None of these people aspire to get ahead within an organization through intelligence, initiative, or creativity; they have realistically assessed that they could not.

Sadly, the informal economy is more advantageous than salaried jobs even for many who have university educations. Julián and Rosita Sánchez, a couple who have sold food on the street from buckets for the last twenty-eight years, have earned enough money to buy a house and put their children through college. But they told me they would prefer for their offspring to follow in their footsteps than pursue professions, pointing out how low salaries are.

They are right. For example, if one of their kids somehow makes it through medical school, at least in the beginning he will only be able to find a job in a neighborhood clinic at a salary of less than four hundred dollars a month, and he might never make his way to the lucrative private practices that tend to be the exclusive province of doctors who were raised among prosperous families. Every day in the windows of employment agencies, jobs are posted for college graduates who speak two languages, with salaries running between four hundred and nine hundred dollars a month.

Some people in Mexico City don't earn salaries at all. I spoke to a woman who pumps gas at one of the state-owned Pemex stations. She told me that although her boss declares to the government that he pays salaries to all of his employees, this is in fact a tax dodge utilized by many of the gas station owners. She lives on tips only, usually between twenty and forty-five cents per customer. However, combined with a monthly bonus of $110, this is more than she earned as a seamstress and a cook.

Calculating levels of poverty in Mexico City is a complicated endeavor. Julio Boltvinik, a sociologist with El Colegio de México, one of the city's most important research universities, has developed his own index. While most people in his field use only a monetary key to measure poverty, Boltvinik's system is based on three elements: salaries; necessities that are left unfulfilled (among them health care and health insurance, housing, education, basic domestic equipment, garbage collection, telephone service, and sanitary conditions); and leisure time.

This last element is often overlooked by poverty researchers, and is the most deficient for many Mexico City residents. Most people here who commute three or four hours a day back and forth in overcrowded public transportation are of course from the working class. Including their commutes, many of their workdays last between twelve and fifteen hours.

Boltvinik calculates that 61.9 percent of Mexico City lives in poverty, and that 15 percent of its residents are extremely poor. "Between the 1930s and the 1980s, Mexico City was much more self-sufficient. There was light and heavy industry, but it has almost disappeared entirely to the *maquiladoras* [piecework factories] in the north. Those jobs never paid well, but at least a steady stream of work was available.

"Basic necessities, like education, housing, and health services, are improving. But salaries are getting lower. They are falling all over the world due to globalization, robots, and the weakness of unions. In the 1970s there was a greater middle class here. More people belonged to unions, had health benefits, paid vacations, and so on. But with the neoliberal model, salaries go down and working conditions have become more precarious.

"Still, it's better to be poor in the city than in the country. Here there is less malnutrition. People always eat. In the cities more people die of cold than of hunger."

It would be a simplification to see the problem of inequality in Mexico City as merely an imbalanced distribution of wealth. Inequality is evident in endless manifestations.

Take gender, for example. Depending in which section of the Federal District they live, working women only fill between 22 percent and 35 percent of supervisory or management positions. Politics is very much a boy's club. Of the sixteen delegations that make up the D.F., six have fewer than 10 percent women politically representing them, including several that have no women representing them at all. Four delegations have between 10 percent and 20 percent female representation, five between 20 percent and 33 percent, and only one has more than 40 percent.

However, these sorts of statistics reveal none of the details of what

a woman has to put up with due to gender inequality in a macho society. Sexual harassment is not only tolerated but is also *el pan de
cada día*—the daily bread—of women in Mexico City, no matter
what social class they belong to.

A friend who has written several books and edited a magazine for
seven years was looking for a job not long ago. A girlfriend of hers,
who knew the editorial director of the Mexican wing of an important Spanish publishing conglomerate, arranged a lunch at which the
three were present. Throughout the meal, the director and the two
women exchanged small talk and briefly discussed the possibilities
my friend might have within the corporation. The man behaved like
a perfect gentleman until after they had finished eating, when my
friend stood up and excused herself to visit the restroom. The man
grabbed her wrist and said, *"Dime, ¿esas nalguitas tienen dueño?"*
(Tell me, does that little ass belong to anyone?)

A single mother who worked as a secretary in the insurance business was informed that the company needed to drastically cut personnel, and hers was one of the positions set to be eliminated. She
went to her boss's office and implored him to reconsider, which
prompted him to unzip his fly and suggest that she might be able to
keep her job if she would "get to know the little head."

Another friend has for the past three years suffered what in the
United States would possibly result in a multimillion-dollar harassment lawsuit. Employed by a company that has enormous contracts
with the Mexican government, she works as an administrator planning events and editing the company newsletter. Since she began
three years ago, she has been periodically and systematically hassled
by her boss. On one occasion when they were alone in a conference
room, he pulled her hair and kissed her on the neck. When she pushed
him away, he claimed to have been "joking." After an industry cocktail party she had organized in a posh hotel, he suggested that they

get a room. During a meeting before many of the company's key players, he referred to a colleague as her "boyfriend."

Recently, he invited her to his office, locked the door, and explained that he had plans to launch an industry trade magazine. He suggested that she could fulfill the editor's job while maintaining her current position. It surfaced that he wanted to discuss the matter over dinner, a proposition she refused. They remained at this impasse until he finally unlocked the door and let her return to work, never to mention the magazine again.

I asked my friend if she thought her boss believed that after three years of rejections she would one day flip 180 degrees and tumble into bed with him. She said he probably didn't, but simply enjoys the exercise of his power and relishes attempts to frighten her.

He is also buoyed by the knowledge that there will be no consequences. My friend doesn't take any action against her boss because she wants to keep her job, and believes her colleagues would either be unsympathetic or unwilling to support her allegations in a lawsuit.

In the Constitution, there are laws against both sexual harassment and gender discrimination. Moreover, in Mexico City there are many local and federal organizations that are supposedly equipped to help women who are victims—the city ombudsman's office, the National Women's Institute, the Federal District Human Rights Commission, the attorney general's office, and so forth. Not a single spokesperson at any of these organizations could remember even one instance in which a woman who had been sexually harassed had seen her boss punished.

Women are getting their messages not from the utopian education programs of those organizations but from reality. A spokeswoman at the ombudsman's office referred me to a 2004 case that involved Héctor Gálvez Tánchez, a circuit judge in Mexico City. He was de-

nounced by two women who worked for him, for numerous offenses
including unwanted sexual advances, asking them to go out to restaurants or discotheques with him, reproaching them for not greet-
ing him with a kiss on the cheek in the morning, and suggesting they
show up for work in miniskirts. The Federal Judicial Council resolved that Gálvez Tánchez should be fired from his job. But the
judge took his case to the Supreme Court, where his colleagues decided that his accusers didn't have sufficient proof, and they revoked
the council's decision.

The three women whose stories I told are college educated, with
support systems they can count on under dire circumstances. For instance, the woman with the pesky boss has a master's degree and
speaks three languages. Although she earns only a little more than one
thousand dollars a month—on which she lives with her son—part of
her divorce settlement included an apartment, and her ex-husband
pays child support. Most women in Mexico City are uneducated,
have no such layers of protection, and live a hair's breadth from the
margin. It is easy to imagine women in more dire circumstances, out
of anxiety, desperation, or hopelessness, rendering sexual favors to
keep their jobs.

Sexism is evident in all aspects of society, even those one might
erroneously expect to be more enlightened. A couple of years ago
Nexos, one of the two most important political-literary magazines in
Mexico City, invited various women writers to publish texts about
emblematic feminine myths and figures—Circe, the vagina dentata,
Medea, and so forth. The section was illustrated with a cheesy drawing of a woman with wild black hair sucking on a phallic-shaped lollipop. Months earlier, the other important magazine of that kind,
Letras Libres, reviewed fiction by three women writers under the
headline "The Good, the Bad and the Ugly." Readers who knew the

authors in question interpreted the title as an appraisal of their physical attributes.

Age discrimination is another measure of inequality here. Half the cabdrivers in Mexico City are middle-aged men who are downsized accountants, bureaucrats, sales managers, and the like. Some have spent years looking for another job within their professions, and say that at interviews, their potential employers look them in the eye and tell them they can't hire them because they are too old. People who are thirty-five and under are more likely to work for lower salaries; anyone older is viewed as a problem due to their expectations regarding wages and benefits.

Tax collection offers still more clues to inequality. In a 2007 speech, the secretary of public works said that the poorest Mexicans—those earning the minimum wage of five dollars a day in the city—tend to hand over 24 percent of their salaries as a corruption tax. (If they are working in the formal economy, the money will go to a union or an industry organization; if they are selling things on the street it will likely be paid in the form of a tribute to the mafia that controls the sidewalk.) Yet in 2006, Mexico's sixteen largest corporations—including the bread company Bimbo, the TV conglomerate Televisa, Wal-Mart, Kimberly-Clark, and of course Carlos Slim's Telmex—deferred taxes to the tune of $10 billion. According to professor of government George W. Grayson of the College of William and Mary, apart from petroleum earnings, Mexico's tax collection equals 9.7 percent of its GDP—a figure on par with Haiti. (In 2007 President Felipe Calderón passed a tax reform package. Supposedly it will result in a 2.5 percent increase in collections.)

The average annual earnings of the working residents of the sixteen delegations of the D.F. are another illustration of the severity of Mexico City's inequality. In Milpa Alta, the most impoverished, it's $5,968.83; in Benito Juárez, the wealthiest, it's $29,647.55.

Inequality is a constant in the history of the city. Like virtually all indigenous American empires, the power structure of the Aztecs was in the form of the pyramid, with hordes of the impoverished supporting a class of nobles and priests. The Spaniards perpetuated this system. Those who arrived were warriors, priests, or bureaucrats, few of whom were accustomed to making a living through either labor or commerce. Riches were obtained through exploitation, in the form of a tribute system in which the indigenous were taxed by the Spaniards for the privilege of working on what had been their own land. Historians have noted that among the Aztecs, even the disabled, single women, and children were taxed during the years of the Spanish colony.

The War of Independence of the nineteenth century and the Revolution of the twentieth only paid lip service to abolishing inequality; in reality, those who had money and power were indisposed to relinquish them. The system is unlikely to change, at least any time soon. People with money in Mexico City are sustained and enriched by the fact that labor is cheap here. It is impossible to imagine the city without a surplus of poor people to perform that labor.

Santa Fe and Santa Fe

Only two or three million people live in the four central delegations of the sixteen that make up the Federal District. We are the lucky ones. Wealthy, impoverished, or anywhere in between, we have access to public transportation, schools, reliable garbage collection, electricity, and running water. Usually in walking distance, at our beck and call—if we can afford them—are the benefits that make for a comfortable and captivating urban experience: markets, shops, restaurants, cafés, bars, movie theaters, and so on.

The remaining seventeen million or so live in what would be considered the outskirts in nearly any other city in the world. Although some of these citizens live twenty-five miles or more from the center, most are much closer. However, traffic is such a terrible problem that coming and going to central parts of the city usually takes hours.

In some of the environs, services and cosmopolitan pleasures are accessible, but hardly guaranteed. Emblematic of the complications and contradictions of life on the periphery of Mexico City is an area called Santa Fe, about ten miles from the *centro histórico*.

Santa Fe is the most economically active area of the city, yet at the same time it is home to nearly a quarter million people who live near the poverty level. In the well-to-do section of Santa Fe, the price of an apartment per square foot is among the highest in the city, yet even there, residents cannot count on basic services or infrastructure.

Until the late 1980s, Santa Fe was a toxic garbage dump, home to about two thousand people who eked out a living scavenging through the refuse. They lived in cardboard shacks in and around the dump. The area also had huge sand mines, and was a base for Los Panchitos, one of Mexico City's most dangerous gangs.

A few visionaries in the city government wanted to develop the area. The new Santa Fe was largely the plan of Juan Enriquez Cabot, at the time head of a bankrupt agency called Servicios Metropolitanos, which made its income from municipal parking lots in the *centro*. Cabot's idea was to fill the dump, get rid of the sand mines, and create a business district for the corporate offices of important industries.

It was a dynamic scheme meant to transform Mexico City from an industrial to a service economy. At the time, much of the city's income depended on factories that ringed the valley surrounding the metropolis. Most of them produced shoddy merchandise, but were vital due to Mexico's policy of import substitution, an economic strategy in which a country tries to manufacture instead of import finished goods. However, in 1986, the Uruguay Round of the General Agreement on Tariffs and Trade decreased obstacles to international exchange, making import substitution a losing strategy. It was time to close the factories in any event—most were obsolete, inefficient, and choking the city with pollution.

Enriquez negotiated with the garbage pickers for two years, until they finally agreed to leave the dump in exchange for jobs and housing. He contracted plans from the most important architectural and engineering firms, and was able to convince Bimbo, the bread manufacturer, and Televisa, the media conglomerate, to put up headquarters in Santa Fe. The price of the land was $120 a square meter, unheard of at the time. In exchange, an elite zone with First World infrastructure was promised.

Televisa and Bimbo were soon followed by Hewlett-Packard Latin America, General Electric, and Banamex, the country's largest bank. Goodyear, as well as the two leading tequila distillers, Cuervo and Sauza, soon joined the crowd. Today nearly all multinationals doing business in Mexico City have their nerve centers in Santa Fe: Sun Systems, Kraft, Pepsi, Federal Express, Philip Morris, Unisys, and IBM, among many others. (Such enterprises used to have their offices in the central neighborhoods of the city, but after the *centro* was badly damaged in the 1985 earthquake, most spread out elsewhere.)

Marginally, there is a center to Santa Fe comprising a set of office buildings, on the ground floors of which are any number of well-appointed restaurants. You get to this area by car, and can stroll between restaurants, or in and out of an office tower. But to get to another office, or to Santa Fe's enormous shopping mall—the third largest in the world, with eight million visitors a year—you will need to get back in the car. There are no parks, no gardens, and there is nowhere to walk.

A short drive from the corporate area, there has been a boom of residential construction, mainly towers of condominiums painted in a desert palette—caramel, toffee, sand, cantaloupe. Nearly all these buildings have swimming pools, gyms, and small gardens where children can play. There are fifty-five hundred houses and apartments in the residential area, home to roughly twenty thousand people. It has been so successful that there are plans to increase housing by about 50 percent.

The condominiums tend to sell out even before the towers are built, despite the fact that you cannot obtain a liter of milk or a pack of cigarettes without driving to get them. Sidewalks are either non-existent or rendered useless. Nor is it visitor-friendly—as an area with no center, and no public areas, there is no one on the street to give you directions to find an address. You can only drive around in circles, consult your street map, and hope you get lucky.

Almost as soon as Santa Fe became a success, the only road to get there became outdated. Today, the seventy thousand people who work in the corporate area are plagued by bottlenecks both coming and going. The ten miles from the *centro* to Santa Fe take easily an hour and a half to negotiate at rush hour in a car. Those who don't have a car can take the subway to the Tacubaya station, from which they can either take an hour-long ride in a *pesero,* or get in a cab with three other passengers for a dollar fifty a head.

Given how much money Santa Fe is generating for the city, it is surprising that in the past dozen years the government has not built a new road, provided better public transportation, or delivered on the promised infrastructure. Both the residential and corporate sections of Santa Fe are plagued by practical troubles.

Water is piped in to many office buildings and residences, as treatment stations are inactive or insufficient. Drainage is also a problem, and sewers often overflow during the rainy season. Hence, people who live and work in the area complain that the air sometimes smells like shit, harkening back to the days of the dump. Most buildings have their own generators, as electric cables and electric substations are also inadequate.

Much new construction in Mexico City, particularly in its environs, is in the Santa Fe mold. Thousands of apartment complexes—not just for the wealthy, but for the middle class in outlying areas like

Ixtapaluca and Ecatepec—are being built willy-nilly, with no guarantee that service infrastructure will follow.

Santa Fe is actually a tale of two cities. A mile or two from the prosperous section is a more humble area, one of the oldest in the city, known as *el pueblo,* or the town, of Santa Fe.

The panoramic view: Imagine an enormous ravine, empty and green. Now picture a child placing building blocks on either side of the canyon. He is something of a wild kid who has been deprived of his Ritalin, and he has an unlimited number of blocks. Soon he fills the ravine with blocks and begins to extend them endlessly in all directions. The community bursts at its seams; there is always room for one more house, or ten, or a thousand. This is greater Santa Fe, with 240,000 residents.

Walk along the streets inside the ravine—with each child's block representing someone's home—and you get the sense of a city in a perpetually unfinished state. Most of the houses are one- or two-story brick bunkers, some covered in unevenly spread concrete, some nude. Façades are mostly unpainted, or halfway painted, or painted fifteen years ago and settled into a weather-beaten, multicolored patina. Rebar pop out of the roofs, marking the second or third story, as yet unbuilt.

Corrugated plastic roofs are held in place with broken bricks. Most houses have finished metal doors, yet others are fashioned of plain wooden planks with a hole cut for a padlock and chain. Most windows are whole, others are broken or missing. Construction tools and materials—plastic tarps, buckets that look as if someone has taken a bite out of them, metal garbage cans rusted and split, wood cut into planks or chopped into kindling—lie on the sidewalks, or the roofs, or are stuffed in backyards, putting so much pressure on metal fences that they strain toward the streets.

Laundry hangs limp on lines. Children's toys are abandoned. The burnt-out skeletons of cars are parked on sidewalks, as if waiting for someone to take them on a Sunday drive. Stray dogs whimper and wag their tails, or else lie in the sun impassively. The plastic bottles, the orange peels, the ziplock bags filled with what looks like raw liver could indicate either the negligence of the residents, the irregularity of garbage collection, or both.

Some residents strive for beauty. Flowers grow out of plastic buckets; some houses have tiny gardens. Some gray brick façades are covered with colorful graffiti.

When you get to the principal streets of the *pueblo,* Avenida Vasco de Quiroga and Avenida Pueblo Nuevo, there are few restaurants, although there are taco and torta joints. There is no supermarket, but there are mini-marts. Some residents improvise mom-and-pop stores from their garages or living rooms. You can rent DVDs, but there is no movie theater. There's a gym and a mattress store and a place to pick up a roast chicken on the way home, as well as a pawnshop and a tuxedo rental (people get married and have first communions here) and a one-hour photo (to record such events). There is no café or bar with a jukebox, but you might be able to order a beer and listen to the radio at one of the taco stands, sitting in a white plastic chair. As of this writing, Wal-Mart, Starbucks, and McDonald's haven't found their way here.

The *pueblo* of Santa Fe is hardly the worst part of Mexico City. There is a lot of competition for that distinction, but it would probably go to Colonia Presa Sección Hornos, also built in a ravine. The residents of that neighborhood have to evacuate their shacks nearly every year during the rainy season, for fear that they will be washed away. Others live above a mine, hastily covered over, and worry that the earth might shift and they'll fall in.

Mexico City is not Calcutta, Maputo, or Ulaanbaatar. The residents of the *pueblo* of Santa Fe all have running water, electricity, and garbage collection, however irregular. Mexico City isn't so much loaded with poor as it is brimming with people slowly struggling to scratch their way out of poverty. The improvised and informal nature of the community is emblematic of the way a megalopolis functions. Most people in Mexico City—indeed, most people in the world—live in a place much like it.

Getting Around

A traffic jam at an intersection of four-lane boulevards. Cars nose their way forward insistently, an inch at a time, amid a chorus of honks. Hordes of people who have autos in Mexico City spend hours a day like this, crawling from one place to another. If we count only waking moments, quite a few pass more time in transit than in their homes. The vehicle in which they crawl along in the sweaty traffic is almost an extension of their dwelling—their attic, their spare room, their pied-à-terre.

Even if you're the only one in the car, in traffic you're never alone. A galaxy of characters makes its place of business at every stoplight. Four guys in ratty T-shirts and dusty baseball caps, their expressions blurred by the glue they've sniffed, carry transparent bottles of murky liquid in one hand and filthy rags in the other. No matter how elaborately you beseech them not to touch your windshield—shaking your head no, waving your arms back and forth, even shouting at the top of your lungs—most of them become momentarily deaf and blind, and cannot be deterred from "washing" your windows, defying you not to give them a couple of pesos for their trouble when they're done. Or one peso. Or half a peso. Or nothing, and it's on to the next car.

Apart from the window cleaners, maybe a couple of children perform lackluster cartwheels and then rise, their palms extended toward
the drivers. Or a María, a woman in peasant dress, frequently nurs-
ing a baby at her exposed breast, may juggle two balls with her free
hand, an impassive cast to her face. Or you may see a skinny adolescent, who removes his shirt so you can admire each of his ribs, lies on
the ground and rubs his back along shards of glass. The sign he carries mentions that he is not a delinquent and he doesn't commit crimes
for money, implying a veiled threat and your moral obligation to support him. In the 1980s there were a lot of fire eaters, but the brain
damage from the accumulation of swallowed chemicals deterred future generations from this career.

Then there are the entrepreneurs: men and women with boxes
strapped to their shoulders, displaying an attractive jumble of chewing gum, candy bars, key chains, and cigarettes, sold in packs or one
at a time. Others sell alarm clocks, windshield protectors, home-
baked cookies, a set of steak knives. One man—who stands out in
his impeccable blazer, necktie, and wire-rimmed glasses, every gray
hair in place—sells books that instruct readers how to improve their
handwriting.

The last study about how long it takes *chilangos* to get where they
are going was published in 1993, when the average trip lasted sixty-
two minutes. We can infer that it takes much longer now, because
the number of cars in Mexico City has nearly doubled since then,
to about four million. Another million or so tool in every day from
Mexico State. It doesn't matter who you are, how much money you've
got, what your social status is, or how pretty your face. In Mexico
City you will never be exempt from frustrating, nerve-racking, infu-
riating traffic and transit problems.

A *capitalino*'s form of transportation is a clear sign of social class, but not only the wealthy own cars. Although it is difficult to get a home mortgage, and almost impossible for a small business to get a loan, banks and credit agencies make car loans with comparative ease. In well-to-do neighborhoods, where individuals may own two or three cars, there are a staggering number of Mercedeses, BMWs, and Mini Coopers; more annoyingly, SUVs are also on the rise. In less privileged parts of the city, people drive decaying Fords and Chevys held together with Band-Aids and dental floss. The drivers of these cars are mostly brown-skinned, while the drivers of expensive models are almost always white.

In late 2007, Ricardo Salinas Pliego, one of Mexico's most important industrialists, in partnership with a Chinese manufacturer, broke ground on a new plant that will construct and sell cars set to cost between sixty-five hundred and ten thousand dollars apiece. It was announced that *chilangos* will be able to buy them at installments of a hundred dollars a month.

In Mexico City a driver's license costs a little less than forty dollars. To obtain one you stand in line and pay; there are no pesky written or road tests to slow a driver down. Despite their lack of formal education, *chilangos* tend to be proud of their driving skills. They point out how fast their reflexes are, which is critical, given that drivers overtake each other from both the right and the left, without troubling to use their turn signals. (In fact, if someone turns his blinkers on, other drivers take it as a signal to speed up and detain his passage.)

A sign that forbids a turn is interpreted as permission to perform that exact maneuver. *Chilangos* regularly ignore stop signs and red lights. They double- and sometimes triple-park, even during rush-hour traffic. To avoid getting caught by the police going the wrong way down a one-way street, they will drive in reverse for two or three blocks. They talk on cell phones while they drive, occasionally with a baby in their lap and a half-eaten sandwich in the other hand. Seven people per day, or about twenty-five hundred per year, die in traffic accidents.

Except at large intersections, there are few traffic lights. Pedestrians are seen as the equivalent of flies, pesky nuisances that you have to get around: the enemy. Waiting until they cross the street is unthinkable; the only way for a walker to get to the other side is *a lo macho*—balls up.

The public transportation system is underfunded, and during rush hours it is so crowded that its inadequacy is most evident. "Middle-class" people—say, those earning between fifteen hundred and twenty-five hundred per month—don't like to ride public transportation at all. They will do anything to get around in a car, even if they have to go into hock to buy and maintain one. I have heard several describe riding the underground metro as a "humiliating" experience. The complainers are invariably white, and their grievance is class-based, implying the fact that they have other options. Having a car separates them from the huge mass of brown people who can't afford one.

Still, as high-status as a car may be, owning one doesn't get you anywhere more quickly during rush hour. The impeccably clean metro, at only twenty cents per ride, is the cheapest and fastest way to get around. Four million people ride it each day. The metro is subsidized by the government, which periodically threatens to raise the price as high as sixty-five cents, although the low fare has held steady for more than a decade.

The metro has some major problems. For one thing, the city has grown much faster than the subway system, so it's far from comprehensive. Moreover, at rush hour you feel as if all the four million are in the same car with you. Cars usually have no ventilation, so when you exit you might feel as if you've been to a sauna.

In the metro, women have to be on constant alert. During rush hour, it is not uncommon for men to cop a feel. I have heard three separate stories of women whose backs were the recipients of the ejaculate of guys who masturbated while riding. During rush hour, as in Tokyo, a couple of cars in each train are restricted to women and children passengers. In early 2008, buses that allow only women on board began to circulate on three routes as well.

If you're lucky enough not to have to travel during rush hour, the metro is a much less fraught, if not precisely tranquil, experience. On any given ride, you can watch women putting on eyeliner, guys grooving to their Walkmen, a long-nailed beauty meticulously peeling an orange before eating it, lovers in a tender clinch. It was once a form of status for riders to wear T-shirts emblazoned with the legends of the Dallas Cowboys, John Deere, or the University of Texas, but these became terribly common. The current trend is to wear shirts with English-language maxims such as, "Trust me, I'm a doctor," "From 0 to nasty in 7.5 seconds," "Born free but now I'm really expensive," or "My therapist says it's all your fault." I have often wondered whether the people who wear them understand what they are saying.

Musicians—a fellow playing "The Sounds of Silence" on an Andean flute, an ancient singing ballads on a decrepit guitar—keep riders amused. Blind and lame beggars cry for alms. An endless procession of *vagoneros*—the metro's fleet of enterprising salespeople—offer CDs, videos, candy, calendars, pens, batteries, and coloring books.

The minibus—known in Mexico City as a *combi* or a *pesero*—is the principal public conveyance. The Department of Transportation registers nearly ten million rides a day on *peseros,* although this includes people who use them more than once daily. They have only two designated stops, the first and the last. Anywhere else along the route, the driver will come to a halt wherever someone has stuck his hand out. The result is a chaos of stalled traffic.

The majority of *peseros* are at least fifteen years old. Most are built for Mexicans; at a little over five feet nine inches, I am too tall to stand up inside them. The drivers often blast their radios as they hurtle down the boulevards. During rush hour they are crowded to the point of asphyxiation, and even off-peak there are usually no seats.

In 2005, a new system of transportation replaced the *peseros* on Avenida Insurgentes, one of Mexico City's most important boulevards. A cross between a bus and a trolley, the Metrobús, with its designated stops, is a lot faster than the *peseros* were. However, it's only a Band-Aid on a hemorrhage; the rest of the city continues to choke in traffic. In the last months of 2007, they had only begun to construct a second Metrobús route.

Compared to cities in the United States and Europe, street taxis are abundant, cheap, and almost never a problem to find, with the particular exception of Mother's Day. However, during a crime wave that began in the mid-1990s, they became a frequent place of business for robbers and kidnappers, which put a damper on some passengers' willingness to climb aboard.

Before getting in a Mexico City street taxi, one is cautioned that it is best to go through an elaborate pantomime. First you're supposed to check that it bears legitimate taxi license plates, which begin with the letter L, S, or A. (Some taxis bear ordinary, nonprofessional plates, out-of-state plates, or once in a while no plates at all.) Then you're meant to confirm that the number on the license plates matches the number painted on the side of the cab. If somehow your suspicions are still aroused, you check that the driver has displayed his *tarjetón,* an official permit to drive a cab. If you're still not sure, you check that the man in the photo on the *tarjetón* is the same as the one at the wheel.

The most cynical taxi drivers have pointed out to me that this intricate rigamarole is no guarantee against an assault. Others try to evoke sympathy by explaining that they are also frequent crime victims. One told me about a young woman, dressed in the plaid skirt and sweater uniform of a high school girl, who got into his cab, removed a gun from her backpack, and robbed him. If all of this is too daunting, there are many radio cabs and official taxi stands. They're more costly but surely safer.

While on the subject of safety, to protect themselves, taxi drivers tend to hang rosaries and emblems of the Virgin of Guadalupe over the rearview mirrors. They will often cross themselves when they pass churches, sometimes two or three times in quick succession. But they rarely fasten their seat belts, which they perceive as curious but useless appendages, like tonsils. Many have expressed their fears that, were their seat belts in place, a mugger could try to strangle them with the implement, while the skeptics have expressed doubt over whether they actually do any good in a crash.

Once he approaches a destination, a taxi driver's preferred method of finding a particular street is to go around in circles with his window rolled down and ask people: *¿Oye, la Calle de Arenal?* This can easily add fifteen minutes or a half hour to the ride, while the meter ticks. Like Michelin's Paris Plan or London's A to Z, there is a street map in book form with over 150 pages called the *Guía Roji.* But as there isn't much of a map culture in Mexico City, it's useless to most drivers. From time to time I bring it with me when I take a taxi to an unfamiliar neighborhood. While going around in circles, the driver will ask to see the map six or seven times. He will look at it straight on, upside down, and sideways, meanwhile rolling down the window and asking people if they know the street where we are going. If no one answers affirmatively, he will ask to see the map again.

In the company headquarters of the *Guía Roji,* there's a store that sells its various products at retail. Agustín Palacios Roji, the publisher, told me that most people who shop there are foreigners.

Lucha

The stadium, in near darkness, reeks of stale beer, sweat, and dust. Early arrivals demonstrate their restlessness with bells, horns, whistles, rattles. Vendors patrol the aisles, trying to unload beer, potato chips, *cuerito* (boiled, pickled pork skin in plastic cups), colorful masks that cover your entire head, photographs of the most popular *luchadores*.

Wrestling matches are one of the few events that begin on time in Mexico City, and as the announcer calls out names of the first fighters—invariably escorted into the ring by knockouts in shiny bikinis—the crowd begins to roar. The people in the front rows, who pay as much as fifty dollars a ticket, scream at the top of their voices, but those up in the cheap seats (four to eight dollars) compete not only with lung power but with the aforementioned noisemakers. If they are not getting enough attention, they might toss the contents of a bottle of water down on those who have a higher budget for their tickets.

The polemic about the *lucha libre* being staged is irrelevant. When you buy your ticket, you are going to the theater. If every headlock, hold, tumble, and somersault has been rehearsed, the actors are admirably strong, flexible, and limber, and their likelihood of being injured while performing is ominous. Indeed, part of what draws *chilangos* to wrestling matches each Tuesday, Friday, and Sunday is the possibility of an accident happening—a snapped wrist, a broken leg, a bloodied skull.

Until recently, the theater of the *luchas* was mostly played for laughs. A wrestling match in Mexico City was more akin to the slapstick ballet of the Keystone Kops than to the steroid-enhanced testosterone displays of the WWF. As agile as they may have been, the bodies of Mexican wrestlers tended toward spindly legs, potbellies, and flat asses. However, the younger generation, perhaps inspired by their U.S. counterparts, is made up of gym rats, with physiques closer to the classic Greek mold.

Everyone is part of the act. Not just the wrestlers, the bikini-clad card girls, and the beer and popcorn vendors (who often whistle and catcall during the matches). The photographers who run around the ring have to be as acrobatic as the *luchadores,* particularly when dodging the athletes who are flung through the ropes by their colleagues, or when the more emotional fans stampede toward the ring.

The audience members scream so loudly that it is as if they believe the more noise they make, the more anointed they will become as part of the show. Watching the crowd—entire shrieking families, the musclebound stud with the hopelessly bored girlfriend, the toothless grandmother who gets so carried away that she drops the cross-eyed baby—is often more fascinating than the spectacle of the matches.

You may even be called upon to play a role. A man from California told me that one night he accompanied a *gringa*—a tall, buxom blonde—to the *luchas*. She was approached by an assistant to one of the wrestlers, who offered her money to walk down the aisle with the athlete and pose as the girlfriend he had picked up while wrestling in the United States.

Wrestlers are either *rudos* (tough guys) or *técnicos* (good guys, literally "technicians"). Sometimes it is hard to tell one from the other. In both camps they may wear masks that disguise their heads, or else show their faces. Some have hair to their shoulders, while others sport crew cuts. Nor are there discernible differences in their fighting styles, although the *rudos* tend to gangbang the *técnicos* three against one more than vice versa. Audiences are sharply divided, although in general those in the expensive seats cheer the *técnicos* and hiss or scream at the *rudos,* while the cheering section of the nosebleed seats runs in the opposite direction.

Half of the complexes of the Mexican character described by Octavio Paz in *The Labyrinth of Solitude* are evident at a wrestling match. The most obvious is in those masks—solid or striped, shiny or matte, black, white, or neon colors. That so many wrestlers wear them reflects the poet's insistence that a Mexican hides his true nature behind one disguise or another: bravado, machismo, servility, irony, sincerity, and so on. Even the wrestlers who don't wear masks are playing roles, as evidenced by the names they choose for their characters: Mephisto, Bismarck, Aztec Blood, the Mystic, and so forth.

Paz also says that Mexican men can see themselves in only one of two roles: dominator or dominated. Either you're the guy who humiliates, punishes, and offends, or else you're the luckless bastard on the business end of those verbs. Combine this with his observation that sexuality is seen as an emotionally closed male's violent splitting open of a female (or in some instances same-sex) other. Often in the ring, one or two wrestlers will splay open the legs of another, so a teammate can simulate the violation of the injured party's most intimate anatomy.

The wrestler's mask hides the possibilities of sensitivity or femininity, that one of the actors might be something other than a macho brute. During matches, many wrestlers make a show of trying to tear off another's mask, and among the most highly staked battles are those in which the outcome is the ritual unmasking or hair-shearing of the loser. Thus he will be exposed as the shameful (read: feminine) individual he is rather than the glorious character he plays.

The audience members who scream loudest, most consistently, and most brutally at the wrestlers—using the most vulgar and vicious slang, such as *pinche puto* (equivalent to "fucking faggot"), *culero* (a word for "coward" with a degrading reference to the behind), or *pendejo* (asshole)—are always women, while their male counterparts sit beside them approvingly. The women may be venting their rage at a *machista* culture, but at the same time they perpetuate it, as can be seen by the way their children obediently ape them.

Given the sexual ambiguity inherent in the spectacle of the *lucha libre,* one of the most noteworthy characters to emerge from its ranks in recent years is a fellow known as Máximo, who has been wrestling for the past four of his twenty-six years. He sports a pink Mohawk, abbreviated and brightly colored costumes that look stolen from the deepest recesses of Fred Flintstone's wardrobe, and a vocabulary of mannerisms that are distinctly and exaggeratedly effeminate. When he gets down to brass tacks, the buff Máximo is a tough customer, but his entire act is the simulation of a screaming queen.

"Wrestling tends to be completely aggressive, all about strength," he said in the offices of the Arena México, the largest of Mexico City's two wrestling stadiums. "I like to give the crowd a little joy and laughter along with that."

It is perhaps not surprising that Máximo, whose real name is Cristián Alvarado Ruiz, chose a comic character for his wrestling persona. His father, an admirably nimble wrestler known as Porky, sports an absurdly rotund figure and is also one of the ring's comedians. The rude remarks he receives from the crowd don't bother Máximo. "I'm helping the audience vent their problems. If they scream, I know I've done them some good. If they were silent, I wouldn't be serving them," he said.

"I have four types of fans. The first are the gays who come by after the match and, in a respectful way, ask me out to lunch and say they want to get to know me. The second are the guys who are very tough and macho in appearance, but all the same, ask me out and say they want to know me. You sort of wonder about them, but in the end they make me laugh. Then there are the women who come up and ask me, 'Are you or aren't you? If you're not, I want to go out with you, and if you are, I want you to give me the chance to change you.' And then there are the people who yell at me and say I'm a fag, a queer, or a transvestite who doesn't belong in the wrestling world." He sums them up matter-of-factly: "I respect all of their ideologies."

Alvarado is in fact married, but his wife prefers not to see him work. "She tells me she'd rather wait for me at home, where I'll be the man she knows. If she sees me as Máximo, she might get confused and think of me as a girlfriend."

The theater of the *lucha libre* is a long show. Usually there are five matches, which together last two and a half hours. By the end, after so much shrieking, the audience has achieved its classical Greek catharsis. As it slowly filters out onto the street, the collective beast has been calmed.

La Penúltima Copa

The clock behind the bar at El Nivel, the oldest cantina in Mexico City, runs backward, an apt metaphor for the spiritual condition of two of its clients on a recent Friday afternoon. Fiftyish, rumpled, crooked smiles on their faces, they sat with their arms around each other's shoulders, not only as a gesture of solidarity, but to keep from falling to the floor. There were more than a dozen empty glasses on the table. One said to the other, in a voice loud enough to be heard through most of the cantina:

"Seas Domínguez
O no me chingues
Estás pedo"

This is specific, vulgar Mexico City slang. A literal translation would make no sense, but the gist of the remark was that his friend was exceptionally drunk.

The friend removed his arm from the first man's shoulder, dismissed him with a wave, and rose to go to the restroom. As he stood, most of the cantina's patrons scrutinized him with morbid curiosity, to see if he would actually arrive at his destination.

Miraculously, he made his way in a more or less straight line. Yet just before he got to the toilet, he tottered and suddenly dropped to the floor, like an elevator cut from its cables. A white-jacketed waiter pulled him to a standing position and escorted him back to his seat, where he would continue to serve him drinks.

In Mexico City, people drink exuberantly, enthusiastically, passionately—anything but prudently. After a cantina closes, it is not uncommon to see one of its blasted patrons at the closest street corner in an embrace with a lamppost to keep from falling to the sidewalk. A Mexican never orders *la última copa*—the last drink—because that's the one you toss off before you die. Therefore, it's considered more prudent, no matter how late or how many you've already consumed, to order *la penúltima*.

Mexico City is a magnificent place to experience the illicit pleasure of drinking in the afternoon. Most *chilangos* do their drinking in cantinas, which tend to draw their biggest crowds in the traditional Mexican lunch hour between two and five o'clock. Lunch in a cantina will most likely be a drawn-out affair, and it's advisable not to have to go back to work in the afternoon. On Fridays, many patrons tend to stay until they are thrown out. Most cantinas shut their doors by ten o'clock, with only a handful staying open until midnight or later.

Although they are mostly no-frills establishments, lit by fluorescent bulbs, with mounds of cigarette butts on the floor, Mexico City cantinas have as much personality as London pubs, Paris cafés, or New York bars. In a far from egalitarian city, they are the most democratic institutions. Anyone who can afford the price of a drink—which limits the population drastically—is welcome.

The best attract a heterogeneous crowd: bureaucrats in polyester, alone or accompanied by extravagantly made-up women who are clearly not their wives. Guys with thick mustaches and muddy boots, who appear to have just gotten off a turnip truck from Sonora. Smooching couples. Art students and ponytailed hippies, wearing nose rings and huaraches, their belly buttons exposed and sporting elaborate tattoos. Middle-aged boulevardiers in shiny antique suits. Guys with crew cuts who could be drug dealers, federal police, or perhaps both. An evident minority of foreigners, teachers, journalists. On Saturday afternoons, some cantinas even attract entire families, including toddlers and grandparents.

Cantinas have history—El Nivel got its license in 1872. They have tradition—Mexicans are used to drinking in them, while European or American style bars are less common, and usually located off hotel lobbies. There is also entertainment, in the form of itinerant musicians, whose talent varies wildly.

At Tío Pepe, decrepit troubadours play guitars and sing for the customers, who are mostly middle-aged men in suits and ties getting progressively smashed. One afternoon at Tío Pepe I saw a dwarf with a straw hat and a sparse beard who sat on a high stool and sang incantations of passionate love in the nasal tremolo of a Munchkin. He turned out to be Margarito, a former film comedian whose career would soon be resuscitated on a television program.

An angelic *trío romántico* graces the Bar Montejo some nights, each member playing a different type of guitar, adroitly crowding notes into each bar of music, and executing complex vocal harmonies. At La Única de Guerrero, an elegant band of four musicians entertains; this group, which includes a zither, a lyrical violin, and a passionate *bandoneón,* is equally comfortable with a Rossini aria as a Mexican bolero from the 1940s.

My favorite cantina performer was Carlos Andrade, known as

Carlitos to the patrons of the three down-at-the-heels bars where he performed in the Colonia Tabacalera. When I first met him, he was well into his seventies and wore an impeccable tweed jacket with a contrasting wool vest, a dark necktie, and a felt hat with a feather in the band. Yet his dilapidated guitar was held together with brown masking tape and his fingers were bent with arthritis. All the same, he played with remarkable skill and emotion; his voice, while no longer strong, was sweet, sad, and fervently hoarse.

In the 1960s, Carlitos had played the *requinto,* a small, high-pitched guitar, as a member of a trio known as Los Soberanos which, if not among the top two or three groups of its type, had enjoyed its share of renown. Although he preferred not to dwell on the past, he would, when pressed, talk about performing in elegant nightclubs and private parties before movie stars, magnates, and high society. Los Soberanos had been to Las Vegas and worked for ten days at the Frontier Hotel. They were so popular that the manager tried to extend their engagement, but Charlton Heston—at the time head of the performers' guilds—wouldn't allow them to stay on. "We hadn't been residents in the U.S. for three months," Carlitos said, a plaintive gaze in his tired eyes. "Who knows, I might have had a career in Hollywood."

The last time I saw Carlitos was early in 2004. On the cusp of his eightieth birthday, he told me he planned to work one more year and then stop. "All I want is to relax," he said. "I want a couple of more years, and that's it. Old people get in the way."

Perhaps what best distinguishes cantinas from bars in other cities is that they are great places to eat, free with the price of drinks. No city I know is as generous to its drinkers as the D.F. During the afternoon hours, from two o'clock on, one is rewarded with *botanas,* food cooked on the premises. While each portion is not huge, there are frequently five or more different items available to anyone who keeps drinking. The abundance, variety, and quality of the offerings can be overwhelming. For example, at La Mascota on Calle Bolívar (where an annoying waiter insistently tries to raffle off bottles of cheap rum and domino sets) there are always six or seven dishes available— *pancita* (a spicy tripe soup), *carnitas,* chicken in green sauce, meatballs in chipotle, and so on. The waiter will keep them coming until you cry uncle.

This is a ploy to keep you in one cantina rather than going off on a crawl to several. At La Valenciana, a sad-faced waiter named Miguel, like a Jewish mother, will admonish his clients for not eating enough. Waiters sometimes display indignation if they believe one hasn't shown sufficient attention or respect to their establishments. During two and a half hours at a cantina called La Auténtica, a companion and I between us consumed—apart from an avalanche of tequila and beer—cream of chile soup, beef broth, steak tartare, chiles stuffed with cheese, and an enormous pork shank that, once picked clean of its meat, appeared to be a lost dinosaur bone. After coffee, I asked for the check. The waiter, a wounded expression on his face, asked, "So soon?"

Women are welcome in cantinas, although they only have been since 1983, when legislation was passed. (That it took so long is sadly unsurprising—Mexico did not allow women to vote until 1947. This was only at the municipal level; they couldn't vote for presidents, or stand for elections, until 1953.) To this day, a woman alone will invariably get hassled by drunken men in a cantina. If she comes with a girlfriend, they might be approached but less insistently. Typical of a *machista* culture, if she is accompanied by a man, other men will leave her alone.

———

In the novels *Queer* and *Junky* by William Burroughs, and in the Mexican section of Luis Buñuel's memoir *My Last Sigh,* the Mexico City of the 1950s is immortalized as a place where every man carried a gun, and in a cantina you were likely to see one fired, if not get shot yourself, before topping off your first drink. (Of course it is crucial to note that during his stay here, Burroughs was loaded on a combination of heroin, opium, marijuana, handfuls of amphetamines, or, when choicer drugs were scarce, antihistamines—all knocked back with double tequilas. He also murdered his wife here, supposedly by accident, while playing a game of William Tell. Meanwhile, Buñuel was famous for being the king of surrealism.) If it is indisputable that Mexicans have a reputation for violence when drunk, I have never seen anything approaching a fight in a cantina.

However, I once saw a man pass a pistol to his friend under a table. Another time, a solitary drunk, nearly asleep at his table, got up to go to the restroom and fell flat on his face. He broke his nose, leaving an awesome islet of blood on the floor. One waiter cleaned the mess while another helped the man wash his face in the restroom. He returned to the table, sat, and ordered another drink. (Customers don't tend to get cut off in a cantina, no matter how drunk. You would have to commit a serious crime before most bartenders or waiters denied you service, and even that might not be sufficient provocation.)

One Friday evening, at a cantina whose clientele is mainly well-dressed, well-behaved professionals in suits, two men were drinking in their shirtsleeves, their ties loosened. They had most likely been there the entire afternoon. Suddenly, one grabbed the metal napkin dispenser from the table and used it to bash his friend in the forehead. The friend bled profusely and somehow managed to spill his blood along the table, across the floor, and even on the white-tiled wall; it looked like a scene from *The Texas Chainsaw Massacre*. Yet the wounded victim only smiled; within minutes he and his friend were laughing together, their arms around each other's shoulders.

Pulquerías—bars that dispense *pulque,* a drink made from fermented but undistilled cactus, said to have been favored by the Aztecs in their heyday—are no-man's-lands, twilight zones, locales where life goes by in slow motion. Watching the customers, conceptions of what time it is, what day, or what galaxy can easily morph into abstractions.

Pulque has a foamy viscous texture somewhere between spit and sperm. The plain version is as sour as buttermilk, but *pulque* is also offered with a variety of added flavors—seasonal tropical fruits, celery, tomato, oatmeal, or almond, always enhanced with sugar. It is the cheapest alcoholic beverage. An entire pitcher of the unflavored variety costs about a dollar, and a large glass of the most expensive, flavored with pine nuts, will run a little more than two dollars. Hence, it is the favored tipple among the underemployed and other cash-strapped sectors of the city.

Pulque is a heavy drink; I have never been able to put away more than a couple of glasses. Hence, I have no idea what it is like to become intoxicated from *pulque,* although I have spent hours in *pulquerías,* watching with fascination. *Pulque* drinkers tend to be over fifty. If they are younger, they are sufficiently pummeled by life as to appear much older. They will have nicknames, such as Speedy (for the guy who moves with excruciating slowness) or Tremendous (for the fellow a couple of inches taller than a child).

After *pulque* drinkers have consumed a pitcher or two, confusion reigns. As I arrived on my last visit to a decrepit *pulquería* called El 60 Colorado near the Mercado Merced, an old man was complaining to the bartender that his glass had disappeared. "It was right here," he whined, "right next to me. And it's not there anymore. Well, it doesn't matter. I'll pay for it, anyway." His companion said, "God will pay."

The bartender had a more pressing problem: another customer smiling ear to ear who, after finishing off his drinks, confessed that he had no money. "What do you mean?" the bartender asked, with the face of a long-suffering martyr. "You drank thirteen glasses."

In the better class of *pulquería,* women drink alongside men, but to this day, they're still prohibited in some. Those that deny them entrance will usually have a separate cubicle, perhaps four feet by four feet, where women can drink among themselves. This is due to custom more than sexism; there may be a metal trough in the middle of the establishment where the customers urinate—with no doors or other private paneling.

In 1980 there were fifteen hundred *pulquerías* in Mexico City, but ten years later the number had dwindled to five hundred. Today there are fewer than one hundred. The last time I was in the neighborhood, El 60 Colorado had disappeared without a trace. In the old days, you could get nothing but *pulque* in a *pulquería,* but in recent years some came up with the idea of serving beer as well. With greater options, a few *pulquerías* have become popular among a clientele with a tiny bit more disposable income, particularly students, protecting their survival at least for a little while longer.

At the turn of the twenty-first century, some hip cocktail bars opened in the city's most cosmopolitan neighborhoods, and many younger customers, wishing not to drink in the same venues as their grandfathers, began to disdain cantinas. The new bars are noted for extravagant decoration. A place called Cibeles, for instance, could easily be mistaken for a furniture store featuring kitsch living room sets from the 1960s. There are a dozen separate areas—Danish modern, stuffed yellow sofas inherited from someone's grandmother, even a set covered in heavy plastic. A bar in Polanco called El Revés (Backwards) was painted black and gold and had entire rooms of furniture affixed to the ceiling. (It was closed down by authorities for lack of appropriate licensing.) In recent years Irish pubs with names like Celtics, St. Patrick's, Biddy Mulligan's, and the Dubliner have also multiplied.

There are more sophisticated alternatives: the rooftop terraces of the hotels Hábita and Condesa DF, and the Zinco, a jazz bar with exposed brick painted black, low lights, and a red velvet curtain. It was clearly designed by an aficionado of movies about jazz musicians from the 1950s, and was a welcome addition—in a city of twenty million, there are less than a half-dozen venues to listen to jazz on a regular basis.

While the new generation of bars is similar to places that can be found in other cities, Mexico City cantinas are unlike those of any other place I know. When I first came to Mexico City, what I liked most about cantinas was that I was never alone in them. All I had to do was belly up to the bar, order a drink in halting Spanish, and in a few minutes comrades would emerge, usually in some stage of inebriation, inviting me into a game of dominoes or for a lecture on Mexican history and manners.

Even when I only understood half of what my hosts were saying, we always reached some kind of fraternal concord. Frequently they would give me *recuerdos* (souvenirs): an old coin, a key chain, or an amulet.

On the last night of one of my first trips to Mexico City, before I lived here, I was melancholy about leaving and decided to salve my sorrow in a cantina located in an obscure side street of the Colonia Escandón. For five minutes I watched a jabbering drunk make life miserable for the waiter and the barman—who received him with stoic grace, ignoring his insults and planting him in a chair every time he stood and threatened to fall on his face. They continued, however, to serve him.

I was approached by a man who looked like Groucho Marx in his waning years. He invited me to join him and his friends for a drink. His name was Carlos and he had two companions: bald-headed, green-eyed Pancho, also Carlos's age and well on his way to a pickled oblivion, and Samuel, a man in his forties with a ruminative air. Samuel immediately began to talk about jai alai, at the time a popular sport in Mexico. He told me that as a young man he had been a player, but an accident had cut his career short. I asked him what he did now.

"I'm a psychologist," he said.

"Do many people go to psychologists in Mexico City?" I asked, explaining that in New York it was practically as common as brushing your teeth.

"These days, yes," said Samuel. "I have many clients. Mexico City is a good location for a psychologist because it's a factory for crazy people."

Carlos then asked me if I would bring him back to New York. "I'm an old man," he said. "Let me spend my last days there with you."

I tried to discourage him. New York, I explained, was hardly as glamorous as it appeared in the movies. Although it was possible to earn a lot of money, it was unbelievably expensive. There was great tension and it wasn't particularly friendly.

None of this deterred the old man. "Hear me out," he said.

I explained that I lived in a one-room apartment. He again went into his song and dance about wanting to spend his last days in New York. "Hear me out," he repeated.

I told him that Mexico City seemed more relaxed than New York, but this provoked a string of curses about what a rotten place it had become. "Hear me out . . ." Finally, my compulsion to tell the truth was eclipsed by an urgent desire to shut him up, so I told him I'd take him to New York.

His face illuminated as if from an inner current. *"¿Hecho?"* he asked. I wasn't shitting him?

"Hecho."

"¿Por Dios?" Swear to God?

"Por Dios."

He took my hand and placed his forehead on it, as if I were the village priest, if not the pope. This gesture deepened my sense of guilt for lying to him. Later, I found that pledging to take Carlos to New York merely constituted a standard cantina custom called *una promesa de copas*—a drunken promise.

Immediately the old man began to crow obnoxiously about his impending trip. His bald friend Pancho, as if waking from a dream, turned to Samuel and asked, "Do you remember when we died?"

Carlos took off his necktie—an object Samuel dated from the Stone Age—and gave it to me.

At this point, a sinewy man with a mustache staggered to our table and asked if we would let him buy us a round of drinks. We accepted and invited him to sit with us. He drank a shot of tequila in one gulp.

This man, who called himself Héctor, was boisterous. He stole Carlos's eyeglasses, which prompted the old man to employ a series of variations on the Mexican insult *chingar* and threaten to kick Héctor in the balls. The glasses were returned, but Carlos had made such a racket that the management threatened to throw him out (per-haps another *promesa de copas*). Héctor, sitting across the table, gave me a seething look.

"He likes to fight," whispered Samuel. "But don't worry. I like to fight, too. I will protect you." He took my hand and demonstrated the firm grip he'd developed as a jai alai player.

Héctor continued to stare at me with chilly eyes. I wondered if a conflict would indeed emerge. To my surprise, he removed his wrist-watch and gave it to me.

Even by the generous standard of cantinas, this seemed like an extravagant gift. I began to make a speech about how beautiful an object it was, but really I couldn't accept it.

"Take it," Samuel said.

"*Muchísimas gracias,*" I said.

I felt better when, a moment later, Héctor produced another watch from his pocket and unemphatically dropped it into a glass of soda water. This gesture seemed so defiant, impertinent, and baroquely inexplicable that I took off my own watch and gave it to him. Soon after, it undoubtedly found itself marinated in one fluid or another.

Before I left, Samuel gave me a note which, to my surprise, was written in English. It said:

When you remember this night
you will think about this life.
Its night or is the life.
Do you understand?

Paty

The Villa Rica is a low-lit bar with amber lighting, wood-paneled walls, and a jukebox that doesn't have a single song recorded after 1980. It is an example of what are known as *antros de ficheras,* and I have never seen them outside of Mexico City.

A *fichera* is a woman who, despite what is usually a boiler-shaped body, dresses in a short skirt and a snug blouse, and sells her company to a male clientele. Most of a *fichera*'s clients are after nothing more than her sympathetic presence: a woman he can flirt with who will not rebuff his advances; a woman to whom he can recount the various misadventures and misunderstandings of his life; a woman with whom he can dance to the familiar ballads on the jukebox. *Ficheras* earn no salary, but are given tips as well as a percentage of the price of the drinks the customers order for them; hence, most have cast-iron constitutions and, as they say in Mexico City, *toman como cosacos* (drink like Cossacks).

Some *ficheras* are game for further adventures; if the customer pays an exit fee to the management, she will accompany him to a nearby hotel. Still, most customers prefer companionship; *ficheras* are closer to geishas than to prostitutes.

Many men like to visit *ficheras* when they are feeling low. Mexican males, the weight of machismo on their shoulders, are emotionally diffident and cannot express their feelings to the people with whom they are supposedly intimate; a *fichera* is a convenient receptacle for their sorrows and shames. There is a particular *fichera* at the Villa Rica named Paty whom I like to visit, but not to recount my anguish. Like Scheherazade, Paty has a thousand and one stories, and listening to her invariably makes whatever troubles I may have recede in the rearview mirror.

Paty wears enormous eyelashes and thick makeup, changes her hair color on a regular basis, and flaunts her enormous breasts with low-cut blouses. About five feet tall, she tends to sport nine-inch heels. Her smile is wide, perpetual, and, as far as I can tell, genuine. She has been working at the Villa Rica since 1985, her *anno horribilis*, when not only did the earthquake leave her and her family homeless, but her husband was diagnosed with multiple sclerosis (a disease she refers to as "European"). Her salary as a waitress in the coffee shop at Sanborn's wasn't enough to sustain them and her two children, so she began her career as a *fichera*.

One of Paty's regular clients is an ancient Spaniard who owns the Hotel Toledo down the street where the *ficheras* take their customers. He only likes to watch—Paty assures me he hasn't had an erection in the twenty years she has known him—so he takes her to swingers' clubs, where men are not allowed to enter unaccompanied by women.

"But he makes me take off my clothes, and in those places if you're naked, you have to let anyone do what they want. You can't say no. Even when you have your clothes on, they still get handsy with you— with their fingers and everything." She made a face like she had sipped spoiled milk. "Having sex is better because at least they've got a condom on. That guy's fingers . . ." She uses the Mexican's universal expletive for disgust: "*Guácala*. I couldn't sleep that night."

Another man, who always dressed in a suit and tie, would take her to a four-star hotel. Before entering, he would buy a bunch of roses on the corner. He would ask Paty to strip and eat the rose petals. "And that was that. He never got naked; he always kept his boxers on. He'd let me have whatever I wanted from the minibar and would pay me more than three times the going rate."

After losing the 2006 presidential elections, Andrés Manuel López Obrador (who had resigned his post as mayor of Mexico City to launch his campaign) arranged mass demonstrations on Avenida Juárez and Paseo de la Reforma, the two biggest streets near the Villa Rica. Getting around that part of the city became close to impossible, and nearly all the bar's customers disappeared. Paty, who usually earns about forty-five dollars a night, was coming home with less than ten. "The other night a guy came and bought me forty tequilas," she said one night while the protests were in full swing. Not knowing when the next time a big spender would arrive, she drank them all. "After all that, I vomited through my nose, but at least I made some money."

Paty didn't blame López Obrador for her hard luck. "It's God's will," she said. "In the Bible you've got the years of the fat cows and the years of the skinny cows. Right now it's skinny time. God squeezes us, but he doesn't strangle us." She put her hand on my thigh. "You want to go to the Señorial steam baths? They remodeled them. You don't know how beautiful they came out. We can go to a private room. They have cable TV with a porno channel."

Two-for-One at the Pyramid of the Sun

When we arrived at the great marketplace, called Tlatelolco, we were astounded at the number of people and the quantity of merchandise it contained, and at the good order and control that was maintained, for we had never seen such a thing before. . . . Each kind of merchandise was kept by itself and had its fixed place marked out. Let us begin with the dealers in gold, silver, and precious stones, feathers, mantles, and embroidered goods. . . . Next there were other traders who sold great pieces of cloth and cotton, and articles of twisted thread, and there were *cacahuateros* who sold cacao. There were those who sold cloths of henequen and ropes and the sandals with which they are shod, which are made from the same plant, and sweet cooked roots, and other tubers which they get from this plant, all were kept in one part of the market in the place assigned to them. In another part there were skins of tigers and lions, of otters and jackals, of deer and other animals and badgers and mountain cats, some tanned and others untanned, and other classes of merchandise.

Let us go on and speak of those who sold beans and sage and other vegetables and herbs in another part, and to those who sold

fowls, cocks with wattles, rabbits, hares, deer, mallards, young
dogs, and other things of that sort in their part of the market, and
let us also mention the fruiterers, and the women who sold cooked
food, dough, and tripes in their part of the market; then every sort
of pottery made in a thousand forms from great water jugs to little
jugs, these also had a place to themselves; then those who sold
honey and honey paste and other dainties like nut paste, and those
who sold lumber, boards, cradles, beams, blocks, and benches, each
article by itself, and the vendors of ocote firewood, and other things
of a similar nature. But why do I waste so many words in recount-
ing what they sell in that great market? For I shall never finish if I
tell it all in detail. . . . I could wish that I had finished telling of all
the things which are sold there, but they are so numerous and of
such different quality and the great marketplace with its surrounding arcades was so crowded with people, that one would not have
been able to see it and inquire about it all in two days.

—BERNAL DÍAZ DE CASTILLO, *The True Story of
the Conquest of New Spain*

Even before it was called Mexico City, Tenochtitlán was a market
town, the Constantinople of North America. When the Spaniards
got here, they found the Aztecs buying and selling swag from as far
south as what would be Nicaragua and as far north as Baja California; anything that could be sold between the Pacific Ocean and the
Gulf of Mexico was also up for grabs.

Today, the educated class here is quick to criticize the United
States for its voracious consumer habits. At the same time, the Mexicans have been enthusiastic converts to the art of spending. This is a
city where people on the brink of poverty will go into hock to provide
an opulent wedding or a coming-out party for a daughter, with tacos,
tequila, and a mariachi band for the entire block to enjoy. Those

drawing high salaries will invite as many as a thousand people to their offspring's nuptials, and serve French wines and filet mignon.

The merchandise that *chilangos* exchange for their money may reveal the limits not only of their pocketbooks, but of how they imagine themselves. Yet where and how they buy reflects the infinitely improvised, ad-hoc nature of life in Mexico City. With globalization, the panorama of what is available has changed. Forms of shopping popular in the United States have invaded and their presence is expanding. Nonetheless, five hundred years after the conquest, a lot of people are buying and selling in the same way as before the Spaniards arrived.

In the beginning was the *tianguis*: the sprawling open-air markets described so vividly by the Spanish conquerors such as Bernal Díaz in the passage quoted above. They have never disappeared. Today virtually every neighborhood has its *tianguis,* also known as a "market on wheels"—a once-a-week event in which vendors are sanctioned to invade and occupy several streets, where they set up stalls with metal poles and wooden planks under pink plastic tarpaulins. Mostly they sell fresh fruits and vegetables, but there is also cooked food and all manner of *tchotchkes:* cookware, toys, clothes, blankets, and pirated CDs and DVDs. (If it is a worldwide phenomenon, Mexico has distinguished itself in the manufacture and sale of pirated goods. Along with China and Russia, it is annually mentioned in the list of the ten countries with the worst piracy problems.)

In the *tianguis* that is set up a few blocks from my apartment each Sunday, there are three lanes of stalls, and the customers walk in the limited space in between. By noon, when shoppers have arrived en masse, movement can be painstakingly slow. Among the clients, merchants without stands sinuously circulate on foot, displaying their wares from boxes strapped around their shoulders like cigarette girls. In this fashion, a man with a black beret and a gray beard sells Argentine empanadas. Another announces sticky candies called *muéganos* in a growly singsong, while another, with slick hair and a pencil mustache, offers heads of garlic, a few fresh herbs, boxes of toothpicks, and matches.

Like many of the *tianguis* merchants, the mustached man is not above seduction, blackmail, or guilt trips to induce people to buy his wares. He will begin by pointing out how large, round, and fresh his heads of garlic are on that particular Sunday. If you tell him you still have garlic that you bought from him the previous week, he'll say, "Don't punish me. Buy some for your mother-in-law." If you remind him that you are unmarried, he will sigh and say, "I never intended to be here bothering nice people like you. I wish that I could have had an education, so I could be doing something more useful."

Such tactics are common at the *tianguis*. There is a stand where a young man with a pompadour sells cantaloupes. If I ask for one melon, he is always quick to prod me to acquire another for my mother, wife, sister, mother-in-law, etc. At this point, I have told him I live alone frequently enough so that he now remembers, and instead suggests that I buy more melons for my girlfriends—real, imagined, or potential—advising that an extra cantaloupe in the house could be a useful seduction technique, or even an aphrodisiac. If I insist that I only want one, he tells me he has eight children to feed. (He is no older than twenty-five.) Should I decide I want two, he will then whisper in my ear that he will sell me a third at half price. If I refuse to budge, he looks at me as if my limited melon consumption is a colossal disappointment, a broken promise.

At the *tianguis*, much of the merchandise costs more than the same items at indoor markets. In the middle-class neighborhood where I live, people are willing to pay such high prices, while in less affluent sections of the city, the food sold in *tianguis* is cheaper. However, many, if not the majority, of Mexico City residents do without such "luxuries" as fresh fruits and vegetables.

The class system is also evident in the *tianguis* in the way that the merchants address their clients, most often with terms of deference like *patrón* (master), *jefe* (boss), or *güero,* which is equivalent to "blondie" or "whitey." *Güerismo* has more to do with custom or perception than actual skin color; vendors call people *güero* who are browner than they are. The merchants may also be meticulously groomed and dressed immaculately, while his client is unshaven and in sweatpants, but the mere distinction between customer and merchant is cause for the latter's obsequiousness.

Around Mexico City there are various *tianguis* that cater to specialized tastes. For example, the Tianguis del Chopo outfits the small but highly visible Goth, punk, and alternative subcultures. For the past twenty years, each Saturday it has brimmed with people in their teens and twenties, their hair dyed jet-black, in black leather, black fishnets, black jeans, black lipstick, black nail polish, and black sleeveless shirts adorned with clanking metal. The pirated CDs available at the Chopo are more specialized (and more expensive) than elsewhere in the city—collector's editions of Patti Smith, Iggy Pop, metal, ska, and surf, as well as obscure British punk bands from the 1970s. Every fashion item and accessory—immense platform boots with innumerable buckles, floor-length black coats, T-shirts with holes in the appropriate spots—is available.

Most *tianguis* feature at least a small section where people can buy *chácharas*—used items, the utility of which is highly dubious. At the Santa Cruz Meyehualco market in Iztapalapa there are secondhand baby shoes neatly lined up in rows, inflatable rubber King Kong dolls left over from the last movie version, old clothes in grab-bag piles at between ten and fifty pesos a pop, urinals, perfume bottles without any fragrance in them, heaps of remote controls from TVs and sound systems, antique Remington typewriters (their keys now cobwebbed), airplane headsets, spoons that appear to have been bent by Uri Geller, rotary telephones, and those little lamps that say "taxi" on top of cabs.

In the era of globalized capitalism, the panorama of the merchandise at the *tianguis* is changing. With the availability of so many cheap, remaindered, and stolen goods from Asia and the United States, there is less perceived dignity in buying the discards of others. Hence, there are less *chácharas* in markets that twenty years ago sold nothing but. As a result, there is a homogenization of what you can buy at all of the *tianguis*—electric drills; sneakers, sweatpants and terry-cloth bathrobes; plastic cereal bowls with Barbie or the Powerpuff girls; Tommy Hilfiger or Abercrombie T-shirts; fake Louis Vuitton bags.

La Lagunilla is Mexico City's most important flea market, but is disdained by *chachareros* (those who buy and sell *chácharas*). "It's not a *tianguis*," one told me, his contempt evident. "They don't sell *chácharas* they sell 'antiques.'" And indeed, at La Lagunilla it is possible to find an upright piano from the nineteenth century, a perfectly sanded and varnished Art Deco dresser, a 1950s cocktail dress, girlie magazines from the 1940s, or postcards from the era of Pancho Villa. It is an excellent outpost for the affluent or the urban anthropologist, but many of the vendors ask for prices similar to (or even higher than) those in the flea markets of New York, Paris, or London. Even for customers with formidable bargaining skills, the sellers are rarely moved to lower their prices.

Apart from the *tianguis*, most neighborhoods also have large indoor markets. A great example is the Mercado de Medellín in the Colonia Roma, which takes up an entire square block.

There are sprawling heaps of impossibly sweet fruits, picked not a moment before ripening: bananas, papayas, pineapples; mangoes on a stick, peeled, cut into the shapes of flowers, and sprinkled with chile powder. Radishes and scallions and garlic, in adjacent piles comprising the colors of the Mexican flag; mounds of hibiscus petals and chile peppers the color of dried blood; cactus picked clean of its thorns; hogs' heads and chicken feet and bloody slabs of beef.

In another part of the market, stout unsmiling women drive hard bargains for household items: pots and pans of tin and copper, brown ceramic bowls, dish towels, brooms, Tupperware, woven straw garbage bins. Inside and adjacent to the market are hole-in-the-wall luncheonettes that serve *carnitas, cochinita pibil,* or more elaborate *comida corrida* for two or three dollars.

The most legendary market in the D.F. is known as the Barrio de Tepito. The rabbit-warren labyrinth of its dozens of streets, where wares are displayed on tables and hung from metal and plastic posts, is like a *tianguis* multiplied by a ruthless virus. A walk through Tepito is deafening, with a cacophony of CD stands blasting their diverse noises: mariachi trumpets and reggaeton howls, the treacly string section of a pop ballad, the relentless drone of an electronic dance tune.

It is located in what is traditionally a hardscrabble, penniless neighborhood. Oscar Lewis's field research there would ultimately result in his theory of "the culture of poverty," and his book *The Children of Sánchez* is set in Tepito. From the 1930s to the 1960s, Tepito was home to a series of boxers such as Kid Azteca Villanueva, El Púas (Barbed Wire) Olivares, and El Ratón (The Mouse) Macías. The star wrestlers El Santo and Huracán Ramírez were from Tepito, as is football powerhouse Cuauhtémoc Blanco.

In the 1950s and 1960s it was Scavengers' Row. If you dropped your coffeepot and the handle broke, someone in Tepito would solder it back on. Shoes could survive for decades with makeshift leather uppers, and lowers made from the rubber of discarded tires. Even underwear and panty hose would be darned perpetually by painstaking Tepito seamstresses. According to the chapter about Tepito in Sam Quinones's *True Tales of Another Mexico,* if your trousers were falling apart, ingenious tailors could recut what was salvageable and make a smaller pair for your son.

Lengthening the shelf lives of panties and household appliances didn't make for an extravagant lifestyle. In the 1970s, Tepito became the capital of stolen goods. Middle-class mouths watered at the opportunity to buy Lee's and Levi's, a Sony TV, a Canon camera, or a GE refrigerator, products which at the time would have required a trip to the United States to acquire. If these were out of one's price range, one might at least have become a hero to one's child by providing a Barbie doll, a Milky Way candy bar, or a gimme cap with a Dallas Cowboys logo. Huge fortunes were made with contraband in that era.

However, in the 1980s Mexico entered into the General Agreement on Tariffs and Trade and in 1994 signed a Free Trade Agreement with the United States and Canada. Products from the north arrived and in stores cost only a little more than they did in Tepito. The appliances came with inspired embellishments like receipts and manufacturer's warranties.

Thus, Tepito began its most recent transformation. Today, its principal highlights are pirated goods—not only CDs and DVDs, but also software, cosmetics, perfumes, autos and auto parts, medicines, liquor, and vitamins. Remaindered goods that cannot be otherwise moved from stores and factories are also sold in Tepito, as are stolen goods and both wholesale and retail quantities of drugs, principally cocaine.

Clothes are on offer, many with designer labels. Calvin Klein jeans can be had for fifteen dollars, Hugo Boss or Versace shirts for twenty-five. The labels appear uncannily genuine, but are probably made with a scanner; as Frank Abagnale notes in his book on contemporary fraud, *The Art of the Steal,* these days both the real and the fake garments may come from the same factory in Ningbo. Sometimes the pirates are less than scrupulous; you might find jeans with a Calvin Kline or Kelvin Clein label. There is a popular brand of jeans here called Furor; one Tepito stall offers Fuhrer jeans.

What else? Winnie the Pooh or Mickey Mouse bath mats, cheap alarm clocks or makeup kits, flip-flops or colorful barrettes. Stereos, boom boxes, TVs and DVD players, and virtually any conceivable household appliance are also for sale. There is also a section where you can get sex toys, sex books, Viagra, and pornographic films of any stripe.

In short, Tepito offers the same things available at any other market in Mexico City—but a lot more of it. It still makes for a vivid day trip, but many who remember it from its heyday say they are rarely stirred to go any longer.

Supermarkets have existed in Mexico City since at least the 1950s; in Oscar Lewis's 1959 study *Five Families,* the wealthiest of the households sometimes shopped in one. When I arrived here in 1990, while they were more prevalent than before, supermarkets were hardly ubiquitous. The majority of the *chilangos* shopped at *tiendas de abarrotes,* little mom-and-pop stores where you could buy anything from a liter of milk, a hundred grams of sliced ham, a lemon, or a tomato to a lottery ticket, a can of beer, or a loose cigarette. *Tiendas de abarrotes* were expensive and shopping in them part of the Sisyphean experience of most of their customers' lives. If they wanted a jar of mayonnaise, for example, they most likely had only enough money to buy the tiniest, which, ounce for ounce, was the most expensive. Yet they earned so little money that a larger jar was perpetually out of reach.

Today supermarkets, particularly cut-rate ones, are becoming more prevalent all over the city. Hence, there are fewer *tiendas de abarrotes,* and they are close to disappearing from the city's most prosperous neighborhoods. There they are being replaced by convenience stores, such as the U.S. chain 7-Eleven and various Mexican copycats such as Oxxo, Extra, and Super City. Compared to *tiendas de abarrotes,* convenience stores are more brightly lit, of a contemporary design, and keep far longer hours (some never close). They are even more expensive than their predecessors, justifying their prices for the long hours they keep (and the supposed convenience). *Tiendas de abarrotes* have at least small sections of fresh produce, but convenience stores here, like their U.S. counterparts, sell nothing in a natural state, and instead have extensive offerings along the lines of Big Bite hot dogs, instant ramen soups laden with chemicals, and a greater variety of potato chips.

The poorer districts are nearly bereft of convenience stores. This is because they are franchises, and while the mother ship provides the design, the know-how, and the distribution of products, security is the franchisee's problem. In the wee hours they are just as "convenient" to stick-up men as they are to the customer with the urgent need for smokes or soda pop.

In the autumn of 2004, the papers in Mexico City were inundated with stories about the protests surrounding the impending opening of a Wal-Mart near the archaeological site of Teotihuacán. The store would open despite the campaign against it (although it was not actually a Wal-Mart, but a Bodega Aurrerá, the lower-priced superstore of the Wal-Mart Mexico empire). The story of its controversy is emblematic of the changing consumer mores here.

About thirty miles northwest of Mexico City, Teotihuacán was the largest city of the pre-Columbian world; archaeologists estimate that at its heyday in about AD 250 it had as many as 250,000 inhabitants. Its Pyramid of the Sun is among the largest in the world. The city was abandoned around AD 750; today the ruins are a UNESCO World Heritage site.

When ground was broken to build the supermarket, hundreds of demonstrators showed up to complain, some carrying signs that said "Yankee Imperialism" and "Foreign Invasion, Get Out!" The Partido de la Revolución Democrática (PRD), the left-wing political party, filed a suit with the attorney general's office to halt construction of the store. Sixty-three prominent intellectuals and art-world notables—among them writers Laura Esquivel, Elena Poniatowska, and Homero Aridjis, and artists Francisco Toledo, Gabriel Orozco, and José Luis Cuevas—signed a letter published in newspapers asking Vicente Fox, Mexico's president at the time, to cancel the store's opening.

It was an easy letter for them to endorse, given that none lives anywhere near Teotihuacán. For them it was a war of ideology that had nothing to do with practical matters of contemporary commerce. "Teotihuacán is our maximum cultural patrimony, the expression of our history and identity as a people and a nation," said the missive. According to one of the newspaper reports, an artist said, "The struggle for Teotihuacán is a war of symbols. The symbol of ancient Mexico against the symbol of transnational commerce; genetically modified corn against the Plumed Serpent and Mexico's traditional foods; the Day of the Dead against Halloween; skeletons against jack-o'-lanterns."

The reports made it sound as if Wal-Mart shoppers were going to be pushing their carts between the Pyramids of the Sun and the Moon. In fact, the store was built in San Juan Teotihuacán, a town of forty-five thousand inhabitants a mile and a half from the archaeological site. Atop the Pyramid of the Sun, it isn't even visible.

The exponential growth of discount supermarkets in Mexico City in the past ten years has caused no controversy, except for the case of Wal-Mart, which opened its first store here in 1993. It began as a joint venture with Cifra, its Mexican discount store equivalent. In 1997 Wal-Mart bought out Cifra and now controls an entire retail realm: not just the Wal-Mart superstores and Bodegas Aurrerá, but also Sam's Clubs, Superamas (upscale supermarkets), Suburbias (middle-class department stores), and Vips, a chain of cafeterias.

As of 2006, there were 912 of these businesses spread across 145 cities in Mexico. More than a third—358 of them—were in greater Mexico City. Sales were close to $20 billion and 150,000 people worked in them, making Wal-Mart the country's largest private employer. More than half of Wal-Mart employees, and about a quarter of those in managerial and directorial positions, are women. On its website (www.walmartmexico.com.mx), Wal-Mart makes a lot of noise about its commitment to "social responsibility"—the Mexico Philanthropic Center consistently votes it a socially responsible company; the National Institute of Women gives it a gender-equity certificate year after year; it has programs in which it raises money for the Red Cross and the UN disaster fund.

The truth is less rose-colored. In Mexico, Wal-Mart employees and suppliers are subject to the same troublesome treatment as elsewhere. According to an essay by academics José Alfonso Bouzas Ortiz and Luis Oliver Reyes Ramos in the 2007 book *Protective Collective Contracts in Mexico,* workers at Wal-Mart earn an average of about ten dollars a day, double the minimum wage. They are made to sign nonnegotiable contracts that have them work for stores that are individual entities, rather than the combined Wal-Mart corporation; thus, collective bargaining is impossible. Like their counterparts in the United States, their hours, days off, and even their duties can be changed at any moment at the caprice of management.

At an event for academics and labor organizers about collective contracts in Mexico, a Wal-Mart employee (who addressed the crowd wearing one of the store's plastic grocery bags on his head so he couldn't be identified) talked about the exploitative conditions under which he and his colleagues worked. Among his examples was that of a twenty-two-year-old pregnant woman who was made to lug around sixty-pound boxes of fruits and juices. When she asked for a different job, she was switched to the bakery, where she hauled forty-pound tubs of lard and milk. Ultimately, she gave birth prematurely.

Ninety-three percent of the merchandise sold at Wal-Marts here is bought from Mexican providers (although this includes Mexican suppliers who buy and sell foreign merchandise). Walking around the San Juan Teotihuacán store, I was surprised at how many of the products, including nearly all of the clothes, were made in Mexico, sometimes at factories owned by Wal-Mart. "That's because of prohibitive import taxes," an analyst at an investment bank said. "If Mexico ever cuts its import tariffs with China, that will all be over."

A reporter with *Expansión*, Mexico's most important business magazine, told me that being a provider for Wal-Mart is "a deal with the devil. They offer you the possibility to produce more than ever, but exclusively for them. They usually ask for rock-bottom prices and they may take months and months to pay. If they find a company that will produce the same merchandise more cheaply, you're finished. You have to work under their conditions. The power balance is terribly unjust."

(Looking for the corporate point of view, I called Wal-Mart's headquarters here two or three times a week for a month. They gave me the Mexican brushoff. Although they didn't refuse to talk to me—indeed the press officer professed great eagerness to help—they never gave me an appointment, claiming that the only people who could help me were busy with inventory, were out of town for sales conferences, etc.)

In the town of San Juan Teotihuacán, most of the merchants at the *tianguis* and vendors in other stores say that the opening of the Bodega Aurrerá has made no difference to them. Their competition for appliances, such as refrigerators, stoves, and washing machines, is a store called Elektra, which has sold such items in Mexico since 1950. Although its prices are higher than Wal-Mart's, the store offers a dizzying number of schemes to pay for its wares in installments by the week or by the month over a year. It also has its own bank, so I could believe its manager, who said he hadn't lost any of his lower-middle-class clientele.

A vendor at the *tianguis* who sold pots and pans at a dollar a throw told me that he had been hit "hard" but that he sold in other towns on different days of the week to try to make up the difference. The only person who told me that Wal-Mart would most likely spell her doom within a year was the owner of a *tienda de abarrotes*. Although I doubt that these mom-and-pop stores will disappear entirely from Mexico City, the rise of cut-rate supermarkets and convenience stores has already reduced their numbers.

If Wal-Mart is a harsh employer, a double-edged sword for its suppliers, and a threat to its competition, it is a boon for its customers. After the Bodega Aurrerá opened in San Juan Teotihuacán, the same reporters that covered the intellectuals' condemnation quoted shoppers who, awed at the variety of merchandise available at low prices, spoke as if they'd woken up in the land of Oz.

Watching the customers stroll the aisles, it is possible to imagine the same wondrous astonishment that conquistadores Bernal Díaz de Castillo and Hernán Cortés recorded after seeing the market in Tlatelolco. In towns of its size, nothing like a Bodega Aurrerá has ever existed and choices have always been limited. A chicken was bought in a chicken store, a stove in Elektra, clothing at the *tianguis* or in small unfashionable boutiques, and so forth.

Suddenly, in an air-conditioned, fluorescent-lit warehouse, pushing their children in wide-body metal carts, Teotihuacán's citizens are confronted with more options than they have ever imagined: umpteen brands of diapers, breakfast cereals, soda pop. Under the same roof they can buy groceries, an LG refrigerator, a Sony TV set, a Goodyear tire, a pair of sneakers, an impish negligee, and reasonably trendy jeans that are sturdier than those they will find in the *tianguis*. A universe of items they never knew they needed tempts: salad spinners and inflatable cushions, reducing girdles, DustBusters, Snow White or Big Bird shampoo. Unlike the intellectuals, these customers registered no complaints about the threat to their cultural patrimony.

With few exceptions, everything is cheaper in Bodega Aurrerá than in the rest of the retail establishments of San Juan Teotihuacán, of great importance in an economy where so many people live so close to the margin. Still, I wondered how many people who live in the town could actually afford to fill a grocery cart and pay for the merchandise.

After spending an afternoon there, I'm not sure how much it matters. Above all, Mexicans are adaptable. Children are in general more obedient than in the United States; the toddler who says "buy me, buy me" at everything he sees—and there were plenty of him in evidence—is more easily ignored. (Indeed, Mexican children are so polite and well-bred that in 1908 Charles Flandrau wrote, "Had

I the ordering of this strange, unhappy world, I think all children would be born Mexican and remain so until they were fifteen.")

A family of seven, including a grandmother and four children, wandered the aisles for nearly half an hour. When they finally left, they had only bought three inexpensive items. The trip to the supermarket had been a Saturday outing for them, something like a visit to an amusement park.

At the end of 2005, I had a conversation with a Belgian who had lived in Mexico City in the early 1990s while working as a well-paid bureaucrat for the United Nations, and had returned after a ten-year absence to retire. He complained about how the city had become *agringada*—gringofied, Americanized. I began to point out all the ways that the Colonia Roma, the neighborhood where we were talking, remained traditionally Mexican—the enormous market around the corner, the guys who repaired curtains from door to door, the taco stalls across the street from the café where we sat.

Had I been more impudent I might have defended the proliferation of supermarkets. Obviously it is with chagrin that I point to a Wal-Mart offshoot as the most desirable export of U.S. culture in Mexico. The Belgian and I may try to avoid supermarkets, but in this stage of capitalism, we are quirky anomalies who don't matter. The stores of the Wal-Mart empire have become ubiquitous in the city; by 2005, when we had the conversation, they were as much a part of the firmament of Mexico City as the *tianguis*.

Certain foreigners pine for an "old Mexico" about which they have a romantic notion—the Mexico of a Casasola photograph from 1910. You can see them in the public squares of the sections of Mexico City that have maintained their colonial architecture, like Coyoacán or San Ángel, fanning themselves under the trees, surrounded by impeccably preserved houses, cobbled pavements, and even the occasional wrinkle-faced *campesina* walking by with a basket on her head.

But those foreigners, while living in their lovely Casasola print, have enough money to enjoy tapas bars and pasta restaurants, art galleries, jazz bars, and foreign-language bookstores. In their homes they have television, telephones, every conceivable kitchen appliance, and one if not several servants. Most are equipped with computers, cable TV, and high-speed Internet. No doubt many enjoy Prozac, Viagra, and Rogaine.

Mexico is not really a Casasola photograph for them, but is for nearly half the Mexicans, who live on or over the edge of poverty. "Old Mexico" is a charming conceit for those who are sturdily anchored in the twenty-first century. For an impoverished Mexican, "old Mexico" is not quaint or nostalgic—it represents misery and servitude. If your struggle to survive is not much improved from that of your ancestors of a hundred years ago, you probably despise "old Mexico" and dream of supermarkets. The Bodega Aurrerá bestows on its shoppers the fantasy that they are first-class citizens of the First World.

The first shopping mall in Mexico City, Plaza Satélite, was built in 1971. At the time, the neighborhood where the mall is located, Ciudad Satélite, was the suburban fringe of the city, but it was ultimately swallowed and enveloped within the urban sprawl. In the next two decades other notably huge malls opened, such as Perisur and Santa Fe. The trend in the last decade or so has been to build smaller malls in any neighborhood where the market will bear them.

Plaza Satélite, and most of the principal malls that came afterward in Mexico City, were designed by two architects, Juan Sordo Madaleno and his son, Javier Sordo Madaleno. Still others followed their blueprints and as such they have an almost cookie-cutter design scheme. The walls tend to be white or off-white. The aisles are circular or oval, and are built around indoor courtyards, a scheme that in the larger malls repeats itself several times. There are barely noticeable highlights in wood, stone, or fake wood or fake stone construction materials. Department stores are set prominently at the entrances or curves of the aisles. The food court is always at the top level, often adjacent to a multiplex movie theater.

With slight variations, nearly all Mexico City malls have the same stores, principally skewed toward the youthful customer. Many of them are multinationals with headquarters in Europe that one sees in much of the world, such as C&A, Mango, or Zara. (The last-mentioned store is part of the Inditex group, which has more than three thousand shops in sixty-five countries, among them the Bershka and Pull & Bear shops, which sell inexpensive, casual clothing; the more conservative Massimo Dotti stores; and a cheap lingerie shop called Oysho, a Victoria's Secret knockoff. All of them are represented in the Mexico City malls.)

There are also similar offerings from Mexican fashion outlets, and the larger malls have further choices from the United States and Europe: Benetton and Bebe, Dockers and Diesel, Emporio Armani and FCUK. The more expensive house Cartier and Louis Vuitton, Coach bags and Ferragamo shoes. In late 2007, Saks Fifth Avenue opened its third store outside the United States (after Dubai and Saudi Arabia) in the Santa Fe mall here.

For most of my life I had the New Yorker's contemptuous view of shopping centers: loathsome eyesores for unfortunate hicks who live in the peripheries of cities and for practical reasons cannot even buy a newspaper without getting into their cars. The presence of malls within city limits struck me as a worrisome portent of the encroachment of a suburban way of life upon urban centers.

However, after living in Mexico City so long, my attitude has changed, at least a little. Here, shopping malls reduce anxiety for the middle class. One of the principal sources of stress in the city is traffic, which makes it so laborious to get anywhere. The fact that shopping centers have sprouted in so many areas makes them easy to get to.

A few years ago, when I wanted new dishes, pots, and pans, I asked a friend with a car if she wouldn't mind driving me to a little store in the *centro* that seemed to have a whole line of kitchenware stolen from Edward Hopper's *Nighthawks*. She told me she would be happy to help me with the errand, but begged me not to drag her to the *centro,* where we would certainly be delayed in traffic and have enormous trouble finding a parking spot. We ended up at a strip mall close to where she lived, at the Wal-Mart.

The other great fear here is crime. Malls, crawling with security guards, are enclaves of safety. Further, the city's unpredictability can be exhausting, so the inexorable sameness of the malls can inspire a pacifying lull.

There is also an element of social status to shopping in a mall. If the cut-rate supermarkets give their customers the sense that they are part of the First World, malls give *chilangos* with more money the idea that they are part of an affluent contemporary universe.

Particularly for the young, shopping malls in Mexico City are social enclaves. They spend afternoons wandering up and down the aisles, stopping for a coffee in Starbucks, angling for a flirtatious encounter, perusing merchandise they very likely will not buy.

However degraded or diminished, the youths strolling the malls are contemporary versions of Parisian *flâneurs*. In the extensive notes that Walter Benjamin compiled for his unfinished book, *The Arcades Project,* an examination of the shopping arcades built in Paris in the first decades of the nineteenth century, he quoted *The Illustrated Guide to Paris,* which described the arcades' "glass-roofed, marble-paneled corridors" lined with "the most elegant shops," so that each arcade was "a city, a world in miniature."

Key to Benjamin's reflections was the figure of the *flâneur*, the city's aimless wanderer, the "botanist of the sidewalk" popularized by Charles Baudelaire and other less well-remembered French writers of the nineteenth century. Alternately envisioned by Benjamin as a ne'er-do-well, a gambler, a whoremonger, a journalist, and even, at least by inference, as Benjamin himself, the *flâneur* is a figure whose mind and five senses are constantly stimulated by his improvised rambles around the city.

If the arcades were "worlds in miniature" in the universe that was Paris at the end of the nineteenth century, shopping malls are undoubtedly our own little planets in the globalized galaxy at the beginning of the twenty-first, however less elegant and architecturally pleasing.

Those Parisian shopping arcades were the apotheosis of modernity in the 1800s, yet today when one walks through them one is imbued with nostalgia for a distant past. I wonder if similarly, in fifty or a hundred years, we will be able to wander in the shopping malls of Mexico City and marvel at their architecture, design, or construction. Will they take on a quaint or picturesque charm as other forms of shopping and architecture replace them? Is anything in them salvageable?

For its kitsch value, I would reclaim a mall in the north of the city called Mundo E. It has the same stores as all the other malls, but on top of the shops, its high-ceilinged aisles are decorated with faux balconies with shuttered windows, as if they were two-story buildings. They appear vaguely Old World, not unlike the Hollywood versions of Paris or Vienna from the 1930s. Indeed, you can almost imagine one of the European character actors of the period, Jean Hersholt or S. Z. Sakall, opening one of the shutters in his bathrobe and bidding you good morning with a Central European accent.

The plaza in Mundo E where the multiplex cinema is located is its showpiece. Under a painted sky, the center of the square has a fountain with an obelisk in the middle. It is surrounded by more of these two-storied balconies, dotted with Roman urns. Even the plastic trees in this court look as if they are wilting or drying up in the heat. Yet it is an oddly agreeable place to have a coffee and people-watch.

The most pleasing new mall in Mexico City is Antara, which opened in the swanky Polanco district in 2006. Occupying 48,500 square meters in what was formerly a General Motors plant, Antara's most striking feature is how little it interferes with the urban landscape. A split-level semicircle, it is three stories high (much lower than many of its neighboring buildings) and its surface of beige limestone combines gracefully with the surrounding streets. The walkways are more generously wide than in most of Mexico City's malls, and there are more choices of places to sit.

Unsurprisingly, Antara was designed by Javier Sordo Madaleno. He is also one of its owners. In various interviews the architect described the center as "a small city within a great metropolis," evoking the portrayal of the arcades in *The Illustrated Guide to Paris*. However, the mall that opened in 2006 was only the first phase of the project; phases two and three involve the construction of three towers, one with condominiums, another with office suites, and the third a hotel. It remains to be seen how much they will intrude on the cityscape.

Sordo Madaleno's plans are above all ambitious. While Antara may appear site specific, he has said that it is a "repeatable success" and has even referred to the mall as "a brand" that could be extended with distinct lines, and has "possibilities in other areas of business." If he gets his way Antaras may sprout up all over the world in the next generation.

If an anthropologist were to examine the shopping habits of the wealthy in Mexico City, he or she would conclude that they are conspicuously conservative, with hardly an iota of audacity or boldness. El Palacio de Hierro (the Iron Palace), which opened its doors in 1891, is the most exclusive department store here. In 1997, hoping to update its image as a fuddy-duddy institution for aging women, it hired an advertising agency to develop a campaign to attract younger customers. The resulting ads, plastered on billboards and bus stops all over town, depicted ivory-skinned women with fine European features, impeccably coiffed, painted, and clad, staring defiantly at the camera. Accompanying taglines included, "It's easier to conquer a man than a mirror," "One sentence separates a girl from a woman: 'I've got nothing to wear,'" and, "There are two things a woman can't avoid: crying and shopping for shoes." Dominating the design of each ad were three little words: *Soy totalmente Palacio* (I'm totally Palacio).

The campaign created a vast controversy. Its cleverness was perceived as a guilty pleasure by opinion makers, who at the same time condemned its image of women as manipulative bitch goddesses with insatiable buying habits (other catchphrases included, "The wonder of shopping is that you always find what you weren't looking for," and, "Luckily we're the weaker sex: the stronger pays when we go shopping").

Performance artist Lorena Wolffer created a didactic countercampaign that featured a darker-skinned woman more typical of the streets of Mexico City, with the tagline *Soy totalmente de hierro* (I'm totally iron). One ad depicted her frowning on a *pesero* as the straphanger alongside breathed down her neck, with the phrase, "The problem is that you think my body belongs to you." Another showed the woman scowling in rage with a burning billboard at her side: "No ad campaign can silence my voice." Another simply asked, "Who teaches you to be a woman?"

A brief walk through the store's aisles revealed that there was no polemic whatsoever to be gleaned from the merchandise. Among the women's clothes, most collars were high and respectably buttoned, hemlines were low and ladylike, and even in the juniors' section most jeans were high-waisted. Most of the garments looked like they had been designed for middle-aged women or young women who dress prematurely like their mothers, while the tackier items (an orange-and-pink plaid dress, a strawberry leather jacket) seemed to be intended for women of a certain age who, looking at the mirror on the wall, still see the fairest of them all.

In the men's department there was nothing a male couldn't wear to a business lunch at the city's most conservative restaurant, except for items in the casual section with safe brand names like Polo, Dockers, and Levi's. Even in housewares it looked as if most of the dining sets and furniture had been chosen by someone's grandmother.

Contrary to the conformist merchandise, the ad campaign kept on going for a decade, despite palpably running out of gas. The taglines seemed ever more labored as the years passed—"Life is a runway," "I'd give you my life, but I'm using it," "Envy is a beautiful feeling when I provoke it." In the spring of 2007 they finally launched a new campaign, this time with just two words per ad—either *Totalmente Marte* (Totally Mars), *Totalmente* Lounge (the latter word in English, referring to loungewear), *Totalmente Blanco* (Totally White), or *Totalmente Negro* (Totally Black)—the last two referring to the colors of clothing and not skin. Some ads featured nothing but head shots of young men and women who looked as if they were hired from a modeling agency in Spain or perhaps Scandinavia. There was even one of a green-eyed baby; you could practically hear it gurgle. With these white, First World faces, the store seems to keep feeding its customers' vision of who they would like to be.

Despite the encroachment of shopping centers, Wal-Mart, McDonald's, Office Depot, and convenience stores, Mexico City is still a place where, along one street in the *centro histórico,* store after store sells lighting fixtures. On the next street they sell bathroom fixtures. Around the corner, raw chickens; a few streets over, wedding dresses; on another street, free-floating heads, limbs, and torsos of dolls to be later assembled by their buyers.

These are the same sort of organized divisions noted by the Spaniards at Tlatelolco. In the *brujería* (witchcraft) section of the Sonora Market you can buy an amulet that will help you find work, a candle that will bring back a straying lover, a bar of soap that will help you sell your car, or baby chicks painted phosphorescent colors for a child's birthday party.

Throughout the day and early evening, various merchants trawl through the streets of residential neighborhoods. The candied-sweet-potato salesman lets you know he has arrived with a shrill steam whistle, while the knife sharpener alerts you to his presence with a pan flute. Men pushing carts attached to bicycles pedal about, in a plaintive drone peddling Oaxacan tamales (it's actually a recording voiced through a speaker). Others alert you to their arrival by simply screaming: he who sells five-gallon plastic jugs of drinking water; the man who repairs rattan curtains; and the odd contraction *¡llegaaaaas!* which tells you the gas man has arrived. I have no idea how far back this form of street sale goes in Mexico City, but it is described by Frances Calderón de la Barca in her 1840 book, *Life in Mexico.*

At the Vicente Guerrero *tianguis* each Thursday in Iztapalapa, a universe of *chácharas* is peddled. The very idea that it would occur to someone to buy the merchandise—dust-covered beer bottles, watches with cracked faces that haven't run in years, books that appear to have been dropped in a toilet and then left in an attic to dry—boggles the mind. But there they are, in full force week after week. Those who are hungry while shopping can stop at Doña Azucena's stall for a bowl of *migas,* a soup invented in Tepito in its most impoverished days. It's made principally of day-old bread and pork bones, seasoned with *chile de árbol,* an herb called *epazote,* and garlic.

People who complain that Mexico City has become *agringada* are in fact revealing that they never stray beyond the affluent neighborhoods. However globalized, the city resists becoming the stereotype of a place that has lost its identity or become ruined due to contemporary capitalism. There are probably many reasons, but the principal one is poverty. Globalization functions for the middle class and the well-to-do, who increasingly find themselves living, working, and shopping in enclaves modeled after their counterparts in the United States. The poor cannot afford such spaces, and globalization passes them by.

Our Rodeo Drive

On a September afternoon, the Louis Vuitton boutique on Avenida Presidente Masaryk opened its doors to a handful of its best clients, offering a few novelties and a show of the fall-winter collection. Among the shoppers was a man with gray hair and a mustache whose companion appeared to have only recently reached legal age. A fellow in a suit and tie patiently sipped Moët Chandon while his wife—hovered over by three patient and smiling assistants—looked over nearly every item in the store. A kid in his early twenties spoke on his cell phone while trying on shoes, completely ignoring the salesman who laced them for him. A few mother-and-daughter combinations arrived; the moms tended to look over the classic items, while their offspring checked out the more contemporary accessories, such as a multicolored mink handbag that cost just under fifteen thousand dollars.

The gray-haired man bought a bag for his consort, removing from his pocket a staggering wad of five-hundred-peso bills. Many of Louis Vuitton's customers—indeed, many of the customers in the various boutiques that line Presidente Masaryk—pay in cash. This could indicate that they work in businesses that handle hard currency. On the other hand, it might mean that they don't want to leave traces of their purchases: perhaps the man with the young girl is married to someone else. There is also a possibility that someone who carries around thousands of dollars in cash is a drug dealer. In any case, after the salesman rang up the handbag, the man and the girl left the store, climbed into a BMW 3251, and disappeared, leaving in their wake on the sidewalk a cluster of chauffeurs and bodyguards. Security, both private and public, is ubiquitous in the neighborhood.

At the dawn of the twenty-first century, multinational purveyors of luxury goods began to realize that Mexico is the most stable economy in Latin America and that, while half of its populace lives in poverty, around 10 percent of its more than hundred million citizens have an enticing amount of disposable income. At least a couple of million of those people live in greater Mexico City, so some of these brands, such as Louis Vuitton, Cartier, and Chanel, opened flagship boutiques on Avenida Presidente Masaryk (the local equivalent of Rodeo Drive, Fifth Avenue, or Bond Street). In addition to Vuitton, a dizzying number of international luxury brands are represented on Masaryk, including Mercedes-Benz, BMW, and Audi; Hugo Boss, Max Mara, and Ermenegildo Zegna; Brioni, Bulgari, and Burberry; Ferragamo, Fendi, and Furla; Cartier and Chanel; Tiffany, Hermès, and DKNY.

At first the brands had an uphill climb. Traditionally, Mexicans who have enough money to spend five thousand dollars on a watch are also in the habit of getting on a plane to buy it in Europe or the United States. You gain points on the social scale by mentioning that you bought a garment on a trip to Houston or San Diego, or better yet, Paris or New York. Indeed, in the Mexico City boutiques of Louis Vuitton and Cartier, customers of that stripe tend to buy one item under emergency circumstances (say, that handbag she absolutely needs for an important party) and do their heavy-duty shopping in other climes. Their freer-spending niche customers are among the nouveau riche, politicians, and drug traffickers.

Polanco, the district where Avenida Masaryk is situated, has long been the most centrally located upscale neighborhood in Mexico City. Many of the best restaurants in the D.F. are there, and patronizing them is a delightful escape, however temporary, from some of the city's harshest moments. After a few glasses of wine and a spectacular meal, you can almost believe you've had your lunch in Europe or New York. (The bill reflects the similarity.) However, once out on the street it isn't long before you are confronted by a reality check: the kid selling Chiclets in traffic, the phalanx of brown-faced security guards who protect the area, the parade of maids who take care of the luxury apartments.

Montse's Trip

Her face is oval and nut colored, with the enormous eyes of a gazelle. Montse's expression is serious, cautious, pensive. Once in a while she drops her guard and smiles enchantingly. Her black hair, straight and thick, is covered by a beige knit cap. Every once in a while, she sticks her fingers inside to scratch her skull and remove some lice, which she smashes obsessively on the pages of a magazine wrinkled from the rain. Insistently, she also scratches her skeletal body. She is so thin that, with her baggy clothes, it's hard to tell if she's a boy or a girl.

Montse lives atop a stone platform in Pushkin Park, on the border between Colonia Roma and Colonia Doctores. She is thirteen, and has lived in the street since she was ten. She shares the platform with six or seven companions (two of whom are her brothers, Luis Enrique and Jesús Eduardo), a white dog with black spots called Stains, and the multitude of fleas and lice. They sleep on top of three mattresses, covered by various blankets donated by sympathetic neighbors. Montse is the only girl in the group.

Her breakfast comes out of a can. The can contains Limpiador Dismex, a toxic liquid that dissolves glue, available in any hardware store for two dollars. The sale of such products to minors is against the law, but Montse has found that the personnel of certain shops in the Colonia Guerrero are kind enough to provide it for her under the table. She moistens a piece of toilet paper with the liquid, lays it in her palm, and covers her mouth and nose with her bony hand. This is how her trip begins.

"My mother's in jail for robbery and attempted murder," she says. She speaks slowly, deliberately, with a monotonous voice, altered by the drug. "She tried to kill her sister." Montse's mother and aunt were partners in robberies to get money to buy drugs—any drugs they could get their hands on. Montse's father plays the trumpet with a mariachi band in Plaza Garibaldi, but he doesn't get along with his children because he disapproves of their drug use.

The sort of substance that Montse inhales damages the brain, the liver, the kidneys, and the heart. Ten or twenty years ago, Mexico City street kids sniffed glue, which was bad enough, but this generation of inhalant is far more destructive and addictive. A body as young and resistant as Montse's will keep functioning for a few years, but if she continues to use the drug, its decline and collapse are inevitable.

When the weather is cold or rainy, Montse and her companions cover themselves with plastic or run underneath the balconies. "Or we just tough it out," she says. Life in the street has its advantages. "I can do whatever I want any time I want. No one tells me what to do." There are, however, difficult moments. "Sometimes the boys come and hit us. They come from other neighborhoods, and sometimes they beat us up. There are a lot of them."

Even though she looks like a gust of wind would send her flying across Avenida Cuauhtémoc, Montse insists that she eats every day. "At first, after getting high, I couldn't. I got nauseous and vomited. Now that hardly ever happens. People from the neighborhood, from the street stalls, from the *tianguis,* give us food. They give us the fruit they can't sell. Sometimes the police give us food, the same food that they eat. I like anything that doesn't have vegetables or onions."

Despite what she says, one morning I saw her biting into a doughnut covered with chocolate. She couldn't swallow it. She spit out the first bite and gave the rest to one of her friends. She covered her mouth and nose with the little paper.

Pushkin Park is a stone's throw from the Plaza Romita, the principal location where Luis Buñuel filmed *Los olvidados* in 1950. A restored version of the film, which deals with the brutal life of street children, was shown at the Cannes Film Festival in 2005 and released in Mexico City just after. What is most striking about the movie today is how little has changed. With the introduction of toxic inhalants, the problem of street children here is worse than in Buñuel's day, when they only amused themselves with alcohol.

The various organizations that try to help street children in Mexico City estimate that there are between three thousand and thirty-five hundred such kids. An additional ten thousand to fifteen thousand work on the street, shining shoes, selling chewing gum, or juggling at traffic intersections, but they tend to live at home with their families. Those who choose the street usually have lived through such extreme violence at home that the sidewalk, with its dangers and hardships, rats and vermin, seems like a better option.

Children are sources of income for impoverished families and often the violence is related to work. They're sent to the street, and if they don't bring home the required quota they are beaten. Girls are often hurt by parents and brothers who feel they haven't performed domestic chores adequately. Sometimes they're raped.

Among the organizations, Casa Alianza (the Latin American branch of Covenant House) has the largest budget and most comprehensive facilities, including homes where the kids can live until they turn eighteen. Pro Niños de la Calle is a day-care center where the kids can arrive in the morning, have a shower and a meal, wash their clothes or even get new ones, and watch TV or play games until sundown, when the doors are shut. Casa Yolia deals exclusively with girls, many of whom are pregnant. All have the best success rate with kids who have been on the street a short time and haven't descended too heavily into drug use. The rest are most often too far gone, not only from drugs, but from violence and such a sustained lack of affection that it is impossible to get through to them.

Each day, Montse consumes a half-pint can of *Limpiador Dismex*. If she doesn't get it, she is desperate. She spent a year in a halfway house without taking drugs, but then told her wards she needed to go back to the street to "help" her brothers. At thirteen, she already has a boyfriend—one of the boys who sleeps on the platform with her. "He hits me," she says. "But he doesn't hit me hard. He gets mad because I don't eat." Once in a while they sleep in a hotel near Plaza Garibaldi. For about eight dollars they are kings for the night, with hot water and cable TV. The crust of dirt on her skin indicates that she doesn't experience that luxury too often.

If she wants a bath or a hot meal, she knows where to go: "Casa Alianza, Visión Mundial, Pro Niños de la Calle," she says. She imagines leaving the street one day with the help of one of these foundations. She'd like to live in another state, near a beach. She wants to be a nurse, but can't say why.

Montse claims to have heard about kids who have died, but hasn't seen them up close. Yet when she goes into more detail, death could hardly have come nearer. "Some people die because they do drugs and don't eat," she says. "Others drown. There was a kid who got run over and died right there," she says, pointing to Avenida Cuauhtémoc. "And Aarón, rest in peace, died in a hospital from an overdose." Aarón was her previous boyfriend. When she found out, at first she couldn't believe it. She didn't cry but says she was very sad.

I ask her if she would like to have children of her own. She smiles and her face transforms into that of a child, rather than a street child. "When I was little I had a lot of dolls and carriages. I dreamt of myself with babies. I'd still like to have a baby. But not in the street."

Mexican Lexicon, Part Two

N *o hay* (There isn't/aren't any). An alarmingly frequent answer in Mexico City when you go to buy something—from hard-to-find items like an out-of-print book or a padded envelope, to presumably less scarce commodities like a roll of paper towels, clothes hangers, or a box of aspirin. The response is sometimes delivered with officious brusqueness, at others with charming guilelessness. The clerk at the pharmacy might smile broadly and ingenuously explain to you that, wouldn't you know it, there was plenty of aspirin yesterday, and indeed it will be stocked in abundance tomorrow. But for the moment, *no hay*. Once, I attempted to buy a pack of Marlboro Lights for a friend. "Hard or soft?" the convenience store clerk asked efficiently. "Soft," I said. She shook her head: *"No hay."* (She had the hard pack. She just liked to say *"no hay."*)

No se encuentra (He/she isn't here). The immutable response when you call a government bureaucrat. It is against an unwritten Mexico City law for civil servants to answer their own phones, and they make it a habit to be unavailable when they ring.

When they leave the office, the hour of their return is a state secret to which their assistants are not privy. Therefore, an inquiry provokes the corollary phrase, *No sabría que decirle* (I wouldn't know what to tell you). The same query importuned five different ways ("Is there anyone in the office who knows when he'll be back?" "Did he leave word in an agenda somewhere?") will induce the invariable repetition of the same answer, until the assistant, frustrated at your insistence, says, "Try calling at one o'clock." At the appointed hour the official has either just left or not quite returned.

Mañana. Mexico's most infamous response, popularized for gringos in a Peggy Lee tune in 1948. It can mean anything from eight o'clock sharp tomorrow morning to a moment or two before the Second Coming.

Ahorita. Related to *mañana* but more complex. *Ahorita* is a word that is rarely used in other Spanish-speaking countries, but employed constantly here. It is a diminutive of the word *ahora*, which means "now." That Mexicans trifle with the word implies that they have a familiar and flexible relationship with its meaning. It also distances them from, and unburdens them of, the responsibility it implies.

There are discernible differences between *ahorita* and *mañana.* Let's say you check into a budget hotel room in the *centro histórico*, undress, step in the shower, and find there is no hot water. You go downstairs to the reception desk. If the clerk tells you that the water heater will be fixed *mañana*, you know categorically it will not happen before the following day. *Ahorita*, on the other hand, is even less specific. If you are told you will have hot water *ahorita*, the relationship to "now" depends on the speaker's tone of voice and the context of the conversation. He may be telling you that it will be fixed within moments, or sometime in the course of the day, or as soon as he damn well sees fit.

If he says *ahorita* with a plaintive smile, holding his thumb and his forefinger together, he is explaining that "now" is an unreliable notion that we have only modest control over—sometimes the little devil just slips out of our hands. If he says it dispassionately, with a stone face, he is implying that unforeseen circumstances sometimes stretch the word "now" to mean "later"—and hopefully, in this instance, it will at least be "soon." And if he says it defiantly, with some indication of heat or temper, he is insinuating that not only is he the master of "now," able to bend it to his will and power, but that he can bend you, too. If you ever want to take a hot shower again, get out of his way.

Ahoritita is a diminutive of the diminutive, usually employed with some charm as a pacifier. Under special circumstances it can be stretched out to *ahorititita*. In those instances, it's best to forget about the shower, go to a cantina, and order a drink. If *ahorititita* is the response to when your next drink is coming, go to another cantina.

Jesus of Iztapalapa

In a glass-encased altar stands a life-size skeleton in a purple velvet robe. Its skull, ornamented with a pageboy wig, gazes eyelessly. Each finger of its hands is adorned with rings, its neck with gold chains. Surrounding its figure are skeleton statuettes and bills and coins of various currencies. Outside, at its feet, the skeleton's worshippers have left a miscellany of offerings: cognac glasses filled with tequila, flowers, candles, bottles of soda, packs of cigarettes, lollipops, plates full of eggplant. The offerings are meant to cure illness, attract abundance, improve sales in business, or bring back a straying lover.

People pass by constantly to pray to this figure, known as Santa Muerte (Saint Death)—alone, in twos and threes, sometimes entire families. There are altars to Santa Muerte throughout Mexico, particularly along the border and in the northern states. But this shrine—on Calle Alfarería around the corner from the Tepito market—is the most important in Mexico City. Its worshippers are said to include prostitutes hoping for protection against disease, children praying their fathers will be released from jail, and all manner of miscreants angling to escape arrest or eager for the death of their enemies. Cops on the take are also said to be regulars here.

On the first day of each month the believers arrive en masse, setting plaster statues of Santa Muerte on tables or atop squares of fabric on the sidewalk. Hundreds of visitors walk around and leave treats for the saint at these makeshift altars—chocolate coins, fake currency, cigars, shots of rum, Barbie dolls. Others walk around with spray cans of cheap perfume, with which they liberally douse the figurines. As the afternoon passes, the street becomes increasingly crowded. By nightfall when the prayers are chanted—"I come toward you prostrate, so that you will meet my needs; thank you for the favors I've received"—there will be about five thousand people, blocking traffic on the surrounding streets.

Officially disdained by the Catholic Church, Santa Muerte is the newest saint in Mexico, having been taken up by thousands, if not millions, since the beginning of the millennium. A woman named Enriqueta Romero founded the Tepito altar in September 2001, although she claims to have venerated Santa Muerte since 1964.

There is only legend about the saint's initial apparitions in Mexico. One story has it that the image of Santa Muerte first appeared in the early 1960s on the walls of someone's shack in Catemaco, a town in Veracruz known for its adherence to witchcraft. Others claim that there were Aztec acolytes of Santa Muerte in Tenochtitlán, the pre-Hispanic version of Mexico City.

According to the 2000 census, slightly more than 86 percent of Mexico City residents identify themselves as Catholic. But as the devotion to Santa Muerte indicates, for many *chilangos,* it is a sui generis, syncretic form of Catholicism—the imperfect melding of indigenous rite with Catholic ritual that began in the 1520s when the Spaniards toppled the Aztec temples and built their churches over the ruins. People all over Mexico City pray to saints. They'll attach their likenesses to chains around their necks or carry little cards with the saint's picture in their purses or wallets. This form of idol worship is a hybrid of Mexican popular culture with official Catholic dogma.

The Church has no problem with the cult veneration of saints, except for those, like Santa Muerte, that it does not recognize. The adoration of a saint who represents death is not surprising in a country that acknowledges mortality on a friendly, familiar basis each November 1. (The tradition of the Day of the Dead, in which families honor and remember their departed, has existed in Mexico since the Olmecs, the country's oldest pre-Columbian civilization. There are few places where one can get as clear an idea of what the holiday is about as the graveyard next to the church known as La Cuevita, the oldest and most important in the Iztapalapa section of Mexico City. During the day and throughout the night, families gather at each grave site, remembering the dead as they picnic and drink among incense and candles, extravagant bouquets of flowers and festoons of brightly colored balloons. Mariachis hire themselves out to play the favored songs of the deceased.)

At Tepito's shrine to Santa Muerte, on a typical first of the month, some of the congregants cultivate a rough look. Numerous young men have adopted the appearance of Los Angeles gangbangers, openly smoke marijuana, display hairstyles dyed and pointy with gel, and wear T-shirts with the sleeves removed, the better to show off their skeleton tattoos. The day I observed, at one moment one began to cheerlead the crowd in the following chant: *Te ve, te siente, la santa está presente* (She sees you, she feels you, the saint is among us).

But most of the faithful—including a teenage girl who hobbled along Calle Alfarería on her knees—appeared to be among the ordinary hard-luck hordes of Mexico City, without any of the evident flash of criminals. Regardless of the Church's official rejection of Santa Muerte, all of her followers to whom I spoke said they were Catholic, although they differed about whether or not their favored saint was actually a part of, or independent from, their professed religion.

All of them referred to their experience with Santa Muerte—who is also known as La Flaca (Skinny) and La Güerita (Little Whitey)—as if she were any other garden-variety saint of the church. They explained that they'd had a problem—drug abuse, family squabbles, or discreetly undefined "emotional" troubles—and that a friend or family member had suggested they pray to Santa Muerte to rescue them. "She's gotten me out of a lot of jams," said a middle-aged lady with curly hair and a black stretch top. "But you can't just think about what she gives you. You have to bring things back to her—tequila, flowers, maybe a cake."

One of the largest statues was commandeered by a young woman with light brown hair, smooth olive skin, and sad, heavy-lidded eyes. She reflected on death worship. "It's part of life," she said. "To venerate death means that you adore life, because death is the only thing that can take life away from you."

Santa Muerte is revered not only by those who congregate at her altar. After I left the Tepito shrine, I got into a conversation about the saint with the cabbie who drove me to a safer neighborhood. Soon after we began to talk, he opened the second button of his shirt to display medallions not only for La Flaca, but also the Virgin of Guadalupe and Saint Jude.

The latter—known as San Judas Tadeo here—has been Mexico City's unofficial saint since the mid-1970s. In a metropolis called home by so many desperate poor, it is hardly surprising that "the patron saint of lost causes"—or, as he is known here, the saint of "difficult and desperate cases"—is so popular. (Indeed, some of Santa Muerte's followers have indicated that they switched to her from

Saint Jude. At a march in support of La Flaca in 2005, a reporter from the Associated Press asked one of the congregants why she prayed to Death instead of Saint Jude. "He's got his hands full already," she said.)

Saint Jude's Day is celebrated on October 28. Yet on the twenty-eighth of each month, an enormous throng gathers in his honor outside the Temple of San Hipólito, an eighteenth-century Baroque church on the border of the Colonia Guerrero, a neighborhood known for its high crime rate. So many thousands arrive that platoons of patrol cops are needed to prevent people from spilling onto Paseo de la Reforma and stopping traffic. On the twenty-eighth, the pews are removed from the church, which can only hold fifteen hundred people, and the masses are broadcast onto the street through enormous speakers.

The congregants—like Santa Muerte's followers—are evidently from the economically strapped sectors of the city. The night I observed, a few young men wore caps that identified them, in English, as the Tepito Kings, but most of the rest of those gathered seemed like ordinary citizens, the majority having arrived in family units. Offerings are exchanged: I was given a rose, a ribbon with the saint's name meant to be tied around my wrist, a tiny bag of chips that included a prayer to Jude and a ten-centavo coin. I was also handed a portrait of Jude by a man in clown makeup, and a lollipop with a piece of paper attached, suggesting that I return the following twenty-eighth with twenty-eight shirts to give away to the flock.

Saint Jude is also purported to be the patron of both the city's criminal element and its judicial police (who in many cases overlap). The *judiciales* have been photographed by the press observing masses in his honor, and for a magazine where I worked, a young writer named Sergio Tellez-Pon wrote about his encounter there with an observant thief one twenty-eighth of the month. The robber told Ser-

gio that it is good luck to find an image of the saint while robbing a
house, and that he comes to the church every month to pray that the
cops don't take him to jail (which he referred to as "Reino Aven-
tura," an amusement park outside of the city).

"You're not going to rob me, are you?" asked Sergio.

"You don't have anything worth robbing," said the thief.

Another Mexico City saint that has become hugely popular in recent years is San Charbel, a Lebanese Maronite who was enshrined
in 1977 by Pope Paul VI. Born Youssef Antoun Makhlouf in 1828,
he adopted the name of Charbel when he became a monk at twenty-
three, and spent the last twenty-three of his seventy years as a hermit
on a hill near the Saint Maron's Monastery in Annaya. Charbel is
depicted as a white-bearded figure in a black hooded robe with his
eyes perpetually downcast; according to one of his biographers, he
never looked up, except for the occasional heavenward glance. Legend has it that he was once among a group of monks that suddenly
found a poisonous snake in its path. Charbel politely asked the viper
if it would be so kind as to wend its way elsewhere, and the animal
followed his suggestion.

There are about four hundred thousand Mexicans of Lebanese
descent and their largest concentration is in Mexico City. They were
the first to embrace San Charbel and include masses in his name in
their churches, but his fame soon spread among other Catholics. Despite the saint's life of abnegation, he is meant to be especially good
at fulfilling favors. One writes one's wish on a ribbon, hangs it in one
of the churches of Charbel's followers, and the results are supposedly
swift and sweet.

Even people who aren't particularly observant—or don't practice
in the traditional manner—are among Charbel's Mexico City flock.
I first found out about the saint from Miguel Ángel Zamora López,
a balding man with a wry smile in his early fifties, who spends his

afternoons roaming from cantina to cantina, selling pirated DVDs out of a satchel at twenty pesos apiece. One afternoon, he left me with a small card—called *una estampita*—that on one side bore Charbel's image and on the other a "prayer to obtain favors."

I wanted to find out more about San Charbel, so I invited Miguel Ángel for a drink. He told me he hadn't touched alcohol in seventeen years, so we settled on coffee. He offered me a roundabout version of how he had found the saint. When he was a small child, Miguel Ángel was placed in the care of a couple, supposedly friends of his parents, who subsequently moved without informing his mother and father of their progeny's whereabouts. At eight years of age, he began to drink vodka with pineapple juice and smoke marijuana. He went on his own after primary school, and worked handing out flyers for street photographers.

At seventeen, he found a job as a handyman at the city's railroad yards. "On the night shift we all worked with a bottle in our pockets," he said. Ten years later, he married a nurse, among whose clients were influential politicians, who helped find Miguel Ángel a job in the mailroom of a government ministry. He continued to drink on the job, but somehow managed to survive a decade before he was fired.

"I left home after that," Miguel Ángel said. "I didn't care anymore." He worked as a *viene-viene*, assisting drivers while they parked their cars and watching over them for a voluntary tip. For two years, he spent whatever he earned on drink and slept on the street. Finally he found his way into an AA halfway house. Once he was sober, his wife allowed him to move back with her and their son, and he began to sell movies in cantinas.

At a certain point, sales were particularly bad and Miguel Ángel found himself struggling with debt. In one of the cantinas, he saw a companion from his street days, a man who had survived by collecting empty bottles and selling them by the kilo. Except now the fellow was cleaned up, dressed in an expensive suit, sitting next to a stunning blonde, a bottle of champagne chilling in a bucket at their side. He told Miguel Ángel that he had achieved his success thanks to San Charbel.

At first dismissive, Miguel Ángel ultimately concluded that writing a wish on a ribbon and going to a church couldn't do him any harm. He went to one of the Charbel churches, in Polanco, a prosperous area of the city. "That night, I slept as if I were blessed," he remembered. "The next morning, I felt healthy. The sun seemed more radiant than ever before." Sales improved immediately. Now Miguel Ángel gives out San Charbel *estampitas* and pamphlets to his favored clients. He hasn't returned to the church, although he is considering another visit because sales have lately been slow.

"You go, you give it a try, maybe it works and maybe it doesn't," he said. "The worst you can do is not do anything."

Popular and beloved as Charbel, Jude, and La Flaca may be, the Virgin of Guadalupe attracts by far the greatest devotion and loyalty among *chilangos*. She is not only Mexico's patron saint, but was declared Patron of the Americas by Pope John Paul II in 1999. On her feast day, December 12, she attracts about seven million worshippers from around the world to her shrine in the north of the city.

There is no tangible evidence that she was ever more than an image painted on a cloak, conceived to persuade the Aztecs to convert to Catholicism. Legend has it that in December of 1531, in the hills in Tepeyac outside the city, her apparition was spotted by a humble native called Juan Diego (who likely never existed either, but was nonetheless declared a saint by the crowd-pleasing John Paul II in 2002). Prostrating himself at her feet, she declared herself the Virgin Mary of Guadalupe. She asked Juan Diego to tell the local bishop, a

Franciscan friar named Juan de Zumárraga, to build a temple for her on that very spot.

No records left by de Zumárraga mention Juan Diego. According to the myth, the cleric was not inclined to believe the peasant and asked him to return with a tangible sign of the Virgin's existence. Juan Diego went back to the hill, where Guadalupe appeared again and pointed to some flowers, their existence miraculous due to seasonal frost. She suggested he present them to the priest as evidence. The peasant wrapped the flowers in his cloak and when he unfolded it before the friar, her image was imprinted on the garment. The cloak still hangs in the basilica, and is viewed by thousands each day.

Many have speculated that her face was painted an olive tone (unlike the ivory skin prevalent in Spain's sacred art of the era) to help convince the indigenous Mexicans that she was one of them. Other followers have come up with wilder conjectures—that her left foot is moving under her cloak (the indigenous traditionally worshipped through dance); that the face of Juan Diego can be seen in the folds of her garment, and so forth.

On any given day there are between two and eight peregrinations to the shrine. In most cases special masses—which cost between one hundred twenty and four hundred dollars, depending on how many singers and organists are involved—are given in the names of the pilgrims. Among the followers during a recent month were bicyclists from the town of San Isidro el Tanque; employees of the Le-Roy Laboratories; a group of podiatrists with the last name Hernández; the inhabitants of the Crisantemo 13 Housing Project; the most faithful dwellers of the hamlet of Tlalixtaquilla in Guerrero State, and an extended family called Estrada.

The last time I stopped by, the merchants of the Mancha Uno market in the Naucalpan district had arrived for an official visit, and before their mass had gathered at the huge plaza outside the shrine.

They had set up their own altar and announced their presence with a thirteen-piece marching band that sounded more fitting for a bull-fight ring than a sacred temple.

The shrine, which holds ten thousand, was packed. People from various social classes and age groups—crying babies, napping ancients, the impeccably dressed, and those wearing fraying T-shirts that had been handed out free during political campaigns—sat in pews or stood near the entrance.

Many in Mexico City consider themselves *guadalupanos*—followers of Guadalupe—whether or not they are observant Catholics. For instance, it isn't uncommon to see a tableful of drunks declaring themselves *guadalupanos* in the sort of cantina where Miguel Ángel hands out *estampitas* of San Charbel. (It is often said here that "not all Mexicans are Catholics, but we're all *guadalupanos*.") In fact, there is a cantina in the Coyoacán section of the city called La Guadalupana. The image of the saint is omnipresent in the city: on bath towels, coffee mugs, the label of a popular cooking oil, and so forth.

A Mexican's declaration of his *guadalupanismo* can be a form of nationalism, a symbol of his pride in his country as much as an affirmation of his faith. Unsurprising in a country with a matriarchal family structure, being attached to the Virgin also triggers feelings of the maternal caress, of blissfully leaving responsibility in the hands of a nurturing, forgiving mother.

Among Mexico's Reform laws of the mid-nineteenth century were the separation of church and state, the nationalization of church property, and the secularization of such functions as education, marriage, birth, and burial. In 1992, laws were passed to soften the perceived hostility between the government and the Church, but according to the Constitution, priests and religious organizations are still prohibited from intervening in political issues or supporting political parties, candidates, or associations.

Nevertheless, Mexico City Cardinal Norberto Rivera is a staple in the newspapers and on television, offering his opinions on nearly any subject to reporters. In the spring of 2007, the city's Legislative Assembly voted on a bill that would legalize first-trimester abortions. Never was the supposed separation between church and state so publicly violated. Mexican bishops threatened that Marcelo Ebrard, the mayor of Mexico City, and any legislator who voted in favor of the initiative would be excommunicated. Even Pope Benedict XVI offered his two cents, saying that excommunication of the lawmakers "seemed" to be within Catholic rules.

After the law was passed on April 25 of that year, Cardinal Rivera called it unjust and suggested that doctors, as a matter of conscience, refuse to perform the surgery. At the time of this writing, an association of Catholic lawyers continues to fight the law and Congress has threatened to prosecute some priests for defying the Constitution. Jose Luis Soberanes, the ombudsman of the National Human Rights Commission, took the issue to the Supreme Court, with the explanation that allowing abortion is unconstitutional. While the issue is in the courts, however, legal abortions are taking place.

Meanwhile, at the Basilica of Guadalupe, they began to distribute *estampitas* to anyone who contributes to the collection baskets. On one side is a depiction of the Virgin, and on the other, the following "prayer for the defense of life":

Beloved mother of the Mexicans, Santa María of Guadalupe, pray to the Lord that we understand that all existence is special. From its conception to its natural end it's an undeserved gift of your love and never an inconvenience, and there is no right or reason to justify its premature interruption. You who in your bosom bring the creation of life, we plead that you help us to value, love, and defend it, so that we will never dare to return without opening your extraordinary gift, your invitation to life, Amen.

During Holy Week, there are various manifestations of the Passion in and around Mexico City, notably in the plaza of the Basilica de Guadalupe, in the Cuajimalpa and Naucalpan districts, and in the Reclusorio Oriente, the men's prison on the east side of town. None of these representations is as well known or well attended as that of the Iztapalapa district, which has reenacted Christ's crucifixion annually since 1843.

Throughout the week, scenes from the Bible are staged in the district's central plaza and oldest church; in 2007 it was reported that Iztapalapa attracted three million visitors. On Good Friday, when the crucifixion was re-created, a million people flocked to the area.

The body of José Emmanuel Guillén, who stood in for Jesus, doused in stage blood and mounted to its cruficix, made the front page of the tabloid *La Prensa* on Resurrection Day. Nearly every day of the year, *La Prensa* has a bloody corpse on its cover, usually due to a nasty car accident, gang violence, or drug-related revenge. These photographs are frequently taken in Iztapalapa, which has the distinction of being the district with the highest crime rate in the city. Residents of the area are quick to point out that the central section of Itzapalapa, known as the Ocho Barrios, is quite safe, and that most of the misdeeds are committed in the peripheral zones. Nonetheless, the mere mention of Iztapalapa is enough to cause anxiety in many a cabdriver, and some refuse to go there at all, particularly after dark.

Guillén, a twenty-two-year-old accounting student, gave the impression of reticence, aloofness, and an almost overwhelming seriousness, perhaps appropriate for Jesus. Tall, slender, olive-skinned, and handsome, with heavy lids and bags under his eyes, he seemed distant, as if it were irritating to share the earth with mere mortals.

We spoke at the home he shares with his parents and a sister. His father is a doll manufacturer whose factory makes about thirty thousand dolls a month. The Guilléns live in a large house, which also includes a patio, a workshop, and even a donkey. Their living room is dominated by a 52-inch television set and an even larger rendering of the Last Supper, while shelves are loaded with dolphin, ballerina, and angel figurines in glass, plaster, and plastic.

Guillén claimed that from childhood everyone from the Ocho Barrios dreams of participating in the Passion, regardless of what role he or she may be designated. Whether or not this is an overstatement, evidently Guillén nurtured that desire, having impersonated a leper, a "Hebrew," and the apostle Thomas during three different years before he was selected to play Jesus by the Holy Week organizing committee. Guillén competed against fifteen other men for the role.

To qualify to portray Jesus, you have to be a churchgoing native of the Ocho Barrios, over eighteen, devoid of piercings, tattoos, a wife, or even a sweetheart, and must assure the committee that you have no vices. To train for the nearly three miles he would have to walk while bearing a two-hundred-pound cross on Good Friday, Guillén worked out with weights in a gym, ran in Iztapalapa's green areas, and walked under the blazing spring sun in the afternoons. However, he emphasized that most of his groundwork was spiritual. He prayed every morning that his faith and love for Jesus would instruct him how to impersonate Christ. "Before rehearsals I deliver myself to God and try to act according to His will," he said.

Another reporter, accompanied by a photographer, was in the Guillén house at the same time. After the interview, there was a photo session, in which Guillén stood with a crucifix in his hand and looked heavenward. The cross was tiny and silver; although Guillén's father produced a substantially larger one that would have made a more impressive photo, the young man refused to hold it because he said it wasn't his.

Dressed in black pants and a white shirt, Guillén looked like a café waiter. His Jesus costume wasn't ready, so the photographer asked whether he would be willing to remove his shirt. Reticent, the young man telephoned the organizer of Holy Week. According to the photographer, after their conversation, Guillén said that if he wanted shirtless photos, *"tenemos que arreglarlo"*—it would have to be arranged—which is virtually synonymous in Mexico City for "you'll have to pay for it." This might have been his way of postponing, and hence refusing, to strip to the waist.

Guillén's otherworldly qualities served him impressively as Jesus. Dressed in a wig, a fake beard, and a white tunic, he seemed in a different league from his colleagues, who mostly spoke their lines in a listless monotone and were reminiscent of teenage students obliged to participate in a high school play.

Some of the extras—Nazarenes in purple robes, Hebrews in short tunics and sandals, Roman soldiers with fake swords—exposed basketball shorts underneath their robes, took photos with their cell phones, or munched on *tortas* during the events. Indeed there was a carnival aspect to the whole affair; the people who came to Iztapalapa seemed more interested in gawking, eating, and drinking than making any sort of show of spirituality. During the week, there seemed to be a lot more action around the food stalls (stewed corn with chicken feet is a singular Iztapalapa delicacy) and the kiddie fair, with its carousel and cotton candy, than in the staged pageantry mounted on two platforms. One rostrum was painted in red and gold and the other in purple and white; they looked like gaudy wedding cakes.

On Good Friday it took an awfully long time for the scene of Caiphas's judgment of Jesus to get started, with endless sounding of the trumpets. Yet when the scene began, the crowd, many sucking on lime and raspberry ices, seemed mesmerized. It was as if they were watching a movie of something familiar, a story their parents had told them about distant relatives. There was also the excitement of being in the vicinity of a famous person.

Jesus, of course, hardly speaks as he is interrogated by Caiphas and the false witnesses testify against him. Yet Guillén projected an incredible solidity and dignity as, in chains, he was pilloried and pushed around by the Roman soldiers.

As he was beaten, there was much stage blood (imported from Los Angeles, according to Guillén). You could feel a sadistic thrill among the throng as his back was whipped to a pulp and his face dripped red from the crown of thorns. Guillén, now carrying the cross, began his three-mile walk through the sweltering streets of Iztapalapa, accompanied by throngs of extras, most on foot, a few on horseback. The crowds were so dense on the side streets that one could hardly breathe, let alone move. But there was no doubt that the Holy Week proceedings elevated Iztapalapa's normally sordid reputation, however temporarily.

I caught up with Guillén about two months later. The experience had been joyous. "I wanted to play Jesus since I was a child," he said. "I remember telling my father. He said, 'Go for it, be a good boy, behave. You might have a problem with height.'" Guillén's father is only five foot six, but Guillén is five foot ten. He is the only reasonably tall member of his family. "Maybe Jesus intervened so I could do this."

There seemed to be a world of difference between the severe, tense-shouldered young man with whom I had spoken while he was rehearsing and the relaxed youth with the ready smile who later greeted me in the plaza of Iztapalapa. It was as if a battleship had been lifted from his shoulders. I couldn't help commenting that he seemed much more tranquil and easygoing than he had at the earlier date. "A lot of people have been telling me that," he said.

His fame was minor and short-lived. After Holy Week, he felt a certain sense of nostalgia, comparing the experience to what girls must feel after their *fiestas de quinceañeras*—the Latino equivalent of the sweet sixteen party. "You've prepared for a really long time and then it happens and in one day it's over. What are you going to do on Sundays? We rehearsed for three months." He had been briefly depressed. "You don't know what you are going to do with yourself after all that emotion and elation."

Playing Jesus changed Guillén's conception of Christ. "I stopped thinking of him as this God with powers. It strengthened my vision of him as a man, as a human being, and all the suffering he went through."

In any case, he must have done something right. While I was in the process of correcting the galleys of this book, I read in the newspaper that Guillén had been chosen to repeat his performance as Jesus in Holy Week of 2008. Playing the role twice is almost unheard of in the annals of the Passion of Iztapalapa.

A well-worn joke here:

Q: How do we know that Jesus was Mexican?
A: Because he lived at home until he was thirty-three, he never had a job, his mother believed he was God, and he believed that she was a virgin.

Winners

The greatest demonstration of faith I have ever witnessed here had nothing to do with Jesus, a saint, or any other manifestation of Catholicism. It was in a cantina called La Mascota during the 2006 World Cup match between Mexico and Argentina.

Much was at stake; the winner would qualify for the quarterfinals. At noon, even before the game began, La Mascota was packed. In the preceding days, Mexico had played three times with little distinction, beating Iran 3 to 1, tying with Angola at 0 to 0, and losing to Portugal 2 to 1. Yet with the blind belief customary of sports fans around the world, everyone at the cantina was sure that Mexico was going to beat Argentina, a team with overwhelmingly superior skills. (Mexico has never gone beyond the quarterfinals in the history of the World Cup, while Argentina has won twice.) The annoying waiter who was raffling off cheap bottles of rum said Mexico would triumph with a score of 3 to 1, and the parents of one of the friends I was with—academics with the National University—were similarly convinced. Customers at the neighboring tables voiced comparable opinions.

While Mexican footballers may not be up to their foreign equivalents in play, their salaries, although not as high as their European counterparts, are far better than those of superior players in South America. Their salaries are not public record, but Juan Villoro, a writer who has published books and myriad articles about football, through a bit of trickery was able to mull over the payroll of Mexican players and says their average wages are around two hundred thousand dollars per year—a sum that far outstrips the quality of their game.

While only a few Mexicans play in leagues outside Mexico, Villoro notes that there are five hundred Argentines playing outside of Argentina. That's enough for two entire Argentine leagues. For those players who stay in Argentina, the average salaries are less than twenty thousand dollars annually.

The Mexican players' jerseys are studded with the logos of Coca-Cola, Adidas, and other corporate sponsors, and the star players earn additional millions of dollars in endorsements. They are constant presences in all forms of media here. Given this ambience, it's perhaps easy for Mexicans to believe that the teams are world class, despite the harsher reality that their standing indicates.

In part because so much money is involved, football is played nearly all year round. In any social gathering, cantina, restaurant, or schoolyard, it is the object of obsessive conversation, on par with politics. In Mexico City the most popular team is the Club América, although the Pumas of the National University and the Cruz Azul also have legions of followers. Whenever there is an important game, traffic can be stalled for hours on the way to the stadium, and the fans of the winning teams whoop it up on the subway or on the streets, often congregating at the Monument of Independence on Paseo de la Reforma to celebrate.

During the opening of the World Cup game, Mexico played more gracefully than I had ever seen them play before, and I wondered whether my skepticism had been unjust. They dominated the ball and left Argentina dazed. After only six minutes, team captain Rafael Márquez scored a goal against the befuddled South Americans. However, four minutes later, Argentina tied the score.

During the first hour of the game, Mexico continued to play better than usual. The French sports newspaper *Le Volé* said that the team's action at the beginning of the match was among the best of the entire World Cup. But they weren't agile enough to score another goal, and ran out of energy in the second half. Argentina, not playing at its best, was just good enough to defend itself and assure its triumph with a goal in overtime.

As perhaps is already clear, I am not a sports aficionado. However, people who follow football here assured me that ultimately the Mexicans played typically: in the end, they did not control the game, and merely followed the play of their opponents.

A pall was cast over La Mascota. Defeat had been snatched from the jaws of victory. The patrons were vanquished, their expressions panicked or perplexed. It was as if they had been confronted with the inexistence of God or a favorite saint. The waiter hung his head. My friend's mother, disconsolate, wept bitterly. For days afterward, *chilangos* would parrot an ironic catchphrase: "We played like never before, and lost like we always do."

Sex Capital

It isn't Rio: there is no overtly sexy vibe on the streets of Mexico City. Apart from a few trendy neighborhoods, where both men and women wear tight or low-slung jeans and tops that reveal cleavage, Mexicans tend to shroud their bodies in loose and shapeless clothing. Tight pants are becoming more popular among women, but even in the suffocating heat of the dry season, you almost never see one in a skirt or a dress. If you do, she is most likely a foreigner or a nurse.

Women say that they stick to jeans and trousers because a glimpse of leg provokes leers, catcalls, and snake hisses from males. Men in Mexico City used to be known for their *piropos,* extravagant compliments along the lines of "What happened in heaven? Angels are walking the earth," or "I wish I were cross-eyed, so I could see you twice." Today that brand of patter has been replaced by slurpy kissing noises and the ubiquitous *¡mamacita!*

Female sexuality is a land mine here. Explicitly or implicitly, most women are brought up to believe that its free exercise is equivalent to having the scarlet letter tattooed on their buttocks. Women with more initiative use it circuitously, creating situations that give men an opportunity to use their own enterprise to get them to bed. No

matter how willful, many feel they must go through an elaborate cha-
rade to make it clear they had nothing to do with the scheme. While
giving oral sex, a *chilanga* might come up for air to remind her partner
that an hour earlier she had no intention of going to bed with him.

To hear them talk about it, men are equally anguished about sex.
Listen to their braggadocio in cantinas, or watch them act up at parties, and you get the impression that every male has a terribly hard
time keeping up with the ten million women in Mexico City, each of
whom is not only fair game (regardless of her marital status) but also
one in an endless line waiting to succumb to his irresistibility. The
only women out of bounds are their own mothers. Yet in these same
cantinas and parties men are usually too drunk to do much of anything if they get lucky. More often they stick with other males, sometimes with their arms about each other's shoulders, making jokes
about what a fag the other is.

Of course it is a thorny proposition to try to make sense of the
sexuality of twenty million people. But it's even trickier when that
sexuality is baroque, misleading, confusing, surprising, and secretive.

Tall, stout, with dyed blond hair and painted eyebrows, Anabel
Ochoa has a nose that is not only bent but upturned. In the studio
where she conducts her radio program, she's dressed in shiny silver
exercise pants that look as if they were stolen from an astronaut, and
a striped dress shirt, possibly borrowed from her husband. Enough
buttons are opened to expose tanned, freckled cleavage and a raspberry brassiere. She wears thick swaths of gray eye shadow and jet
mascara. When she reads e-mail from her listeners, she puts on eyeglasses that have kitsch black frames with rhinestones.

Despite the sign in the studio that in no uncertain terms prohibits
smoking, she lights one cigarette after another during the three hours

of her broadcast. Consequent to her tobacco habit is a deep and sump-
tuous voice, with the lisp and brusque tones of Spain's Basque region
(from where she immigrated to Mexico more than twenty years ago),
a voice that alternately growls, barks, and purrs. Camp and larger
than life, Ochoa could be a character in an Almodóvar movie.

A man named Rodrigo has sent her an e-mail inquiry. He wants
to know whether sperm has regenerative properties for a woman's
skin. "I know where you're going, my friend, Rodrigo," says Ochoa,
her voice vibrating as if she were licking honey off the listener's body.
"You like to come on your wife's face and you're trying to convince
her that there is something enchanted about your sperm." She laughs
brusquely, and as her tone rises one can imagine Señora Torquemada
in a one-woman Inquisition.

"You rascal. This is a phallocratic culture and you men act as if
your penises were Harry Potter's magic wand. My friend, if there
were antiwrinkle properties in semen it would be on sale in the cosmetics counter of every department store in the world. Let me set you
straight: Semen doesn't kill you and it isn't fattening and it won't
poison you. There's a little fructose in it but not enough to have any
nutritional value if you're hungry. If you and your wife like facials,
go ahead. And if you find that yours has antiwrinkle properties, I
want to become your business partner."

Beside her on the table is an enormous stack of paper. "I'm behind
by about a thousand e-mails," Ochoa says during a commercial break.
Yet for much of the show she responds to neither messages nor calls,
and extemporizes about whatever strikes her fancy, including shameless self-promotion for her own self-help sex books. Among her riffs:

- "Masturbation is stupendous, but if that's what you do all
  the time, what kind of a future do you have? Remember,
  your hand will never fall in love with you."

- "When you go to the movies and there's a shootout, you know that they're not firing real bullets from those guns. So why should you believe that pornographic movies are real, with all those huge members and multiple orgasms? If watching porn gets you hot, enjoy it, but don't compare yourself or your partner with the actors."

- "When my daughter was little, I found her looking at a pornographic Internet site with Barbie. Imagine! You do a Google search for Barbie and you end up looking at porn. I don't like Barbie to begin with. She has those big tits, the tiny waist, and no vulva, and even worse, goes out with that moron Ken. But porno with Barbie? I don't believe in putting locks on the Internet or the TV. You have to have a sane, healthy conversation with your kids and prepare them for what they'll inevitably see. To prevent them from seeing it, you'd have to gouge out their eyes." (With her deep and melodramatic tone, it is possible to imagine her, Medea style, doing just that.)

- "Remember, if you have one hundred orgasms a year, it will add ten years to your life!"

Although her sense of humor is charming and singular, there is nothing extraordinary about Ochoa's advice, which mostly comes from common sense and basic sex education. What is surprising is how few people in Mexico City are willing to speak as openly and plainly as she.

It isn't as if there are no other sex-advice sources here. Indeed, in the past dozen years, there's been a deluge of them in nearly every newspaper and magazine. Most radio stations have at least one show similar to hers, and some have several. Many TV talk programs (even some broadcast during daytime hours) invite sex therapists to counsel on a regular basis. However, the difference between Ochoa and her colleagues is her frank speech. Most of the others talk and write about sex in sober, studious tones, as if their research has been entirely theoretical, with no actual field work. A few women columnists write warmed-over versions of *Sex and the City* that are all tease, with little confession or revelation. Certainly none of them is as freewheeling and uncensored as Ochoa. Mexico City is famous for its *doble moral*—anything goes in private, as long as you maintain a respectable public pose. Given such communal taboos here, it isn't coincidental that a foreigner became the trailblazer of sex advice.

All these spaces in the media indicate a vacuum of knowledge about sex, and a great hunger for that void to be filled. The venues are safely anonymous; the letters and e-mails are unsigned. Many demonstrate an astonishing ignorance. A tabloid daily called *Metro* publishes an advice column known as "Tía Remedios." (*Tía* means "aunt" in Spanish, and *Remedios* is not only a woman's name but also the word for "remedies." Any person for whom it is characteristic to dispense advice is known as a Tía Remedios.)

Recently, a correspondent inquired whether urinating after unprotected sex could prevent pregnancy. Another wanted to know how likely she was to get pregnant after unprotected anal sex. Yet another asked if an ordinary contraceptive pill would be useful the day after having unprotected sex. Ochoa receives similar letters, so I asked if she ever got the feeling that people who wrote such missives were putting her on.

"I get the letter about pregnancy from anal sex nearly every week," she said. "Mexicans don't have the vaguest idea about basic anatomy." (Verónica Maza, another advice columnist, agreed, adding that she received a letter from a nineteen-year-old who had made a mutual decision with his girlfriend that they were ready to have sex. He wanted to know where he was supposed to penetrate her.)

The questions and answers in the "Tía Remedios" columns can be fascinating inasmuch as they illustrate the problems, traumas, and complications of sexuality in Mexico City.

> *My husband has* mamitis *[an exaggerated attachment to one's mother], so my mother-in-law is in my face all the time. I've told him that she's got to let me have my space. Do you think it's bad that I said that to him? Should I complain to her, or should I wait for my husband to do the right thing?*
>
> Your husband will never do what you think is the right thing, because his mother is the sacred author of his life. You need to change what's going on in your relationship with her. Maybe you could be very sweet to your mother-in-law to confuse her. Change your tactics, because your husband will never— I repeat, never—do what you want so you can have your space.

Over the course of a day or two, the basics about human reproduction are explained to Mexican students when they are twelve or thirteen, but sex education as such doesn't exist in schools here. In 2006, biology textbooks were published with a section that included material about sexual orientation, masturbation, prevention of sexually transmitted diseases, and contraception, but parents' associations and Catholic groups were successful at preventing their distribution.

These upright parents—particularly mothers—are a significant impediment to the fulfillment of their children's sexuality. The day I visited Ochoa at the radio station, one of the e-mails to which she responded was emblematic. A mother wrote asking for advice regarding her daughter's husband, who suffered from premature ejaculation. The query nearly sent Ochoa into paroxysms.

"Why are you telling me about your daughter's husband's penis?" she snarled. "Does he know which dates of the month you menstruate? Does your daughter come crying to you at night about how he comes in a minute? Do you all sit around the breakfast table the next morning and say, 'Hey, Speedy, want a café espresso?' Leave her alone! Her sexuality belongs to her!"

On the surface, the Mexican mother is an angelic untouchable figure venerated by her husband and children. In Mexico City, most children—even when they are middle-aged and accompanied by their own families—continue to have lunch with their mothers every Sunday. Typically, the mother is a more ambiguous creature, often meddlesome and guilty of emotional blackmail, who spoils her sons while victimizing her daughters.

"Mothers educate their daughters about sex," says clinical psychologist David Barrios, who has counseled couples and the sexually dysfunctional in Mexico City for twenty-four years. "They see their mothers as a divine moral authority, with an all-seeing, punishing eye. They are told that pleasure is forbidden and sex is for making children. If you have sex for pleasure, you're not fit to be a sainted mother. Women hear their mother's voice when they have sex."

According to the psychologist, the ominous mother figure is one of the reasons for the high incidence of anorgasmia among women here. Mexican mothers also cause complications for their male offspring. Boys are usually pampered and babied in the home, taxed with no domestic responsibilities while their sisters shoulder many. Most men want to marry women who will similarly spoil them, yet have difficulties square-rooting the sexuality of a woman who treats them like their mother. If a single man has great sex with a woman, he is likely to discount her as a prospect for marriage. His logic is that a woman who enjoys sex would like it with any man and is as such a *puta,* likely to betray him and unfit to bear his children. Meanwhile, a woman who abhors sex, or professes to consider it only as a vehicle for procreation, has far greater potential as a spouse.

The ambiguity of the mother figure is reflected in Mexican slang. To say that someone or something *no tiene madre*—literally, has no mother—is as high a compliment as one can give. To say that something *tiene poca madre*—has very little mother—is sometimes praise and sometimes pejorative, depending on the context. *Me vale madre*—a phrase that makes no sense when translated literally ("I care as much as a mother")—means that one doesn't give a damn. On the other hand, the word *padre* (father) is always a complimentary adjective.

If these last few paragraphs imply that mothers deserve to be condemned while fathers should be let off scot-free, nothing could be further from the truth. Mexican families are matriarchies because fathers are frequently absent, and men who live with their wives and children tend to offer economic support but little in the way of emotional or practical guidance. Male adultery is nearly universal, accepted openly or tacitly. This is one reason that mothers cling so tightly to their children; they get no physical or emotional satisfaction from their husbands.

The offspring of these shady figures are not blameless, either. The majority of sons and daughters in Mexico City live with their parents until they marry. While this tendency may be understandable among the starving class, it is almost equally common in well-to-do families. The "children"—who are treated as such well into their twenties and thirties—freely admit that the idea of having to take care of their own laundry, shopping, and cooking, not to mention paying their own rent, holds little attraction. As such, sex is limited to furtive encounters when parents are away, in the back seats of cars, weekends in Cuernavaca or Acapulco (women most typically tell their mothers they are traveling with girlfriends), and hot-sheet hotel rooms.

The latter are ubiquitous in Mexico City, used not only by the young who live at home, but also by the married or otherwise compromised, and couples looking for a break in their routine. The economically challenged can rent a room of the bare-bones, cracked-mirror variety for seven or eight dollars, while those with fewer limits to their budget can hire ones with Jacuzzis, mirrored ceilings, or even a bed suspended from on high by ropes. One motel, on the highway to Cuernavaca, has a suite known as "the Beach," a small warehouse with a pool and a sun roof, the floor of which has been inundated with sand.

By the time they get married, these overage children supposedly enter adulthood willy-nilly, with no preparation. Women are trained that it is far more acceptable socially to suffer than to experience pleasure. Men make great theater out of their machismo, but in truth identify far more closely with the mothers who spoiled them than with their fathers, who probably treated them unkindly if not unjustly, were absent emotionally, and cheated on their wives.

Every couple of days "Tía Remedios" prints a letter from a woman, usually young, in the throes of an affair with a married man. In Mexico City, I have never felt as magnetic to women as when I presented myself as another's husband. After I divorced, while I didn't suddenly resurface in monk's robes, the aura I generated when I wore a wedding ring disappeared.

When I mentioned this to psychologist Barrios, he suggested that women might have been attracted to me because my marriage represented experience, and the possibility of sexual satisfaction they felt less likely to receive with a single man. Women have mentioned that married men are attractive for representing sex with no strings attached.

There's another element in operation I'd call the Catholic imperative. Just as many Mexicans can barely taste food that hasn't been seasoned with chile, a sizable swath cannot get off, or is barely satisfied, if there isn't at least a whiff of sin involved. It might be just a vague taste—say, going to bed with someone in the same social circle, a close friend of a close friend. Someone else's wife or husband is unquestionably hotter—say, a married colleague, in a hotel during lunch hour. But your best friend's spouse, or your sibling's, can take you through the roof.

It is hard to figure out the frequency with which women commit adultery—they are far more discreet about it than men, who cannot go so far as pinching a woman's bottom without telling all their friends in the cantina the following day. A woman typically will not even tell her best friend (although she might own up to a shrink, a hairdresser, or some other disinterested party who hardly figures in her life). Anecdotes and rumors abound—personal trainers in gyms are supposed to be servicing half the married women in Mexico City. In monied circles some say that wives go for the most attractive chauffeurs and bodyguards.

Adultery in Mexico City is understandable in the context of people who have spent their adolescence and young adulthood—perhaps ten or twenty years—having sex in illicit or prohibited places, often with the threat of being discovered in the act. Married sex, ordained by the family, the state, the pope, and Almighty God, might well turn out to be underwhelming.

Mexican families are the polar opposite of those in the United States that virtually throw their children out in the street once they reach legal age. In a culture that has no confidence in its institutions, the family is the only cohesive unit. As such, Mexican families are preternaturally tight. Although this closeness is primarily manifest in a lack of privacy and busybody interference in personal affairs, roughly one in six letters in the "Tía Remedios" columns are written by people who are having sex, or are considering sex, with relatives.

One column published two letters, the first from a married man who had sex "constantly" with his aunts and cousins, and wanted to have sex with his wife's cousins. The second was from a thirty-five-year-old man, married to a twenty-year-old, who also had sex with his forty-year-old mother-in-law and "didn't know how to stop." Tía Remedios always advises these pen pals to avoid sex with relatives, whom she refers to as "sacred material."

Another inhibitor toward the free exercise of sexuality is what Mexicans refer to as *pena*—which in Royal Academy Spanish means "distress" or "grief" (as one might feel upon the death of a relative), but is used in Mexico to connote shame. (The word for "shame," *vergüenza,* is appropriately used in the context of what you feel after having done something wrong.) Alarmingly, Mexicans claim to feel *pena* over nearly anything.

For example, when I edited a section of a magazine, I used to commission two articles each month. Frequently, contributors would contact me six months or even a year after their pieces had been published, and in an extremely roundabout way—after asking how I'd spent the holidays, wondering aloud about an idea for another story, and soliciting an opinion about the latest political scandal—would mention that they'd never been paid for their work.

"Why didn't you tell me before?" I'd always ask.

"Me dio pena," was the inevitable response. "I was ashamed." If you are embarrassed to ask for the money you are owed for work you have long completed, or if you would rather sink into a hole in the ground than tell a waiter that the food he's served you is inedible, or if it would send you into spasms of humiliation to tell someone who has just cut in front of you in line where he is supposed to stand, then imagine the complications of telling a man where your clitoris is and how

you best like it stimulated. In 2006, 78 percent of Mexican men and 71 percent of women, responding to a Pfizer-sponsored survey, said they were sexually unsatisfied. But to put the cards on the table, or ask out loud for something that might improve the situation? *Qué pena.*

Partly because male adultery is so prevalent, most women innately mistrust men. Anabel Ochoa points out that since marital relations are so often unsatisfactory, women look for material manifestations of a man's supposed love: from flowers or a movie ticket to a house, a car, or a diamond ring. Many men don't trust women, either—especially those who like sex. Better to be with one who just lies there, and have affairs or see prostitutes. Obviously the situation of mutual mistrust doesn't lead to communication, and with neither trust nor dialogue, a couple is unlikely to have a satisfying sex life.

Miscommunication can be terribly baroque, and practically pre-destined. Various men told me that many *chilangas* are willing to go to bed with them, but they usually had to initiate things; if they pro-posed a sex act apart from the two or three most common ones, the women had never tried it before. At the same time, women said that regardless of their age, men wanted to believe they were inexperi-enced, and often felt obligated to at least imply their innocence. Women complained that men would say anything to get them into bed, yet men opined that women ask for at least an implicit promise of commitment before they are willing to have sex.

Many of Ochoa's listeners seem to write to her as a way of avoid-ing a talk with their partners. The day I visited, she read an e-mail from a forty-seven-year-old woman named Berta, who wrote after having unprotected sex with her husband, with whom she had been separated for a year and a half. She wanted to know where she could be tested for venereal diseases.

"When will anyone ever ask me about these tests before they have sex?" Ochoa bellowed. "Berta, if he has something, then you have it too, and when you go to the clinic maybe they'll give you a two-for-one discount. When are you going to understand? When husbands go away for a year and a half, it usually isn't to a Trappist monastery. And if that's where they went, watch out for what they did with the priests."

I'm married with two children, a three-year-old and a five-year-old. While riding the subway, I've realized that when someone rubs against me from behind, I feel vibrations, as if I liked it. What do you recommend? Do I need a lubricant for my first time?

You can ask your wife to anally penetrate you, with one or two fingers, depending on your tolerance, or for her to use a vibrator made expressly for this kind of penetration. If you want another man to penetrate you, you'll need a water-based lubricant and protection to avoid an illness you could pass on to your wife. We're talking about infidelity here; if you don't care, that's your business. But think about whether you would like it if you found out that she were unfaithful to you.

Circumstantial evidence of male bisexuality, homosexual confusion, and even panic is overwhelming in Mexico City. Across the board, from the most highly educated and supposedly liberal classes to day laborers on the sidewalk, men insistently and constantly make fun of each other's sexuality. If you walk a certain way; if you speak too loudly or too quietly; if you gesture with your hands as you speak; if you are surrounded by women or absent of their company; if you order certain drinks or foods, then you are undoubtedly a *puto*, a *joto*, a *maricón*. To this day, many Mexicans believe that if they take the active part in an encounter with another man, that they are straight—the guy who is penetrated is the fag.

I have a slovenly writer friend who constantly referred to a mutual acquaintance (with the looks of a soap-opera actor, always well-dressed, every hair in place) as gay. This went on for years until at one point I mentioned that a woman we knew had been to bed with the supposed homosexual. She claimed the encounter had been incredible. "These days the *putos* are tricking us," my friend said. "They even go to bed with women."

An old joke:

Q: *What's the difference between a straight Mexican and a gay Mexican?*
A: Three tequilas.

When I moved to Mexico City, many taxi drivers pointed out the streetwalkers as we passed by. They advised me that if I saw a beautiful one, she was undoubtedly male. Indeed, there are far more transvestite prostitutes on the street than actual women (who are more commonly found in massage parlors, table-dance bars, the classified ads, and the Internet). One of the sidewalk transvestites, who went by the name of Martha, told me that 100 percent of her clients—those who knew her gender identity from the beginning, and those who professed to be surprised after she warned them—once in bed went for her penis.

In the evening after a long afternoon of drinking, it is quite ordinary in a cantina to see men with their arms around each other's shoulders, boozily professing their love for one another. "It's very common here for a married woman to believe that her husband might have an adventure with another man," says Anabel Ochoa. "At a party, or after a bar hop, the most macho guy can go off with another man and the next day, it's as if nothing happened."

The sex columnists, educators, and psychologists I interviewed for this chapter cautioned against coming to any conclusions about overwhelming queerness in the male population. They warned that much of Mexican sexuality is fluid, complicated, and resistant to labeling.

Some suggested that the homosexual fixation is a manifestation of the anxieties suffered as a consequence of machismo. Their descriptions made it almost possible to feel some pity for men here. It turns out that the pose of machismo is difficult to keep up, both figuratively and literally. Except when they are very drunk, men are forbidden from showing signs of affection, tenderness, fragility, or vulnerability. With so many women feigning passivity and needing to be "conquered," psychologist Barrios points out that men "have to be sexual athletes with incredible erections and have to produce pleasure for the woman."

Ochoa agrees: "Women are passive about their sexuality. They believe in penises that either give them orgasms or don't." This is probably the biggest source of the overwhelming performance anxiety experienced by men. And of women's sexual dissatisfaction: the psychologists and columnists whom I consulted estimated that between 40 percent and 70 percent of men in Mexico City suffer from premature ejaculation.

If the nature of women's complaints about men is not unique to Mexico City, their grievances are certainly ubiquitous here. Women say that *chilangos* are excellent at seduction: "To get you into bed, they'll pull the stars from the sky," says columnist Verónica Maza. Once the stars are at mattress level, however, *chilangas* complain that men forgo foreplay and want to go straight to penetration; that little attention is paid to their bodies apart from breasts, buttocks, and vaginas; that they are clueless or slapdash about a woman's pleasure. A man will push a woman's head toward his penis when he wants oral sex, and will try to initiate anal sex by pretending he has arrived at the back door "accidentally." Various women I talked to told me that they had had positive, even ecstatic, experiences with Mexican men. However, even among them, many complained that they felt men were distant—that on an emotional level they weren't really there; that they could have been with any woman at all.

In the past decade there has been a huge increase in sex shops in Mexico City, and sex toys are also sold via cable television, mail order, and even at private gatherings for women not unlike Tupperware parties. Edelmira Cárdenas combines sex education workshops with the sale of dildos, vibrators, and other such apparatus. She also has her own shop and a nightly cable television show, where she pitches sex toys as if they were the most mundane household items imaginable.

When asked what her best-selling items were, she mentioned a vibrating dildo, which, she claimed, stimulated the clitoris, the G-spot, and the first third or so of the vagina (the most sensitive part, she assured), all at the same time. The item would produce one orgasm after another, she promised, each more explosive than the last. She admitted that her apparatus was of no help for the problem of the skewed communication between men and women.

As unsatisfying as it often may be, there is nevertheless a lot of sex in Mexico City. Those twenty million people have to come from somewhere. Anabel Ochoa remembers that soon after she arrived from Spain, a man at a party asked her if she would like to go to the bathroom with him. She wasn't sure she'd understood and asked him to repeat himself. "Come to the bathroom with me for a little while," he said, as if he were suggesting a trip to the moon on gossamer wings. "I promise, we won't take up too much time." She laughs at the memory. "He was offering me a premature ejaculation."

"People get horny and have encounters very quickly, without premeditation," says Ochoa. "Managers and employers sometimes make it an obligation at work. There is a lot of promiscuity on the job, and you have to combine that with [the tendency toward] infidelity."

Women's apparent passivity doesn't preclude them from having sex. "Women say, 'I did it because he was so insistent,'" says Ochoa. Barrios has conducted workshops with teenage girls, who often admit to having sex they say they didn't want. "I always ask why they didn't say no, and they say, *me daba pena*." They were ashamed. "There is a high incidence of marital rape in Mexico," he adds. "You have to 'do your duty' or it's forced on you."

"Quantity is cultivated more than quality," says Ochoa. "There may be a lot of sex, but it's much harder to find a couple that has a rich sex life." Indeed, the panorama for many couples is bleak: men who stop having sex with their wives once their children are born; people who live together for decades who never have sex with the lights on or on top of the bedcovers; and what Barrios refers to as *coitos chinpuncuás*. He explains: "All too frequently, sex in Mexico City is done in the half light, only half undressed, without caresses, words, kisses, closeness, or complete body contact. There's a fast penetration and it's over in three strokes."

In the last dozen years or so, in addition to the franker discussion about sex in the Mexico City media, there has been more openness, albeit surreptitiously, in the schools. People under twenty-five told me that during high school, although they had received no more than the requisite couple of days' description of their reproductive appara-

tus in biology class, they had all been provided with some extraoffi-
cial information about sex and sexuality from other teachers (usually
those who taught the humanities rather than science).

This same generation—like kids all over the world—has grown up
with the vast sources of information about sex and sexuality available on the Internet. So while the young may be suffering from the
same neuroses, anxieties, inhibitions, and indiosyncrasies as their
older counterparts, their distress is at least on a smaller scale. Notably, some younger women appear to be less repressed about asking
for what they want in bed, and it turns out that even macho men can
be pretty good at following instructions if their sexual invincibility is
on the chopping block.

Nowhere is the generational difference more evident than in the
gay and lesbian populations. Although Mexico City is traditionally
one of the few places in the country that gay Mexicans veer to (Gua-
dalajara, the port of Veracruz, and some of the famous beach resorts
are others), in the early 1990s, the capital was a dangerous place to
be homosexual. There were at least a dozen gay bars, but on any
given night they were subject to police raids, during which customers
would be taken to the closest police station en masse and made to pay
bribes before they were released. Even more frequently, as they left
the bars individual clients became victims of extortion by patrol cops,
forced to withdraw the daily limit from cash machines.

Incidents of violence against homosexuals were common; in the
early 1990s, several noted AIDS activists were murdered. A homicide
that might have been qualified as a hate crime in the United States
was often characterized as a crime of passion in Mexico City. Aggres-
sors were sometimes let off with a slap on the wrist or set free with
no consequences.

When I arrived in 1990, there was one lesbian bar, which closed within a year or two. Lesbians were mostly hidden and nearly always (like their male counterparts) married and with children.

It would be a mistake to overestimate the advances; homosexuality is only tacitly accepted in most of society here. Still, progress is evident and significant. Today, the Zona Rosa neighborhood is a sector of tolerance where both gays and lesbians—most of them under thirty—not only have bars, restaurants, and cafés where they congregate, but also can walk on the streets hand in hand, their arms around each other, and kiss openly. All of this was unheard of fifteen years ago. Apart from the Zona Rosa, in the rest of the city, some bars that cater to gays are scattered here and there. Those for lesbians can be counted on the fingers of one hand, and one would still have digits left over to scratch one's head; there are, however, various bars where lesbians and gays share the same space.

In the early 1990s, the majority of gays and lesbians wouldn't dare tell their families or colleagues about their sexuality, for fear of chastisement or even banishment. If today their existence isn't precisely accepted, it is most often at least tolerated. Various young people of different social classes told me that they had confessed their sexuality to their parents and although the topic was never discussed in depth, they continued to live under the same roof *en famille,* which at least represents a tacit understanding. In the workplace, openness about one's homosexuality is similarly tactful—it is frequently known but rarely a topic of conversation.

Because of the freer discourse and access to information, as well as the efforts of human rights organizations and a few forward-thinking politicians, assimilation is much easier today than ever. Various homosexuals and lesbians under twenty-five told me about how much they had suffered when they first recognized their sexuality, typically in their mid to late teens. It turned out that their suffering lasted for between six months and a year or so, after which they were able to find a community of like-minded people (often among their high school classmates), as well as a committed boyfriend or girlfriend. A few even had parents who accepted same-sex lovers on a friendly basis, if not precisely as part of the family. Most seemed only vaguely aware that many of their older counterparts passed decades, if not entire lives, living much more anguished lives of secrecy.

In the early 1990s, among the roster of gay bars were a couple of beer halls on Calle Cuba in the *centro histórico,* the Viena and the Oasis. In those days, if you had walked in uninitiated you would have had no idea that you were in a gay bar. The customers looked like any other men on the sidewalks or in the metro—nothing about their dress or body language revealed their sexuality. Even in their hookups, they were discreet, sitting together at tables without touching. Today these same beer halls exist, but you are just as likely to find guys with hair gel and shirts unbuttoned to the navel as you are men who look like accountants or bus drivers. The latter are likely to be dancing on top of a table with a seminude waiter.

Other bars, such as the notorious Spartacus in Ciudad Nezahualcóyotl (which has the appearance of a small-town disco), have darkrooms for sex, and Tom's Leather Bar on Avenida Insurgentes features naked dancers with erections on top of the bar.

In 2007, two laws and a cultural event in Mexico City pointed toward progress, however slow or ambiguous. Firstly, *la ley de convivencia—* the law of cohabitation, known commonly as "the gay law"— recognizes same-sex couples who have officially registered with the government. Mexico City is one of the few places in Latin America to have passed such a law; there are a few other exceptions in South America (Colombia; Uruguay; some cities in Brazil; and Argentina).

However, the Mexico City law grants same-sex couples no significant rights they didn't already have. For example, it stipulates that gays and lesbians can leave their possessions to their same-sex partners when they die, and that they can let their partners make medical decisions for them if they go into a coma. However, these options were actually open to them prior to the law's passage, and to exercise them they still need the same legalized documentation as before.

The law does not grant the same privileges of Mexico's Social Security system that are allowed to married heterosexuals, such as medical insurance or housing credits. The most optimistic see the passage of the law as a first step toward a more comprehensive package of rights.

Mexico City also became the only place in the country where it is legal for a woman to have a first-trimester abortion. (Most Latin American countries, including the rest of Mexico, allow abortion only in cases of rape or if pregnancy threatens a woman's life. It is legal in Cuba, and in Chile and Ecuador morning-after pills are legally available.) The Mexico City law is particularly significant, given that dangerous, back-alley abortions are hugely prevalent among the impoverished classes.

In May 2007, the New York photographer Spencer Tunick, who travels the world and photographs nude populations en masse, came through Mexico City and over eighteen thousand people showed up to bare all for him. Much was made of the fact that this was the largest number of people ever captured by the photographer, as if it were a sign of sexual liberation. Given that there are so many people in Mexico City, the record is unsurprising; in other cities, Tunick captured a greater number of residents proportional to the size of the population.

Further, three out of four participants in the Tunick shoot here were male, as compared to other cities where the division was more or less equal. After shooting all the participants, Tunick asked the men to leave so he could take some pictures with women only. A large number of males waited around and, after the shoot finished, jeered and catcalled at the women as they gathered their clothing.

Given so many confusions and frustrations attendant to sex here, it is perhaps predictable that prostitution is widespread. In the streets around the Merced Market, you can find working girls with bodies shaped like tamales who will charge about twenty dollars for a *coito chinpuncuás* in a flea-bitten hotel room. On the Internet Argentine models offer their services for as much as one thousand dollars an hour.

Laws regarding prostitution in Mexico City are typically murky. Supposedly it is legal—except in brothels, bars, nightclubs, and cabarets. This limits permitted activity to the sidewalks and outcall services, advertised not only on the Internet but also in all of the newspapers. However, as in many aspects of the city, legality appears to be open to broad-minded interpretation. The employees of massage parlors, coyly known as "spas" or *estéticas* (beauty parlors), routinely offer sex to their customers. (In the spas a customer can get a half-hearted massage, but if you go to one of the *estéticas* and ask for a haircut and a manicure, they'll look at you like you're from Mars.)

Some of the high-end table-dance bars operate under restrictive rules in which a customer cannot even touch the woman who is writhing on his lap. Still, it is frequently said that many of these women will leave the premises or meet a customer outside for astronomical sums of money. Other such bars are much more lax, offering few or no limits for the paying client; some have back rooms where anything goes.

The most sordid locale for prostitution that I have seen in Mexico City is the Callejón de Manzanares, an alley near the *centro histórico,* where dozens of women languidly walk around in a circle while being ogled by a horde of working-class gawkers. Every so often, one of these men will make a signal to a girl, and go off with her to a cubicle where the cohabitation costs ten dollars.

In the mid-1990s several nightspots opened near the Plaza Garibaldi, an area of the city known for mariachi bands in the open air, dive bars, and blaring neon signs, equally tantalizing for its inexpensive pleasures and unsettling dangers. Cheap drinks and live sex were the principal attractions of these bars-cum-nightclubs. The most famous was a cavernous dungeon called El 14.

Imagine a scene painted by George Grosz, peopled by figures with brown skin. The principal clientele were off-duty soldiers, who came alone, in groups, or occasionally with women. Most were in uniform, although those who weren't were easily identifiable by their crew cuts. El 14 wasn't obviously a gay bar, but it was understood that some of the guys were available to civilian men, usually at a price. So it attracted slummers from well-heeled areas, hoping to either pick up a piece of trade or at least gaze at many. The entertainment consisted of male strippers, whose acts were followed by a couple of doughy, glowering women who got naked onstage and took on all comers.

That last word is a figure of speech. The night I showed up at El 14, none of the various customers who stripped to the skin and climbed aboard, bright-eyed and bushy-tailed as they may have appeared, could muster an erection. It all seemed like a vaudeville joke, with the audience catcalling the luckless volunteers.

A half hour after the entertainment, nearly the entire audience

suddenly stood up and ran, making an en masse beeline for the back
door. The military police had arrived, and the soldiers had to take a
powder; they were not allowed on the premises while in uniform.

The era of these clubs would meet its end in 1997. Left-wing
mayor Cuauhtémoc Cárdenas was rumored to have imposed an unwritten law that clubs with live intercourse would be closed down,
although oral sex onstage was permitted. (It is one of Mexico City's
aberrances that its leftist politicians are also its most repressive; the
other parties are more sympathetic to free enterprise.)

A few years into the new century, a mini-shopping center opened
near Plaza Garibaldi, called—in English—Sex Capital. Built on three
levels, the lowest is a warren of shops that sell dildos, lubricants, vibrators, tiger-print tangas, blow-up dolls, etc. It's a mystery how
these stores stay open; the times I have passed through there were
hardly any customers. The top floor has a cheesy sex museum and a
table-dance bar.

The middle floor has proven to be a popular attraction and fills up
most afternoons. There are two stages among a cluster of white plastic tables and chairs. Customers—some men alone or in groups,
plenty of couples—are seated and served beers and fast food. (Hot
dogs are listed in the menu under the rubric "doggie style," and piz-
zas advertised "from 12 to 16 inches.") They settle in to watch a
stage show of two or three strippers.

The episodes of audience participation between the strips are far
more involving, and seem to be the main reason for most of the audience's presence. An emcee trawls the audience offering free beer to
the man who can recite the longest list of pseudonyms for vagina—
papayita (little papaya), *chile con crema* (chile with cream), *cosita
dulce* (sweet little thing)—or the woman who can do the same for
penis—*camote* (sweet potato), *plátano macho* (plaintain), *guayabo*
(guayaba tree). The most audacious, regardless of their body type or

fluidity of motion, clamber onstage and strip to their underwear, all the while performing suggestive gyrations.

Audience members are encouraged to vote, with their voices, for their favorites. On a recent afternoon, a group of—wouldn't you know it?—off-duty soldiers yelled, hooted, whistled, and even lifted tables and chairs in the air in support of a woman whose body resembled a one-story building, and who wore panties so voluminous they looked like a diaper.

Another novelty of the last few years is the emergence of a swinger scene. Various partner-swapping venues exist. In the largest suites of a hotel in the Colonia Doctores (a neighborhood notable for its trade in stolen car parts), every weekend there are swinger parties, some themed (doctors and nurses, vampires and werewolves) and others free-form.

The city's most famous swingers club, in operation since 1993, is located around the corner from the Secretariat of the Interior. Decorated with Christmas lights strung from the ceiling, with an annoying smoke machine, it looks a bit like a down-at-the-heels discotheque. Men are not allowed to attend this place alone, so I asked a journalist friend to accompany me. We were seated in the back, next to a table where a man wearing a gray suit had his head up the floral-print dress of his companion, who moaned in ecstasy. Most of the couples were less impatient and warmed up by dancing to eighties music. The appearance of a couple of male strippers, their penises erect, also contributed to set a certain mood.

The place is known to habitués as Pedro's Club, appropriate given how protagonistic a role its owner, Pedro López, plays. Before he arrived onstage, an announcer mentioned through a microphone that Leonardo da Vinci had been censored, and Salvador Dalí had been censored, but Pedro López would not be held back. At first López, a slender and diminutive man in his early forties, whose e-mail address implies a disproportionately extensive member, warmed up the audience by offering free champagne to the first woman to offer up her bra, her panties, and so forth.

Upstairs, there is a salon with couches where people can get to know each other, perhaps through a friendly chat or simply by dropping their jeans, leaning over, and initiating intercourse while standing up. Next to the salon is a room in near darkness where an orgy takes place.

Strict protocol is observed. Participation is not obligatory; the word no is enough to stop a stampeding rhinoceros. Pedro told me that if a couple shows up several times and is not interested in anything beyond voyeurism, they are disinvited. He wants real couples—if a man shows up with a different woman on three or four occasions, he will be discouraged from returning. The women tended to be made up, coiffed, and perfumed, and wore attractive outfits, at least until they felt compelled to remove them. The men were decidedly less attractive; I can only hope that they are good providers.

The reporter who accompanied me noted that certain codes of machismo prevailed, despite the supposedly libertine setting. Women did not initiate sex. Indeed, five centuries after the indigenous Mexicans traded their women to welcome the conquering Spaniards, the female of the species is still wampum here. Each tended to wait passively to be chosen, after which she would look toward her partner for an overt approval of the arrangement.

Entrance to Pedro's Club ranges between twenty and forty dollars per couple, depending on the night of the week; additionally, there is a thirty-five dollar minimum. Hence, swinging is a luxury, prohibitively expensive for the city's masses.

One day while showering I stuck a toothbrush in my anus and had an orgasm very different from the usual ones. I'm not

*homosexual, but I don't know if this type of practice is homo-
sexual or not.*

Anal stimulation is not an exclusively homosexual practice.
Men and women who consider themselves heterosexual can
also enjoy it, if they like. The only limits are when a situation
stops being pleasant and causes physical harm.

Reader: If a Mexican offers to lend you his toothbrush, think twice.

Wim Wenders with Skin

The Hilton hotel chain makes more money from the rental of porn movies in their rooms than they do from their minibars. Eighty percent of AT&T's broadband business is generated from porn. Most of General Motors' business from their DirecTV business is porn. That's a lot of money."

A charismatic thirty-four-year-old Mexican who calls himself Maldoror believes there are golden eggs to be hatched from his dream: to become Mexico City's porno king. He and his partner Tirielle imagine an empire that includes film production, live Internet sites, erotic soap operas for Sky TV, individual stills and scenes being sold at newsstands, at porno-industry trade shows, on the Web.

We talked at a humble cantina on the edge of an unsafe neighborhood. So far, their production company, Barro Ardiente, had only completed one film, *Fetiches Mexicanos 1* (the plan is to produce a series of twelve). An hour-long effort divided into four scenes set in apartments and hotel rooms, Maldoror claims that the amateurish quality of the effort was intentional: "That's the trend these days, to make them look homemade, as if they were people from the street." (It is indeed the trend in Mexico City. At numerous street markets you can buy DVDs that are supposedly shot with hidden cameras at short-stay hotel rooms around town. Most of the time, when you get home you find that, far from anything pornographic, the package contains a pirated version of the latest effort from Adam Sandler or The Disney Company. Presumably the street vendors rely on the fact that few unsatisfied customers will return and ask for their money back.)

Maldoror sold the rights to *Fetiches Mexicanos 1* to the United States and several Eastern European countries. They needed to guarantee that all of the women in the movie were Mexican. Most porn stars are blond and blue-eyed; men who like to see Latinas have turned Mexican porn into a fetish niche.

Apart from their plans to shoot the other eleven episodes of *Fetiches Mexicanos,* Maldoror and Tirielle also want to make a series of movies based on classics of erotic literature—*The Story of O,* the Marquis de Sade, Georges Bataille. They won't be restricted to Mexican casts for those films. "We'll use whoever shows up," says Maldoror. "We don't care if they're like Wim Wenders movies, with everyone speaking different languages."

It will be easier to shoot with an international cast. Mexico has no tradition of a porn industry. Maldoror says that in a book of the history of pornographic cinema, the handful of Mexican entries featured women and animals. It took him and Tirielle "years" to convince four actresses to appear in their maiden effort.

"We looked for them in table-dance bars, in brothels, anywhere you can imagine. In the end, they found us." For example Bárbara—who has Chinese characters tattooed in her pubis which mean, among other things, love, God, and eternity—approached them while working as a model at an erotic fair, where they'd set up a stand. Another, an eighteen-year-old called Giselle, was referred to them by a friend who runs a body-piercing studio. Maldoror, Tirielle, and a couple of their friends filled the male roles.

They blame Mexico's *doble moral* for their difficulties in finding women to fill the roles in their movies. However, until they get the empire going, women don't have much of an economic incentive to work in the industry. Maldoror and Tirielle can offer between one hundred and three hundred dollars for a day's work, depending on what a woman is called to do during the shoot. However, the days of employment are few and far between. In a table-dance bar, a woman could earn that much money various nights of the week without having to actually have sex with anyone, let alone allow the coupling to be recorded for posterity and sold outside every subway station in Mexico City. Even a prostitute can do her job without having to worry about her family or acquaintances finding out.

The latter is an undeniable problem: within two weeks after DVDs of *Fetiches Mexicanos 1* hit the street, the mother of Giselle was informed by a neighbor about her daughter's burgeoning career. Mom, a Jehovah's Witness, threw Giselle out of the house. Maldoror and Tirielle found her an apartment and are helping her get by.

She is the only woman in the first film to have agreed to appear in *Fetiches Mexicanos 2*—perhaps because, as Humbert admitted of Lolita, "she had nowhere else to go."

The Last Cabaret

The neon sign outside the Club Savoy depicts a glass of champagne. Not of the elegant fluted variety, but the squat saucer-shaped type, the goblet apocryphally reputed to have been inspired by the bosom of, alternately, Marie Antoinette, Mesdames du Pompadour and du Barry, Diane de Poitiers, and Helen of Troy.

The neon wineglass is a nod to better, bygone days. The Savoy—the last cabaret in Mexico City—is located on a street of crumbling buildings, sinister and deserted at night during the club's business hours. Under the neon sign, at the entryway, are photographs of the singers, dancers, and strippers who are the luminaries of the Savoy's show. Their sequins, feathers, and bouffant hairstyles, as well as their pouty *moues* of insinuated seduction, suggest a time-tunnel journey that is sustained once inside.

The clock stopped in the Savoy around 1959. Most of the dancers in the show have the round and sturdy bodies favored in that era, and the clientele is principally composed of men in the timeless dark suits of bureaucrats. (These versions are of synthetics and can be bought off the rack at three for the price of two, with an extra pair of pants thrown in, at nearby shops on Avenida Insurgentes.) Until a renovation in 2007, the walls were adorned with murals, of Mexico City monuments on one side, and of stars, planets, and flying saucers on the other. Those dated from the club's first incarnation as La Ciudad de los Marcianos (Martian City) in the early 1950s, when space travel was still a dream.

Tables form a semicircle surround the Savoy's apron stage. One night between shows, I watched a woman in a skintight orange gown seated with a gray-suited pencil pusher. A waiter replenished her glass of sparkling wine from a bottle reposing in an ice bucket. What most impressed me was her affected, widemouthed laugh, which made her head shake and her platinum-blond hair quiver. I could hear her cackle all the way across the room. Even in the darkness of the Savoy it was evident she was of a certain age; precisely which age remained a mystery. Soon she stood up. There were geometrical shapes cut from the sides of her dress, exposing smooth tanned flesh. She disappeared into the dressing rooms.

A few minutes later, after the beat of a piped-in drumroll, she re-surfaced as Claudia Tate, the star of the show. Her curves nearly bursting from a sparkling-ruby gown, she strode onstage, her smile simultaneously sweet and suggestive, her dark eyes shining with a startling blend of hope and tragedy. She began to sing with infectious energy.

"*¿De qué manera te olvido?*"—How could I possibly forget you?— she cried, waving her abundant hair, enhanced by extensions. It was as if she were singing to multitudes in a stadium rather than the handful of impassive customers in attendance that *viernes de quin-cena,* one of two Fridays a month when Mexicans get paid. It's a song that everyone in the city has heard a thousand times, but after a couple of drinks, during the instant that Tate looked me in the eye, I could nearly believe it was a first.

She was backed by prerecorded music. The Savoy has a live four-piece band, but the management only pays it to play while the customers dance with bar girls in between shows.

She enchanted me. In between shows I presented myself to her as a reporter and invited her to lunch the following day. She stood up to scrutiny under the unforgiving fluorescent lights of a seafood restaurant at the Mercado de Medellín. Her body, encased in a snug tiger-print blouse and white Capri pants, seemed a miracle of genetics and gravity, devoid, as far as I could tell, of reconstructive surgery. Her visible skin was smooth and soft. Yet there was a weary bitterness in her eyes impossible to contain, and a network of lines around her mouth from decades of chain-smoking.

But once. In her golden era in the 1970s, Claudia Tate performed in only the cream of the cabarets in a Mexico City crawling with them: El Social, El Cadillac, El Capri, Las Fabulosas, La Cartier, El Folies Bergere. Her suitors tried to impress her by nonchalantly spending appalling amounts of money.

"In those days," she said, "a bottle of Veuve Clicquot cost twelve hundred pesos [about one hundred dollars at the exchange rate of the time]. Dom Pérignon cost two thousand pesos. But these gentlemen wouldn't buy one bottle, they'd buy fifteen or twenty. We had a deluxe clientele. They wanted to seduce us, but with style, with taste."

She prefers not to mention names. "Athletes, politicians, businessmen. They're men who are alive and married—who knows if they're happily married, but they're married."

Tate claimed that one night during her heyday, the president of Mexico sent a squadron of soldiers to the cabaret where she worked to pick her up and take her to their leader. She roundly refused. The owner of the nightclub begged her to go; if she rebuffed the politician, the business might have been closed. "Send your mother," said Tate. "Or your sister. I'm not going."

Around the time Tate was born, according to Armando Jiménez in his book *Sitios de rompe y rasga en la Ciudad de México* (which loosely translates as *Dives and Dumps of Mexico City*), there were forty-four cabarets within a thousand-yard radius of the Savoy. In the entire city there were hundreds. Among the most notable was El Burro, where the emaciated composer Agustín Lara entertained, wearing a dinner jacket and a scar that traversed the right side of his face, supposedly the result of being caught in flagrante delicto by a jealous husband. At La Linterna Verde, a curvaceous Chicana called Tongolele, a white stripe in her wavy hair, made her debut in 1947 before she became a star of movie musicals. In a dive called the Leda, Diego Rivera and Frida Kahlo rubbed shoulders with streetcar conductors and auto mechanics. In El Golpe, showgirls alternated their gyrations with boxing matches inside a ring. The names of some of the clubs indicate a proclivity toward the exotic East or Middle European schmaltz: El Bagdad, El Cairo, El Estambul; El Molino Rojo, El Gran Vals, El Imperio.

These clubs inspired a series of films in the forties and fifties, soap operas with musical numbers, with titles such as *Aventurera* (Adventuress), *Pecadora* (Sinner), and *Pervertida* (Perverted). The stories were more or less identical: an essentially angelical young woman, usually from a small town, comes to Mexico City and is corrupted by a gangster who has connections in a cabaret. She begins work there, singing and dancing the rumba in provocative costumes. Toward the end, she will pay a dear price for her fall. Even in their day, these films had a camp element, and their moralistic message was taken with tongue in cheek by at least some of the audience.

During the 1960s, Mexico City's cabarets declined after hard-line, law-and-order mayor Ernesto Uruchurtu mandated that they had to close their doors at one in the morning. It wasn't until 1966, when he left his post, that they enjoyed a renaissance. Soon after, Tate made her fame as a *vedette*. Among her contemporaries were Gloriella, who wore a minuscule bikini underneath a fur coat; Olga Breeskin, who played the violin dressed in little more than feathers; and Lyn May, "the Chinawoman from Acapulco."

In those days, Tate was offered more work than she could possibly accept. In addition to cabarets, she performed in vaudeville theaters, on TV programs, and in movies with titles like *Sex vs. Sex, Sex Among the Poor,* and *Sex Makes Me Laugh.* But the big money was in cabaret. She said a "first-class *vedette*" cleared about two hundred fifty dollars per day, and that her admirers paid not only for fifteen bottles of champagne, but also her costumes, her musical arrangements, her wigs, and her shoes. "Sincerely, it was in exchange for nothing, because they liked me. Of course, they wanted something out of it, and as they say, 'Good things come to those who persevere.'"

Tate, who adopted her stage moniker after the murder of Sharon Tate, worked in Vegas-style revues that included a sixteen-member chorus line, singers, and comedians. While she posed naked in certain men's magazines, she never did so onstage. She wore scanty costumes "with a lot of feathers" and bit by bit took almost everything off. "I ended up with little bikinis and tangas that covered my nipples and pubis—I insinuated, nothing more. That way we remained *artistes.*"

When I saw Tate in the Savoy, the show consisted of four chunky chorus girls, a couple of off-key singers, three strippers, and a guy who warbled mariachi numbers to prerecorded music. In between shows, Tate shilled drinks, sitting with customers who sometimes got too forward for her tastes. She blamed some of her younger colleagues who, she claimed, gave hand jobs under the tables. "This was never a first-class place, not even in the 1950s." She inhaled on a

Marlboro, accentuating her frown lines. "Today, it's a third-rate joint with fifth-rate salaries."

When I first visited Mexico City in the late 1980s, I was fascinated by the many still-surviving, if decadent, cabarets, which represented to me a universe from before my birth. The culprit of their downfall is unmistakable. In 1992, just before the North American Free Trade Agreement was signed, the capital adopted a custom of its northern neighbor and opened its first table-dance bar.

The stakes for this sort of entertainment were raised abruptly and vertiginously. Not only could a customer see a naked woman, he could also pay her to sit in his lap while she writhed and contorted. In some places, touching was not only permitted but encouraged. Upstairs and backstage at other *teibols,* as they're called here, the menu of services was even more abundant, reaching the limits of the male imagination. Like certain deadly viruses, in short shrift the *teibols* had multiplied exponentially.

For the cabarets, they were the kiss of death. Sergio González Rodríguez, a cultural critic and nightlife columnist, explained: "They closed the breach between the spectator and the onstage object of desire which, no matter how close, was always very far away. The act of possessing a female body at a distance, mediated by a floor show, became a palpable, achievable reality for a modest sum of money."

González Rodríguez merely refers to the client's point of view. The economic reality for the owners is staggering. In most Mexico City table-dance bars, the customer pays about twenty dollars for contact with a dancer during one three-minute taped song. The house tends to keep half the "modest sum." Multiply that by so many songs, by so many women. Add the profits from bar tabs—the dancers, known as *teiboleras,* mercilessly shake down their clients to buy them successive, dizzyingly overpriced drinks—and deduct the musicians' salaries. Table-dance bars are money factories; in comparison, a cabaret's earnings are closer to those of a taco stand.

As in so many other industries, Mexican *teiboleras* have seen their earning capacity compromised by globalization. By the late 1990s, word had spread to South America and Eastern Europe about how much money could be made here. Today, the women working the high-end table-dance bars are principally from elsewhere. Czechs, Hungarians, and Russians—with their blond hair, high cheekbones, and sculpted frames the very embodiment of what is out of reach to most Mexicans—are in particularly high demand.

The places where they work are the most expensive in the city. They tend to writhe to music with what are, at least in Mexico City, exotic rhythms, performed by singers I can only imagine are the Britney Spears and Shakira equivalents of Latvia and Estonia.

Most of the Europeans work three months (earning no salary, only the 50 percent of the dance tickets that the house doesn't keep, plus tips) until their tourist visas expire. They visit home, bringing presents for their families and entertaining their friends with stories of their Mexican adventures. Then they come back. At first they were the wetbacks of Mexico City, working without permission. But by the new millennium, members of Congress, some perhaps economically encouraged by bar owners, passed legislation that gave foreign *teiboleras* legitimate work visas as entertainers.

Given such competition, it is a miracle that the Savoy still exists. When I last spoke to her, Claudia Tate had become fed up and quit the business.

Eating on the Street and Elsewhere

The true journey, as the introjection of an "outside" different from our normal one, implies a complete change of nutrition, a digesting of the visited country—its fauna and flora and its culture (not only the different culinary practices and condiments but the different implements used to grind the flour or stir the pot)—making it pass between the lips and down the esophagus. This is the only kind of travel that has a meaning nowadays, when everything visible you can see on television without rising from your easy chair.

—Italo Calvino, "Under the Jaguar Sun"

La Central de Abastos—the largest market on the planet, according to the Mexico City government—is a nocturnal infraworld where the busiest hours are the darkest ones before dawn. At five in the morning its concrete passageways are as densely crowded as the inner-city highways during rush hour, and perhaps even more dangerous. As you navigate these aisles, an army of roustabouts trots behind, in front, and at your sides. Each man pulls a handcart atop which dozens of boxes of fruits and vegetables are balanced. They move at a trot just short of running, and if they want to get past you, they whistle shrilly. The chorus of these squeals—along with the percussive rumble of the wheels of their carts—is the musical accompaniment to the panorama. If you don't get out of their way, you could get trampled. Each time I have visited, I have imagined photos of my bloody corpse on the front page of the tabloids, with the headline "Flattened by Onions."

About 30 percent of the country's food is sold in La Central, and any description of how Mexico City is fed must begin here. On the eastern edge of the D.F., La Central is spread out over more than 750 acres. On a daily basis thirty thousand tons of food are trucked here from the rest of the country, and sold to three hundred thousand customers—mainly people who sell in smaller markets, to restaurants and food stands all over the city.

Zola could have written a novel set in La Central. Spend a morning in this market and you feel you have arrived at another city, another universe. Every bank in Mexico is represented within its confines, each protected by a cop with a submachine gun. About $8 billion a year changes hands, mostly in cash; as such, merchandisers are prime prey to kidnappers. One vendor handed over half a million dollars to have his son released from captivity. He had that much money lying around at home; it was his float.

The inequality of Mexico City is once again represented in the architecture and design. La Central is elevated and constructed in the form of a quadrilateral. On the ground level there is ample open-air space for immense trucks and trailers to park and unload merchandise. But when the architect, Abraham Zabludowsky, designed La Central in the early 1980s, he was evidently thinking only of the truckers and not the *cargadores*—the poor devils who use those handcarts to pull the food back and forth. Along the aisles there are an infinite number of steep concrete hills. The *cargadores,* pulling their small mountains of twenty or thirty boxes, have to climb and descend hill after hill. It is brutal work, a donkey's labor; watching them, one thinks of the Aztec slaves who carried the stones to build the pyramids. Various have died during a day's labor.

People who own the stalls may have half a million dollars lying around at home, but the *cargadores* do not even earn a salary. Indeed, to rent their handcarts, they have to pay a little over a dollar a day to a character known as El Chino, a former street child and *cargador* himself. The workers vary between twelve and seventy years old. They charge between twenty and forty cents per box, depending on how heavy the load and how far it has to be carried. An old man calculated that he earned about seven or eight dollars for a day's work.

Hard labor at slave wages harken back to Tenochtitlán, the Aztec capital, while the nocturnal chaos, lit by buzzing neon, is reminiscent of *Blade Runner*. La Central is a gastronomic purgatory, a limbo between the farms, seas, and ranches from where the food comes, and the plates from which it will be ultimately consumed.

There is a constant buzz of vendors' voices:

"Precio, precio" (Low prices, low prices) . . .

"¿Qué le lleve?" (What'll you have?) . . .

"¿Cuánto quedamos?" (How much do you want?) . . .

Enormous heaps of bananas, mangos, papayas, melons, potatoes, carrots, string beans, huge sacks loaded with every type of chile, herbs tied in bulky bundles atop spread newspapers. Each pile has its own exclamation-pointed sign: *"¡Mírame!"* (Look at me!) *"¡No lo piense!"* (Don't think about it!) *"¡Anímese!"* (Act now!) *"¡Aproveche!"* (Take advantage!) And my favorite: *"¡100% chingón!"* (Roughly translated: "This is the bomb!")

If we are what we eat, La Central is an X-ray of our entrails, the gastric juices coursing through our digestive system. Back in the city, we can see the pretty shells and skin of the food that *chilangos* ate.

There is a cornucopia of good things to eat in Mexico City, and most of them are found on the street. The sidewalk is a *chilango*'s pit stop, his permanent picnic. He likes to eat standing up, the aroma of sizzling meat mingling with those of exhaust fumes, putrefying garbage, dust, and sweat. At any of the twenty-four hours of the day, flocks of citizens swarm around one white-painted metal *puesto* (stand) or another, balancing some foodstuff over brightly colored plastic plates, or waiting patiently to do so.

Such a lot of food is consumed alfresco for various reasons. Importantly, weather permits it throughout the year. But the most crucial basis for street feeding is economic. The owner of a *puesto* pays virtually no taxes; in exchange for permission to set up shop on the street, he gives the government a pittance. He passes his windfall on to his customers, who eat bountifully for low prices.

The cornerstone of street food is the taco. There is absolutely no ingredient on the planet that Mexicans will not stuff inside a tortilla— from sliced beef or mushrooms to the bolder flavors of tripe and tongue, brains and bull's testicles. You can also have tacos stuffed with *gusanos de maguey* (earthworms), *chapulines* (grasshoppers), and *escamoles* (ant larvae, also known as Aztec caviar). These insects are considered delicacies and most frequently combined with guacamole, onions, and hot sauce.

Mexico City has no indigenous cuisine, but if there is such a thing as a municipal dish, it would have to be tacos *al pastor*. A variation on Middle Eastern *shawarma*, it is made from pork, marinated with various spices, including garlic and a heavy dose of annatto, which gives it a shrill orange color. The slices of pork are mounted atop each other to form a huge orb, and impaled on a metal stick, which revolves around a vertical charcoal grill. The fire from the grill is turned up as orders are placed, and the *taquero* slices from the most fully cooked part to fashion the taco, which is adorned with cilantro, onion, and a slice of pineapple.

Tacos *al pastor* are fast food, but even quicker is the taco *de guisado*—tortillas heated on a grill for a moment or two and filled with previously cooked items that are kept warm on a steam table. They are not for people with sensitive digestive systems. Among the most popular *guisados* are beef liver and tongue. The less intimidating variations include meatballs in a spicy *chipotle* sauce; sautéed strips of poblano chiles, their fire softened by cream gravy; potatoes sautéed with sausage; or scrambled eggs mixed with string beans. All *puestos* have bowls of both green and red chile sauce to further ignite their products, and sliced limes are always available.

Even more popular are the stands at which a fire is lit under a round metal basin, within which huge slabs of *suadero* (a cut of beef from the lower part of the rib), extensive tubes of *longaniza* sausage, festively curling tripes, and chunks of pork marinated in chile all sizzle in the same deep grease. The *taquero* daintily dips the tortillas in the fat before heating them, chops the corresponding meats with which to fill them, and, before serving, asks his customers if they want the tacos garnished with "vegetables." (He's referring to chopped onion and cilantro.)

If I had to choose a favorite taco, it would be those stuffed with *carnitas,* which are *puerco profundo*: hunks of pork shoulder or butt, mixed with the rest of the pig—liver, heart, snout, skin, even reproductive organs. They are seasoned, braised in water or milk, subsequently fried, and then chopped into bits before being made into tacos. The squeamish order *pura maciza*—only the white-meat flesh of the pig, unadorned by those parts that have to do with bodily functions. But the *surtida,* a mixture of everything, is delectable.

Chilangos say that you can tell a lot about people from how they eat their tacos. Given that tacos are supposed to be fast food, it is re-markable how slowly *chilangos* consume them. *Chilangos* are also immaculately clean, even dainty, eating their tacos with care and small bites, so that the filling doesn't spill from the ends. (I hope they don't judge me too harshly on the street. I usually make an unholy mess out of a taco, with the *guisados* spilling all over the plate and the tortillas often falling apart.)

In general, there is a climate of distrust in Mexico City. *Chilangos* are always on the alert for those who might try to scam them. Yet re-markably, street tacos are sold through an honor system. Neither the man who makes them nor his cohort who collects the money keeps track; when you are finished they ask you how many you have con-sumed and charge you accordingly.

Another popular street item is the quesadilla. Similar to a taco, it's a thin half-moon of dough stuffed with one delicacy or another. *Queso* is the Spanish word for cheese, and as the name indicates, quesadi-llas are traditionally filled with it. In most of Mexico, that's *all* they're filled with. In the capital, however, any self-respecting quesadilla stand offers multiple options for fillings: sautéed squash flowers, *tinga* (shredded pork or chicken in a tomato-based sauce), mush-rooms, or *huitlacoche* (a dearly beloved corn fungus, aka the Aztec truffle). Quesadillas are most frequently deep-fried, but for the diet-conscious there are also stands at which they are cooked on a *comal* (flat grill) with only a minimum of oil.

A *torta* is Mexico's answer to the sandwich, and if it isn't exactly a work of art, it is by all means a handicraft. A roll is split in half and heated, while the filling is cooked on a grill. It might be ham, chicken, or cheese; egg, sausage, or a breaded beef cutlet, or a combination of those. *Tortas* are not piled high with meat, but stacked with additional complementary elements: layers of refried beans, avocado, to-mato, onion, and chiles. To call this fast food is deceptive; *torteros* are most often painstaking in their preparations. At one *torta* stand near my apartment, I can almost finish the newspaper between plac-ing an order and being served.

Chilangos fight fervently over which stands or holes-in-the-wall serve the best *tortas,* quesadillas, or tacos *de guisado.* Given the size of the D.F., these arguments tend to be endless, and played out over geographical lines, with people most often defending places in or near their turf. Even within a small area there can be fierce rivalries. A friend who favored the *pastor* at Tacos Álvaro O. in the Colonia Roma—clearly being given a run for its money by Taquitos Frontera down the street—once asked its manager which *taquerías* he thought were his competition. "I have none," he snipped.

Other *chilangos* show their street credentials by arguing in favor of, say, the tripe tacos in some grimy joint in Peralvillo, one of the city's roughest neighborhoods. Or else they champion places that are far away from the central neighborhoods, or on impossible-to-find side streets near the Portales Market, only open on Saturday and Sun-day mornings until midday.

In *Journey to the End of the Night,* Louis-Ferdinand Céline observes, "In the kitchens of love, after all, vice is like the pepper in a good sauce; it brings out the flavor, it's indispensable." If a lot of *chilangos* would agree with his assessment about transgression being a neces-sary ingredient in a satisfactory sex life, nearly all would concur with his views about pepper.

Contrary to the predominant cliché, not every single dish that comes out of a Mexican kitchen has been prepared with such an overwhelming amount of chile that it will set your hair on fire. Most sautéed and stewed fare indeed contains one pepper or another, but often only enough to, as the French author suggests, enhance the taste. Yet all food is served with accompanying hot sauces, and millions of *chilangos* liberally heat up whatever they eat. I don't think Céline would have imagined pepper becoming the vice unto itself, or an addiction: without a generous enough dose, food becomes insipid. Many *chilangos* cannot even taste food without chile.

In the arena of machismo, chile is also a time-tested proving ground. In Carlos Fuentes's *The Old Gringo,* Ambrose Bierce convinces a platoon of Pancho Villa's soldiers that he is a man because of his ability to eat a raw chile without wilting. Indeed, when I mention to cabdrivers how long I have lived here, quite often their first question is if I have accustomed myself to *el picante.*

The most industrial-strength sauce comes from the habanero chile, and is commonly served with food from the Yucatán Peninsula. In the Colonia Condesa there is a Yucatecan restaurant called Xel-Ha popular among Mexico City journalists. Once I ate with a couple of them, and each put heaping spoonfuls of salsa habanera on their tacos of *cochinita pibil* (shredded pork in a bitter-orange sauce). As they ate, heavy sweat appeared on their brows, and by the time they finished, they were gasping for breath on the inhale. Their suffering was evident, yet each extolled the exquisite sensation of *enchilarse*—to become overwhelmed by chile.

Waiters' qualifications of how much fire a dish contains are idiosyncratic. If he says *"no pica"*—it isn't at all hot—it's most likely a little hot. If he says *"pica un poquito"* (it's a bit hot), it's probably a dish that would test the tolerance level of ordinary mortals. If he says *"sí, pica"*—that it's indeed hot—you probably want to avoid it unless you're looking to flaunt your macho credentials.

Mexicans traditionally eat their main meal sometime between two and four o'clock. Because so many *chilangos* work far from home, they eat out every day, which for most of them is an expensive option.

For the struggling class, the most common choice is *fonda*—a modest, unadorned restaurant with plastic-covered tables. There are thousands of them dotting every Mexico City neighborhood. *Fondas* serve *comida corrida*—meals in the style of "home cooking," with four courses at a modest fixed price (between two and seven dollars, depending on the affluence of the neighborhood).

For each course, you have three or four choices. Traditional Mexicans always begin their main meal with soup, which is usually of the thin, water-based variety and rarely served piping hot. At a *fonda,* it might be consommé with chicken and vegetables, fava bean with sausage, or tomato-based with noodles and ham. The second course is usually rice, flavored with garlic and tomato or with poblano chiles and corn. The main dish (pork loin in *chipotle* chile, chicken in a fruit sauce, or breaded cauliflower stuffed with cheese) is accompanied with beans, hot tortillas, and water flavored with fruit. Dessert is underwhelming—usually Jell-O, a cloying rice pudding, or a bit of fresh fruit.

Within most markets you can find *fondas,* tacos, and *torta* stands. Some have more remarkable offerings, like the one in Coyoacán where a man named Cesar González makes pancakes in the form of cartoon characters. First, he "draws" the eyes, the nose, and the mouth with the batter, and once these parts are browned, he pours the batter around them to form the "canvas." Most of the clients are children, but Cesar entertains their parents with portraits that border on the salacious. A woman will ask for a rendering of her boyfriend, and the hot-cake artist will ask if she wants it "loving" or "with details." The "loving" part will be an oversize heart, while the "detail" is a penis that keeps growing. "Let me know how much you can take," Cesar will suggest.

Tacos tend to cost between thirty cents and two dollars, and *tortas* between one and three dollars, once again depending on the neighborhood where you eat them. There are few midprice options in Mexico City, where a meal will cost, say, ten or twelve dollars. However, in this range there are a series of ubiquitous cafeterias designed in a 1960s U.S. style, with harsh lighting, roomy booths, and horseshoe-shaped counters. They have names such as Vips, Toks, Wings, and California; the oldest of them, Sanborns (today also a chain store), has been around since the 1920s.

The food is identical in all of them. You can order Mexican specialties, like *enchiladas suizas* (chicken enchiladas in a mild green sauce topped with cream) or *carne a la tampiqueña* (a flattened steak with enchiladas on the side), or hit-parade standards from the United States, like cheeseburgers and club sandwiches. Nothing in these places will harm you but they are spectacular in their forgettability.

The prices are too high for the poor, but for the middle class it is a sign of status to eat in the proliferating franchises of U.S. fast-food restaurants. McDonald's, Burger King, and KFC are the most popular, but nearly all of them are represented, and their numbers multiply exponentially. (The only one that failed outright was Taco Bell.)

In fancy restaurants, diners appear to have nothing but time. Lunch rarely begins in these places before three in the afternoon and can easily stretch to five, six, seven, and beyond, with the constant petition for one more *digestivo,* one more *café.* Most of the customers at these hours are men with their jackets draped along the backs of their chairs, ties loosened, and sleeves rolled up. Once I overheard the conversation of two of them, government bureaucrats who clearly were not going to get back to work that afternoon. Indeed, one was fielding various cell phone calls from a hospital, where his wife was about to give birth.

Given the crouching waiters, the opulent surroundings, the sybaritic experience, but above all Mexico City's severe imbalance of wealth, extravagant restaurants here strike me as even more indulgent than those in cities where the distribution is more equal. Here, you rarely see the neurotic behavior that marks the diners at a fine restaurant in New York, for example: the panicky expressions while checking watches in anticipation of an encroaching appointment; the scrutiny of who might be at other, better, tables; the forgoing of alcoholic beverages for a bottle of designer water.

High Mexican cuisine, the most sophisticated in the American continent, with its elaborate play of textures, flavors, and colors, truly lends itself to this sort of epicurean, dissolute pleasure seeking. If Mexico City has no cuisine of its own, here one can sample food from all regions of the country, including pozole (a pork and hominy stew) from Guerrero, *mixiotes* (seasoned meat cooked in maguey leaves) from Puebla, *cabrito* (roast kid) from Nuevo León, and *birria* (goat stew) from Jalisco.

Tequila is the traditional *aperitivo* before an extended meal. Many *chilangos* keep drinking it as the repast progresses, or else accompany their food with beer, but *aguas de sabores*—water flavored with fruit—also augment the various essences of the food. Only in the last decade or so have decent wine lists become widespread in Mexico City restaurants.

Unlike countries whose chefs feel the constant, perpetual need to refine and redefine their food, at most well-appointed Mexican restaurants, diners eat the same dishes that their ancestors have devoured for hundreds of years. The city's oldest restaurant (and still one of its most beloved) is the Hostería de Santo Domingo, situated in what was a convent in the sixteenth century, and which opened its doors as an eatery in 1860. Here, an ancient duo of violinist and piano player serenade the patrons with lyrical renditions of "Begin the Beguine" or favorites from the Latin American repertoire, such as *"Frenesí"* or *"Perfidia."* The specialty of the house is the *chile en nogada*. This dish was invented in 1821 to celebrate the saint's day of Agustín de Iturbide, who soon after sampling it would serve ten months as Mexico's emperor.

The *chile en nogada* is a green poblano pepper, blistered and skinned over a direct flame and lion-tamed by the removal of its seeds and veins. It is stuffed with a mincemeat mixture that includes (among many ingredients) pork, onions, cumin, cinnamon, and *acitrón,* a dried and candied cactus. The stuffed green pepper, most frequently served at room temperature, is topped with a creamy white walnut sauce and red pomegranate seeds. Thus dished up, it encompasses the colors of the Mexican flag.

Like the Greeks' definition of drama, the basis of Mexican food is conflict, and the *chile en nogada* is emblematic: sweet combined with hot, cream combined with crunch, various flavors warring to assert themselves. This sensuality is artfully described by Italo Calvino in his short story "Under the Jaguar Sun," about a couple of tourists in Oaxaca, the tensions of whose relationship escalate at a series of restaurant tables. The narrator of Calvino's story wonders whether this riotous blend of flavors might have been motivated by the indigenous Mexican aristocrat's wish to hide—or enhance—the flavor of human flesh, which, before the arrival of the Spaniards, played a crucial role in his diet.

———

There is no such thing as a light Mexican meal. Salads are practically nonexistent on the menus of the traditional restaurants, and vegetables are most often cooked to within centimeters of their lives (or else battered and fried, stuffed with cheese, or flavor-enhanced with lard). Indeed, time-honored Mexican recipes emphasize food cooked thoroughly enough to massacre microbes and bacteria (fitting when you consider that they come from a nineteenth-century menu, when anything resembling the contemporary refrigerator was decades distant). Old habits die hard: today in a steak house or a French restaurant, most Mexicans will order their beef well done, and send it back if even the faintest suggestion of pink surfaces from its sinew.

If it is a fancy of Calvino's imagination that heavy Mexican sauces disguise a cannibal's diet, there is no doubt they were invented for people whose lifestyles afforded them a siesta after lunch. Today, the impossible distances between home and work, the intense traffic problems, and an economy that obliges people to labor during long hours make naps impossible for most *chilangos*.

For these reasons—as well as younger Mexicans' inclination toward the trendy—traditional Mexican restaurants hardly figure in the culinary barometers of hip *chilangos* under forty. These places, like the Hostería de Santo Domingo, El Cardenal, and El Bajío are where they suffer Sunday lunches with their grandmothers, their parents, their brother's bratty children, various maiden aunts, and the latest boyfriend of their connubially capricious sister. They are the last restaurants they would take a date on a Saturday night. Indeed, they couldn't: most traditional restaurants close between six and eight o'clock.

In Polanco and the Condesa, the city's hippest areas, or in Santa Fe and Las Lomas (less hip but even wealthier), you can hardly find a Mexican restaurant at all. The fashionable crowd would prefer to eat tapas in a space where a fortune has been spent to replicate an ordinary Sevillan bodega, or in a faux Paris bistro, or in a sushi bar re-created after their own taste buds.

As such, Mexico City has a range of culinary offerings as varied as any important city; however, the results are uneven. Mexico has a far smaller immigrant population than the United States or Western Europe, so there are relatively few foreigners preparing food for the populace. Therefore, attempts at "authenticity" are elastic. Mexico's closest neighbors, the United States or the tiny war-torn republics of Central America, provide little culinary inspiration.

The city is loaded with excellent Spanish restaurants, most of which were opened in the early 1940s by anti-Franco refugees of the Civil War. These restaurants specialize in dishes like paella, tripe *a la madrileña,* or Asturian *fabada* that are even older and at least as heavy as what Iturbide ate. However, in the last decade or so a half-dozen contemporary Spanish places have taken up the slack with more imaginative, and lighter, fare.

The other predominant foreign food in Mexico City is Middle Eastern. At the beginning of the twentieth century, there was a significant immigration from Lebanon and Syria; as such, there are various places with names like Al Andalus, Emir, and Adonis, that serve faultless baba ghanoush, hummus, kibbe, tabouleh, and so forth.

Other attempts at foreign cuisines are less successful. Even at the most beloved Italian restaurants, pasta is rarely served al dente here. There are four Polish restaurants where farm-raised roast ducks are served, but their other dishes are not nearly as exciting. In the past five or six years a passel of places calling themselves French bistros have opened, but the quality of what is served varies from dish to dish.

In the *centro* there is a Chinatown all of one block long, better for buying paper lampshades, green tea, or black cloth slippers than for dining. Recently, Mr. Chow opened a restaurant here and the Hotel Presidente imported a team of cooks from Hong Kong for a new eatery. Both of these options are incredibly expensive. Near the Viaducto subway station is a more authentic place called Ka Won Seng, where, gathered at round tables, groups of ten or twelve Chinese serve themselves from dishes in the lazy Susan centerpieces.

There is a multiplicity of Japanese restaurants in Mexico City, but sushi chefs would hardly think of preparing a roll that doesn't contain cream cheese, mayonnaise, or jalapeño peppers, or at times, to the delight of their *chilango* customers, all three. There are a couple of more legitimate places, but even these have at least a few cream-cheese offerings to placate the local palate. Thai, Vietnamese, and Indian restaurants barely exist.

Some ambitious chefs refer to what comes out of their kitchens as "nouvelle Mexican." They try to update or revive Mexican cuisine with continental techniques (or, inversely, use local ingredients to add a twist to European food). In the happiest of cases, there's a successful blend; in the worst, a hodgepodge.

The best is called Pujol, where a young chef named Enrique Olvera uses the identical spices to tacos *al pastor* and rubs them on sea bass, accompanying it with a pineapple cream, the result a celestial interpretation of street food. Other such restaurants are hit-or-miss affairs. Some of their dishes are as sublime as what is served at Pujol, but others have sauces or spices that overwhelm the raw material—instances of fixing food that wasn't conspicuously broken.

The most consistent problem with nearly all of Mexico City's upper-crust restaurants is their inconsistency. One meal might be spectacular, while another is disappointing or worse. "You have to know what to order," is the rebuke from those who consider themselves insiders—as if it were fair game to have various stinkers on a menu where the customer spends twenty times the minimum wage for a meal.

I understood some of the problems with supposedly fine dining in Mexico City when, for a magazine article, I took Diana Kennedy out for breakfast, lunch, and dinner. Kennedy is an eightyish English-woman who has lived mostly in Mexico since 1957. Her painstaking research collecting recipes—traveling from town to town on second-class buses, in hired taxis, or her own beat-up car—resulted in what are considered the most authoritative Mexican cookbooks ever published. Yet she is something of a dictator about cookery; if she doesn't have it her way, she can be mischievously malicious.

At Flor de Lis, a breakfast spot famous for its tamales, she practically choked over the dryness of one and exclaimed, "What barbarity! A disaster! I can make them a thousand times better at home." At Águila y Sol—one of the most beloved of the nouvelle Mexican restaurants—Kennedy pronounced a preparation of goat and parmesan cheeses with a vegetable called *huazontle* "ridiculous," because the cheeses were so powerful that you could barely taste the *huazontle*. The tortillas that accompanied the main dishes were "absurd" (for being flavored with chiles and spices rather than neutral). An appetizer at Izote (another nouvelle favorite) was "a horrible distortion of what it ought to be."

Apart from whether or not one shares her opinions about a particular dish, Kennedy outlined certain problems: that the most well-known chefs in Mexico City, as they go around the world promoting themselves at conferences and cooking classes, leave their kitchens in the hands of less-talented underlings. But she claimed that the worst offenders are Mexico City's residents. "There aren't many cultivated palates here," she said. "The situation won't change until the people learn to taste food and not just swallow it. With few exceptions, they don't go out to eat seriously. They go out to have a good time, in search of sensations and to be with their friends."

Service in Mexico City, nearly always courteous and often fawning, is idiosyncratic. It is common to ask your waiter for, say, a glass of water, upon which he will command another waiter to bring it to you. In turn, that waiter will ask another, and so forth, until the order disappears into a black hole and you have to begin the process all over.

Waiters in Mexico City often try to clear your plate before you have finished eating, as if someone in the kitchen stood guard with a whip if he were to bring the dish back empty. On the other hand, he will never convey the check until you have asked for it.

If service has its peculiarities, many *chilangos* who can afford to eat at expensive restaurants assume that waiters are lesser life forms and treat them as such. To get a waiter's attention, it is fairly common to see a man snap his fingers or even make the sort of kissing sound that owners of French poodles produce when they want the animals to stand on their hind legs. Waiters are almost always addressed as *jóven* (young man), even if the waiter is white-haired and hunchbacked.

Given the twenty million who live here, it is extraordinary how few options exist for eating after midnight. Restaurants shut their doors tighter than oyster shells, despite the multitude of people who work at night, and the fact that many bars stay open until the wee hours when they deposit their hungry customers onto the street. Branches of two Parisian brasseries, Au Pied du Cochon and L'Alsace, are open twenty-four hours, and so are a small number of those sixties-style cafeterias.

But aside from those choices, after two in the morning you're back to tacos, either from street stalls (where the *suadero* and the tripes have been simmering in the same grease since the morning) or in holes-in-the-wall that specialize in feeding the city's assorted drunks and after-hours detritus. El Charco de las Ranas (the Frogs' Puddle), for example, is decorated in an orange-colored Formica so bright as to prematurely begin the process of a hangover. It caters to upscale clients and charges nearly as much as a fancy restaurant. Others are dirt cheap, like El Borrego Viudo (the Widowed Sheep), with its dozen snarling murderous waiters, who bring plates of tacos to customers who've parked their cars on the sidewalk. A few other joints serve chicken broth from a huge cauldron, which you can sip by itself or with any piece of the boiled bird, including livers and gizzards.

Ever since I arrived in Mexico City I had been told about a restaurant called Chon, in continuous service since 1924, which specializes in food from the pre-Hispanic era. Each rumor about the menu was more outrageous than the last—that they served monkey burgers, lion's paws, squirrel du jour. It took me more than ten years to finally get there. I cannot say precisely what frightened me; rationally, whatever they served couldn't have been more dodgy than any number of things I'd eaten on the streets.

Although they have five different insects on the menu, they were all out the day I showed up with a couple of friends. For appetizers, there was a paté of *pejelagarto* (a river fish) served on tostadas, and tacos made of shredded venison. The main dishes were more adventurous. There was wild boar in a tomato-based sauce—remarkably tender considering its wildness. We also had armadillo in a sweet mango sauce. Sr. Chon, the potbellied proprietor, explained to us that the dishes of the day depended on what he could find that morning in the San Juan market, brought in from the rest of the country or smuggled across the Texas border. He offered us one more pre-Hispanic dish, under the condition that we promised not to ask what it was until we had finished eating.

This was the hit of the lunch, no doubt due to the mystery of what—or, dixit Calvino, whom—we were eating. It was a shredded meat cooked in various spices, subtly flavored and extraordinarily tender. The closest thing to which it tasted was pork, but I had never eaten from any pig so buttery in texture before. When we finished—leaving not a morsel on the plate—Chon toyed with us for a while before ultimately revealing that we had eaten *tepescuincle,* fresh from Chiapas. There was a slight moment of discomfort—*escuincle* is a particularly ugly breed of hairless dog, the favored pet of Frida Kahlo. With a reassuring smile, Chon assured us that *tepescuincle* was not from the canine but the rodent family.

Onions

C alle Balderas was deserted at one in the morning, except for the odd taco eater at the white-painted *puestos,* lit by bare bulbs. The taxi driver picked me up and began to hurtle down the street at great speed. I tried to fasten the seat belt, but it wouldn't budge from the wall. He began to complain about his fellow drivers:

"You don't have to worry about the drunks until about three in the morning. These people in front of me may have had a drink or two, but that's not the problem. The problem is that they're tired. A lot of people know how to drive, but they don't really know how to handle a car. They don't know the difference between driving at night, and driving during the day, driving when it's dry, driving after it's rained."

As he expounded, he tore down Avenida Cuauhtémoc, switching lanes with abandon, missing the cars at his sides by inches. "They don't know how to stay awake," he went on. "Me, I've been driving for, what?" He looked at his watch. "Forty-nine hours. I've only stopped to eat and to bathe, and to drop off my money at home. I don't like to have a lot of money in the cab."

I turned to get a good look at him. He appeared to be about forty years old, with his hair brushed back, a trim mustache, and huge bags under his eyes.

"I'm not on drugs, either," he said with a smile. "The longest I've ever driven is eight straight days, from Sunday to Sunday." I tried once more to maneuver the seat belt, to no avail. "I have to bathe every twelve hours or so. I have very sensitive skin. If I don't bathe, the collar of my shirt gives me a rash on my neck. But the real secret to staying awake is eating. I eat a lot." He was of a normal body type, not at all running to fat. "In the last twenty-four hours, I've stopped to eat six times. You need to eat for energy. Our bodies are like these taxis. If you don't fill them up, they won't run.

"You know what the real secret is?" he asked, now with a manic look in his eyes. "Onions. If I eat a lot of onions, I can go on and on. At this hour, I usually get some beef tacos at a stand on Calle Bolívar. They know me, and they always pile on the onions. No cilantro, just some extra cheese and a heap of onions." He must have noticed an incredulous expression on my face. "Look, I can't give you a scientific explanation. I've never looked it up, and frankly, I don't care. Try it and you'll see for yourself."

The Best Lies Are True

Four of us were sharing a bottle of wine at a sidewalk table at a restaurant overlooking the Parque México. It was a spring evening and the leaves of the trees swayed in the breeze; it was one of those moments you'd wish to last indefinitely.

Paola's cell phone rang. She asked the person on the line if he had arrived yet. "I'm stuck in traffic in Santa Fe," she added. I wondered if the man on the other end of the phone could hear the house music being piped in from the restaurant.

A half hour later, Paola excused herself—she had to get to her appointment. Liliana tried to convince her to stay: "We're having a lovely time, it won't be the same without you." Paola insisted that she couldn't stand up the man; it was an important business rendezvous. "Come on," said Liliana. "Just call and tell him you can't make it." Sergio seconded the motion, trying a slightly different tack: "Stay a little longer. All I'm asking for is a half hour of your time." Ultimately, Paola would telephone again, lamenting the horrible traffic jam; she and her colleague would have to reschedule.

At that point, I made my own excuses: I had a date fifteen minutes hence. In chorus, Paola and Sergio implored me to cancel. When I said

I didn't have the woman's telephone number to call it off, they suggested I simply stand her up. Using a time-honored peer-pressure tactic, Liliana added, "Paola canceled her appointment. Why can't you?"

At the time, Liliana was working for an outfit called the Foundation for World Ethics in Mexico.

Lying is a central attribute of Mexico City culture. One listens to falsehoods, fibs, half-truths, and untruths day and night.

> *Sorry I'm late. There was a protest march on Reforma.*
> *We'll have to call each other to figure out when we're going to have lunch.*
> *I'm already on the street; I'll be there in five minutes.*
> *I don't usually do this so soon but it feels different with you.*
> *Where did I buy it? I didn't, it was a gift.*

According to a survey by the Mitofsky research group, seven out of ten Mexicans claim they are not liars. Yet the same survey stated that on average Mexicans claim to tell four lies a day.

Lying is passed on from parent to child, practically along with the breast milk. In middle-class families, it is not uncommon for a parent to do her child's homework or for a mother to tell her daughter who has answered the phone, "Say I'm not at home." When the father delivers his child late to school, he will tell him to tell the teacher that an accident created an insurmountable traffic jam.

There is a historical precedent for everyday lying here. The Aztecs had to pretend to the Spaniards that they had converted to Catholicism while still maintaining their own belief system. When the same Spaniards—buccaneers, priests, and bureaucrats, most of whom had no actual experience of a day's work—demanded tributes, the Aztecs had to find ways to cut corners and deliver fewer of the fruits of their labors than had been expected or bargained for. Those Spaniards, who often tried to take more than their fair share of gold, jewels, and precious metals, needed to develop a similar discourse when dealing with those in the motherland who were not receiving as much bounty as they expected.

I've cleared my desk of everything but your project.
Monday, first thing in the morning.
We mislaid your bill.
You didn't get it? I sent it three days ago.
Our system was down in the morning; there was no Internet.

Another reason that prevents people in Mexico City from telling the truth is their mania to *caer bien*—to be liked. They would rather invent something than say words that make them seem self-serving or unsympathetic. They do not consider that they may ultimately seem loathsome if they don't show up for an appointment, if they don't deliver work as promised, if their lie is exposed.

In *The Labyrinth of Solitude,* Octavio Paz wrote, "We lie for pleasure and fantasy, like all imaginative people, but also to hide and to protect ourselves from intruders . . . we hope not only to dupe others, but ourselves. That is where their fertility is, and is what distinguishes our lies from the crude inventions of other people."

Now that you mention it, we had coffee the other day. She looks
    terrible, she's put on a lot of weight.
I left my cell phone at home.
There's something wrong with my message machine.
It's almost ready.
We just kissed.

There are two drag queens who earn a few pesos a day as waitresses in a beer joint in Xochimilco, one of the least well-to-do sections of the city. One, a deaf-mute, has hormones injected on a regular
basis to enhance her breasts, while the other suggests a feminine form
through pure illusion. "The best lies are true," she explains.

Who's Afraid of Mexico City?

The floor of a moving taxi smells like gasoline, metal, and the driver's jittery feet. That's the reek I remember from two hours spent lying in a fetal position with my eyes closed in a Volkswagen Beetle, curled in the space where the front passenger seat had been removed to facilitate customers' access.

I wasn't resting there because I was tired or have eccentric habits while riding cabs. I was the victim of what is known as a *secuestro express* (express kidnapping), a crime all too common in Mexico City at the end of the twentieth century. It happened one night after having a couple of drinks in a bar in the Colonia Roma with Yehudit Mam, to whom I was married at the time.

Our experience was typical. We flagged down the taxi on Avenida Insurgentes, one of the city's widest and longest boulevards. The driver suggested a logical route that included passage through a quiet, ill-lit side street. Once there, after halting at a stop sign, two individuals opened the door and barreled their way inside.

To distract us, they announced that they were Federal Judicial Police looking for drugs. One was large, with the body of a gorilla and the crew cut typical of Mexican cops and soldiers. He wore sweats, while his partner, diminutive and slender, was dressed in a suit and tie.

Once inside, the big guy produced a knife. He told us to close our eyes. If we cooperated, we wouldn't get hurt, but if we resisted he would kill us. The pair took our wallets, watches, wedding rings, and Yehudit's jewelry and raincoat. At that point, they made me lie on the floor.

I had the bad luck to be carrying a credit card. They asked me for my PIN number, and at a nearby juncture the guy in the suit left the cab with the card in his pocket. Another individual, more thuggish in build, replaced him. The two of them sat in the passenger seat flanking Yehudit. The Gorilla draped a simian arm around her shoulder, with the polite explanation that if anyone looked inside, they wouldn't raise suspicions—they'd appear to be sweethearts. In case I got any funny ideas, his accomplice placed his foot against my ass and kept it there throughout the ride.

And that's how we spent the next couple of hours. We drove in circles, presumably on the inner-city throughways, given that the car didn't stop during the trip. My instincts told me they didn't intend to hurt us, but I was terrified that the driver might crash.

Adverse circumstances change one's notions of luck. *Chilangos* would later tell us that we had been "lucky" because our captors were reasonably professional and not drug-addled maniacs. They didn't manhandle Yehudit, let alone rape her; nor did they get violent with either of us (although after I protested a bit too firmly, the Gorilla twisted my arm as if it were a chicken wing, to give me an idea of his physical capabilities).

Two hours is a long time under such circumstances, and we were able to engage in a little Stockholm-syndrome dialogue. The Gorilla was the most voluble. Soon after the joyride began he informed us that what was happening was not his fault but the government's, for turning its back on its neediest citizens and forcing them to steal to survive. Yehudit was quick to point out that neither she nor I had any connection with the regime.

"*Les tocó*," he said, in a perfect illustration of Mexican fatalism. *Your number came up.*

We tried every ploy we could think of, mostly culled from soap operas, to evoke sympathy. Yehudit began by telling the kidnappers she was pregnant, a fabrication that raised nary an eyebrow. To appeal to whatever religious conviction they might have, she incessantly chanted the Lord's Prayer (her knowledge of which was a revelation to me, given that she is Jewish). I told them I had asthma and had forgotten my medicine, and began to wheeze (although not too loudly; I didn't want to overact). "Mother" is a magic word in Mexico, particularly if there are heartstrings to be tugged. I mentioned that mine was ill, and as my father and brother were both dead, I was the only one to take care of her.

Unimpressed, the Gorilla assured us that they all had mothers, wives, and children. Yehudit tried to bargain for the return of her amethyst earrings, explaining that they'd been a gift from her mother, who'd died three years earlier. One of the robbers was about to give them back, but his colleagues vetoed the gesture.

Finally the gang met up with their diminutive, well-dressed accomplice, who had been unable to withdraw cash with my credit card. In retrospect, we were blessed, because I'd made a stupid mistake: I'd given them a bogus PIN number. People who engaged in smartass tactics like that had been beaten to a pulp, and even killed. However, at the time, cash machines were fairly novel in Mexico City and functioned only sporadically with cards from foreign banks.

They released us on a deserted sidewalk in an unfamiliar neighborhood. They warned that we'd be killed if we looked back as their car was leaving. Soon a man who lived on the street arrived. We asked if we could use his phone to call friends to come fetch us.

This happened in January of 1996. Thirteen months earlier, the peso had been devalued by half, and in the subsequent year, reported crime had increased 65 percent in the capital. Friends had warned me that taxi kidnappings had become widespread. Anything but cooperation was a bad idea. Sam Quinones, a journalist, had been "tattooed pretty badly," as he put it, after he put up resistance to the robbers. Juvenal Acosta, a writer friend, got his ear sliced when he tried to kick his way out of a purloined taxi.

"Don't you know who you're dealing with, Juvenal?" the man who wielded the knife asked him. "I'm God. You can't fuck with me. Your fate is in my hands." Juvenal was more infuriated that the guy insisted on calling him by his first name than for claiming to be the deity. Later in the ride, the robbers discovered a cache of *El cazador de tatuajes,* his recently published novel. The leader asked if Juvenal would autograph a copy for his girlfriend.

Between 1995 and 1999, virtually all the people I know here had a similar anecdote of a taxi kidnapping that had happened either to them, a relative, or a close friend.

There were other anecdotes with distinct settings, mostly second- or thirdhand. Armed robbery was (and still is) a commonplace as people left ATM machines after withdrawing cash. While loading his trunk with purchases from the supermarket, a friend of an acquaintance had his head broken in front of his young son, the robbers absconding with the car (and the groceries). Friends of Yehudit told me about ruffians who entered a karate school, raped the female students, and stole the contents of the cash box. (So much for karate's effectiveness.) A friend's cousin was kidnapped and held for ransom—by uniformed policemen. Passing in a taxi, I saw that cops had cordoned off the entrance to a branch of the department store El Palacio de Hierro after a robbery. A colleague heard of an investment banker who'd visited from the United States, was kidnapped in a taxi, robbed, stripped to her underwear, and dumped on the outskirts of the city.

The city felt like a time bomb. *Chilangos* told news reporters that they were terrified of their own city. That the media affects our perception of safety is a commonplace, but the details regarding Mexico City are illuminating. At the time, magazines, newspapers, and TV, both international and Mexican, treated the capital as the poster boy for urban violence, a Wild West of metal, asphalt, and burning rubber, a locale of impossible and insane danger—Mogadishu in Spanish. In the United States at the turn of the twenty-first century, virtually nothing appeared in newspapers or magazines about Mexico City that didn't involve murder, robbery, or kidnapping.

Much of this reportage was exaggerated and poorly researched, if not blatantly irresponsible. For instance, in January 1999, PBS's *Jim Lehrer News Hour*—a program not well-known for sensationalism— broadcast a report about crime in the capital. One of its talking heads stated that there were 15.5 million assaults annually in the metropolitan area.

This number is patently ridiculous: it would mean that roughly three-quarters of the population was assaulted once a year, or that, say, 15 percent was assaulted ten times a year while the rest of us got off scot-free. The "statistic" was met without an iota of skepticism by the program's reporter, even though the source was the American owner of a private security company doing business in Mexico, who would clearly benefit from an inflated perception of the crime rate.

I'm not suggesting Mexico City wasn't a dangerous place at the time or that crime doesn't continue to be a significant problem. Yet at least in part safety is a matter not only of perception but of perspective. Around the same time that the PBS show was broadcast, the newspaper *Reforma* published an article based on a comparative study of danger in Latin American cities—principally culled from homicide statistics—and Mexico City didn't even make the list of the worst fifteen.

This is perhaps unsurprising. At the time of the survey, the major cities in Colombia and Peru were plagued by guerrilla terrorism, drug trafficking, and the frequent convergence of both. Many of the Central American capitals suffered from the combination of civil wars and grinding poverty. Gang violence in large Brazilian cities continues to be a constant. Compared to those places, Mexico City was—and in some cases continues to be—Switzerland.

In the past seven or eight years, far fewer of my friends here have told horror stories—or any stories—about being crime victims. I cannot remember the last time anyone I know mentioned a taxi hijacking. Yet many *chilangos* continue to perceive their city as dangerous, if not terrifying.

The truth is, the great majority of people in Mexico City go about their business every day unmolested. Still, I've often wondered how crime becomes the defining characteristic of a city, and how long it might take (or what has to change) for that reputation to abate.

When I was a kid, New York's economic situation was dismal, and drug traffic and consumption were out of control. In childhood I was trained never to talk to strangers and to watch my back at all times; even so, as a boy I was mugged twice and beaten up once on the streets. Nonetheless, I knew that movies like *Fort Apache, the Bronx* and *The Warriors,* with their comic-book street gangs, and cops chasing drug dealers down dark alleys while trading gunfire, were laughable exaggerations. At the time, despite its problems, New York was a vibrant city that not only functioned but survived and thrived.

So how dangerous is Mexico City, really?

It's almost impossible to tell. There are no reliable statistics. According to surveys, only about 25 percent of crime victims bother to report the incidents to the police; most believe it would be an utter waste of time. They're right. One criminologist estimates that at most only 3 percent of reported crimes lead to convictions here.

Some people refuse to report crimes because they believe the police were most likely involved in the offenses in the first place. They are often right about that, too, although the evidence is more anecdotal than data-based. Police have always been poorly paid in Mexico City. Today, a cop's starting salary is around five hundred dollars per month, depending on the area of the city to which he's assigned. Traditionally, cops have had to pay their station chiefs a daily "rent" for use of their uniforms, guns, bullets, squad cars, etc. In the past few years, it has been said that much of this practice has been abolished; however the "news" has come exclusively from police sources, which at the very least kindle doubt. Cops I spoke to told me they are issued one uniform and need to pay for any others; it's said that many police still "rent" their bulletproof vests and that investigative police pay for their own bullets.

Low salaries, coupled with tools of the trade for which they may have to pay, are virtually licenses to steal. Cops have frequently colluded with criminals—principally thieves and drug dealers—to supplement their incomes. The citizens of Mexico City are another horn of plenty. *La mordida*—literally "the bite," figuratively "the shakedown"—is a time-honored tradition and still an everyday phenomenon. Most often a cop will "bite" when he stops a driver for a real or imagined traffic infraction. To avoid the hassle of a ticket and a trip to the station house, he generously allows you to pay your fine then and there, and puts it in his pocket. He might also extort from small-business owners in exchange for "protection" or some other favor, or from sweethearts in a parked car, who he insists are committing *faltas a la moral* (moral improprieties). Drunks leaving bars at night have been frequent targets.

The quantity of a *mordida* depends on one's negotiation skills. For a minor moving violation it can be as little as a dollar or two (*para el refresco,* so the policeman can "buy himself a soft drink") or as high as fifty dollars if the infringement is serious. Others in more vulnerable situations might be coerced to go to an ATM to hand over their daily limit.

Recent campaigns have attempted to change public consciousness and to encourage civilians to refuse to participate in the bribery process. However, the tradition is so deeply ingrained that most *chilangos* think it's more efficient to hand over cash to a policeman than to try another method. The *mordida* is, in their conception, one of the ways that the city functions.

There are eighty thousand police to protect the eight million residents of the Federal District alone, an off-the-charts per-capita ratio compared to other big cities. According to a *New York Times* report in September 2006, nine thousand police officers were enough to cover the four million residents of Los Angeles, and New York made do with thirty-seven thousand for eight million citizens. Yet the current mayor of Mexico City has promised to augment the number to one hundred thousand during his term.

Mexico City cops come in a dizzying variety: preventive police, investigative police, transit police, tourist police, mounted police, auxiliary police, bank police, diplomatic police, industrial police, and customs police, among others, each corps with its own uniform.

There is no central command, no correspondence between the various agencies, and, most gravely, no accountability.

Given the sham system of law and order, the police are the most reviled, mistrusted, and feared citizens of Mexico City. Since the day I arrived, nearly anyone who has had the chance has told me I should avoid them at all costs; indeed, that I was safer at the hands of criminals than with cops (if I were somehow able to distinguish between them). Police I have interviewed told me that the citizenry routinely shouts insults at them, and I have seen civilians curse them or give them the finger from behind the wheels of their cars. In a rough neighborhood, a cop told me that men habitually suggest he take off his uniform or set aside his gun so they can break his face.

No one I know here would count on a uniformed beat cop to intervene during a mugging or a robbery. Most *chilangos* think it is best to ignore them. Plainclothes undercover cops are even more detested. In 2004, three of them, supposedly on an antidrug patrol outside a school in the Tláhuac section of the city, were lynched by a neighborhood mob. Two were burned alive while the third was beaten so badly that he ended up in the intensive care unit. It is a testament to the climate of mistrust and suspicion here that it took hours for the police chief to intervene, and that no member of the mob was ever taken to task for the incident.

The police consider themselves ill-paid, exploited, victimized by their superiors, pitiable, and misunderstood. Elena Azaola, author of the book *Imagen y autoimagen de la policía de la Ciudad de México* (*Image and Self-Image Among the Mexico City Police*), interviewed two hundred fifty cops for her research. Among her findings was a common belief that with a greater awareness of human rights in Mexican society the civil liberties of the police have been run roughshod. Reading their remarks, one can almost feel sorry for them:

If you're a cop, it's as if you're not a human being: You can't go to the bathroom or eat; the civilians look at you funny if you're at a taco stand. When they see us eating, they yell at us, For this, we're paying taxes? . . . We're human beings, not robots. We can't work like robots. Society doesn't understand that we think and feel like everyone else. We're not made of steel and we're not supermen.

One's sympathy evaporates when one reads in Azaola's study that 13 percent of Mexico City's incarcerated population was once part of the police corps.

The only crimes for which there are even moderately accurate statistics are homicide (because it requires great diligence and/or ingeniousness to make a corpse disappear) and car thefts, which are almost universally reported so the victims can collect from the insurance companies. Even the uninsured almost always go to the police; if they don't, they can be held responsible for accidents that might occur with others at the wheel.

In 2004, there were 710 homicides in Mexico City, as opposed to 218 in Washington, D.C. Yet there are close to twenty million people in Mexico City and only 572,000 in the U.S. capital. Therefore, your likelihood to get murdered in D.C. is far greater than it is here—equally true in many U.S. cities, among them Detroit, Philadelphia, St. Louis, Phoenix, Dallas, and Las Vegas (according to 2004 statistics from the FBI). In 2006, New Orleans—after Hurricane Katrina, with a population smaller than 1 percent of Mexico City's—had a murder rate nearly equal to the D.F. In 2004, there were a whopping 31,247 car thefts in Mexico City, but proportionally, the incidence is once again much greater in Washington, D.C., with 8,136 reported thefts.

By far the most prevalent crime in Mexico City is robbery, often armed, usually occurring on the street. According to official statistics, there were fifty-eight reported per day in 2005. If that number only reflects one quarter of the reality, there were 84,680 in the entire year. That figure represents less than half of 1 percent of the population.

Yet this math doesn't square up with periodic surveys from the newspaper *Reforma,* in which 10 to 15 percent of the population says it has been victimized by criminals within the previous three months. Criminologists' explanation for the discrepancy has to do with the *chilango*'s perception of time. When surveyed, victims nearly always believe that crimes have occurred more recently than they did. In cases where they have been interviewed more comprehensively, they realize the crimes were committed further back in time.

Trying to interpret existing data is a complex process. Most crimes that are reported are never even registered by the police. At the station house, police discourage victims, sometimes going as far as explaining that there is in fact no crime to register.

For instance, if you go to the station house and tell them that a robber stole the sewing machine you inherited from your grandmother, the cop who receives your complaint will most likely ask whether or not you have a receipt for the item. If you do not, from his point of view, you can't prove that the sewing machine had in fact been yours—or that it ever existed—so he will refuse to register the complaint. After some thugs tried to kidnap a journalist's mother—who put up a fight and actually tried to pull a pistol from one of their hands—the police explained that since there had been no actual kidnapping and the gun hadn't been fired, there was no crime to report.

———

In the absence of hard data, people rely on their perceptions. *Capitalinos* are terrified about the possibility of becoming victims, regardless of the actual likelihood. There are a variety of reasons for their dread, but many point to the media.

The Mexicans have a great tolerance—some might even say lust—for *la nota roja* (crime journalism), the bloodier the better. In bookstores one can buy anthologies, sometimes in several volumes, of the greatest crimes of Mexican history. Most people who follow the news watch it on TV, and the networks broadcast about two hours a day of footage of uncovered corpses lying in puddles of blood and, whenever there is an arrest, the snarling countenances of the apprehended (ipso facto treated as guilty).

Tabloid newspapers in Mexico City—which outsell other papers by far—indulge their readers with front-page stories of the same variety, with headlines in 216-point type, such as "Massacre," "Squashed," and "Killer Son-in-law." *La Prensa,* the most salacious of the dailies, not content with reporting the local misdeeds du jour, will sometimes publish crime stories from Nicaragua or North Korea, and once a week opens its nostalgia files and runs a Greatest Hits section of notorious felonies of the past. (An indication that the crime rate might be abating in Mexico City is that in the last year or two, the bloody photos on the front page of the tabloids depict city traffic accidents more often than murders.)

When running for office, politicians also do their best to exploit the crime problem, promising citizens that they (or their parties) are the only ones with the requisite machismo to get tough on crime. Usually they propose legislation for more severe punishment, including life imprisonment or even the death penalty. They succeed in increasing the public's fear, but presumably the delinquents remain little deterred at the possibility of a harsher sentence should they be among the 2 percent who are caught and convicted.

The obvious populations live in fear—women, the elderly, parents. The poor are the most anguished, and are twice as likely to become crime victims as the well-to-do.

Despite these longer odds, the rich, with so much to protect, are petrified. One evening, I had a drink with a woman who, at twenty-nine years old, still lived with her parents in Las Lomas, one of the city's wealthiest districts. Between nine and ten o'clock at night, her mother rang her on the cell phone three times, repeatedly suggesting that she come home before eleven, the hour at which Don Joaquín, their private security guard, went off duty. After that, she would have had to get out of her car to open the garage door, leaving her (and by extension, her family) vulnerable for an entire minute.

As it happens, the Don Joaquíns of Mexico City aren't necessarily guarantors of safety. Private security guards are among the lowest-paid citizens. As such, security impresarios recommend that they be frequently rotated, so they will not last long enough in any job to plan a robbery or kidnapping of their employers.

If statistics about crime are imprecise, it couldn't be clearer that insecurity is a huge business in Mexico City. All over town, fortunes are being spent in exchange for the perception of safety. For about half a million dollars, an outfit called VIP Protection will build you a state-of-the-art panic room, made from bulletproof materials and equipped with cellular communication, water, food, light, climate control, and a first-class first-aid kit. (Other companies offer panic rooms for as little as three thousand dollars, although at that price they're probably akin to the homes of the first two of the Three Little Pigs.)

Between three hundred and four hundred armored cars are sold per month, with annual sales of about $150 million. In 2006, Miguel Caballero, a Bogotá enterpreneur, opened a boutique in Mexico City offering four separate lines of high-fashion bulletproof clothing. The surprisingly sporty offerings cost between three hundred dollars for the safest T-shirt in the world, to three thousand dollars for a suit. Companies such as Kroll Inc., Control Risks Group, and The Steele Foundation offer clients a broad range of "risk management" services, such as background screening, intelligence and investigation, forensics, and the negotiation of kidnaps for ransom.

A celebrated beneficiary of the climate of terror here was former New York mayor Rudolph Giuliani, the crimebusting architect of the "zero tolerance" policy. Some of the city's wealthiest citizens, principally Carlos Slim, put together a $4.3 million piggy bank so the New Yorker could visit, study the capital's crime problem, and fashion a report that would outline ways to lower the crime rate. The ex-mayor made only one public appearance here, in January 2003, barely visible due to the phalanx of bodyguards who surrounded him as he toured some of the rougher neighborhoods.

When his report finally appeared in August of that year, it was roundly ridiculed by the press, which pounced on two or three of the document's recommendations that perhaps made sense in New York, but were tone-deaf to local realities. For instance, Giuliani advised the elimination of such dangerous miscreants as rag-brandishing windshield cleaners, the children who sell Chiclets at traffic intersections, corner men known as *franeleros* who for a few pesos direct drivers to available parking spaces, and street prostitutes (whose labor is in fact not illegal here).

Another of Giuliani's brainstorms was the implementation of Breathalyzer checkpoints at strategic junctions, meant as a deterrent to drunk drivers. An excellent idea in principle, but one man's stop sign is another's green light. *Reforma* published a report (including photos) about cops who sold the information of the Breathalyzer locations to bar owners, who passed the tip on to their intoxicated customers as they left for home. (The police department subsequently avoided this ingenious moneymaking scheme by frequently rotating the patrol cops on Breathalyzer duty. The number of drunk-driving accidents dropped 10 percent in the first year after the policy was installed.)

While the press found it easy to make fun of Giuliani, his report was in fact a useful document. Some of its 146 recommendations may have made little sense here, particularly those that had to do with the management of the streets. Yet three-quarters of its suggestions had to do with updating and reforming the police department, and most of these were spot-on. For instance, he favored the installation of a computerized system that would analyze the statistics of all reported crime, the establishment of an independent Internal Affairs division to combat corruption, and the fusion of the preventive and the investigative police, which work separately and don't share information.

Some of these proposals may seem obvious (and indeed had been previously advocated by nongovernmental organizations that were roundly ignored by the Mexico City government). But they weren't made widely public until Giuliani came here.

Sadly, five years later there is little evidence that much has been implemented. In an interview, Mayor Marcelo Ebrard (whose tenure as police chief coincided with Giuliani's visit) assured me that each of the New Yorker's ideas was either in place or in the process of being established. He said that the average citizen didn't comprehend this, because the work was taking place out of sight in the entrails of the department.

I'm skeptical. It's obvious that the majority of Giuliani's proposals that are evident to the public—such as controlling the incidence of graffiti on the streets, and the modernization of security systems in banks—have not been put into practice at all.

Despite the fact that between two thousand and twenty-five hundred robberies at ATMs are reported every year in Mexico City, there is virtually no security in or around them. You can get in and out of an ATM without swiping a card, and there are rarely guards, cameras, or panic buttons to alert anyone to robberies. If no visible measures have been taken to improve security in the city, there is little reason to believe that we're being protected by unseen ones.

The Giuliani report, nonetheless, served certain purposes, apart from enriching its author. One beneficiary was Carlos Slim, who was perceived as magnanimous for his financial backing of the New Yorker's intervention. Andres Manuel López Obrador, mayor of Mexico City when Giuliani was invited, was seen as serious about fighting crime. As such, the New Yorker's visit fueled the Mexican's presidential aspirations. Marcelo Ebrard, the former police chief, was elected mayor of Mexico City in 2006, in no small part due to the public's perception of him as a tough-on-crime, law-and-order guy.

Although a complicated proposition, with political will it wouldn't be impossible to substantially reform the Mexico City police force. Indeed, some advances have been made within the greater urban sprawl; what remains to be seen is whether or not they are merely temporal.

In the municipality of Ciudad Nezahualcóyotl, part of the Mexico City sprawl although technically in Mexico State, between 2003 and 2006 reported crime dropped about 20 percent. Some felonies, including car theft and street robbery, dropped nearly 50 percent. In January 2003, there were ten express kidnappings, yet in January 2006 there were only three.

It's still a rough part of town. Nonetheless its crime reduction results are better than the Federal District's, with a police force that is, per capita, less than a tenth the size. To get those results, Ciudad Neza didn't need to pay a cent to Rudolph Giuliani or any outside adviser. They were the efforts of a program established by Luis Sánchez Jiménez, Neza's mayor at the time, and his appointed police chief, Jorge Amador Amador.

From the start, Amador made it clear that he wouldn't tolerate corruption in the 750-member force. Twenty-five cops were fired, and about two hundred more, sensing that the party was over, left voluntarily. With local and federal funds, he hired six hundred additional police, augmenting the staff to about eleven hundred, and raised salaries by 20 percent.

All cops had to follow a seven-point agenda. They needed to meet minimal physical standards. They were obliged to spend an hour a day in physical conditioning, either playing soccer or at a gym. They had to take courses in psychology, ethics, the use of arms, and how to be good neighbors and workmates. The least expected element, which made headlines as far away as the BBC, was that they were required to take workshops in literature, in which teachers guided them through anthologies of poems and short stories published expressly for them. (Among other workshop activities were updating sections of *Don Quixote* in police argot, and the publication of some of their own writings.)

Reading in between the lines of what cops in Neza told me, I inferred that while corruption hadn't been entirely obliterated, it had at least been largely suppressed, and that it was looked upon disapprovingly by much of the group, most strongly by the newer members of the force.

Unlike in many parts of Mexico City, Neza's cops were well-groomed and took impeccable care of their uniforms and patrol cars. This self-respect seemed to register with the populace they were policing. I watched as two patrol cops stood guard outside of a school while its students left the building, and the parents treated them with respect rather than contempt. One mother—who had been helped by patrolwoman Aída Virginia Vázquez Cuenca when her child went missing a couple of weeks earlier—even greeted the policewoman with a kiss.

"I don't think of myself as a cop," Vázquez told me. "Technically, I'm an ordinary policewoman and not an officer but I think of myself as one, because I'm willing to risk my life to help other people. I've got a clean record. There hasn't been a single complaint against me." She told me that five hundred neighbors signed a document and sent it to the police chief, angling to keep her in their area.

Vázquez, thirty-eight, burly, and with spiky hair, remembered that when she was a child in Neza, the police sold drugs from a grocery store on her corner. Contrary to that tradition, "I can walk among the crowd with my head held high," she said.

She received me in two modest rooms, where she lived with three teenage children she raised alone. They lived on the top floor of her father's house; he resided downstairs with another daughter. Although Vázquez had little furniture and few amenities, she had prepared a cold oatmeal drink for my arrival. None of my experience in Mexico City had prepared me for her perception of herself and her definition of what a cop should be: "an honorable person, an honest person, and above all a person with a vocation for service."

It is uncertain whether Ciudad Neza will continue with its police program, let alone provide the inspiration for the rest of Mexico City. One of Mexico's worst problems is that elected officials cannot serve more than one term in any given office. As a result, they tend to spend the first half of their tenure doing their job, and the second half using it as a launching pad for their next move. After less than three years as mayor of Neza, Luis Sánchez began his campaign to become a federal deputy. He was elected, and in his new job will probably take Chief Amador to work at some other post. Neza's police department will be someone else's responsibility.

Hence, there's no continuity from one administration to the next. Newly elected officials have their own plans and projects (at least for the first half of their terms). Any long-term political undertaking suffers, and most are simply abandoned. In an interview, Victor Bautista López, Neza's mayor-elect after Sánchez, conceded only with great reluctance and impatience that the previous administration had done anything of merit with the police force. He had his own plans, far grander and probably impossible to orchestrate, to decentralize the entire police department in the greater Mexico City area.

Even if the police force were impeccably efficient and upstanding in Mexico City, it wouldn't make the slightest difference if enormous changes weren't made in the justice system. Once someone is arrested here—if he doesn't have enough money to pay a bribe and be released on the spot—after he is taken to the *ministerio público* (the station house) he is probably far less safe than he would have been in the worst neighborhood of Mexico City.

Mexico City's court system dates back to the colonial era. In those days, the protectorate sent written reports to Spain, where larger decisions about crime and punishment were decided. Today, miles and miles of paperwork continue to be generated by the courts, but as Mexico is no longer a colony, they are sent nowhere and read by no one. They are simply piled up, secured with twine, and stored in basements and warehouses.

Once taken to the station house, twenty or so accused are caged in a bull pen while their "trials" are set. They give evidence, often to people who don't even take the trouble to identify themselves. According to *El túnel* (*The Tunnel*), a documentary about the inefficiency of the judicial system by academic Roberto Hernández, 70 percent of the accused are not even aware of having met a public defender supposedly assigned to their cases. Seventy-two percent are not allowed to make a phone call. The most incredible aspect of the structure, at least to someone accustomed to an American or European trial system, is that 80 percent of the accused never even go before a judge.

Instead, the intermediaries who take "evidence"—sometimes there are no witnesses at all—prepare a dossier that is later read by the arbitrator, who decides from the documents alone whether or not the party is guilty and how stiff a sentence he should serve. In *El túnel,* among the interviewed prisoners is a woman serving six years for allegedly stealing less than twenty dollars. The only "proof" of the theft of another convict was the photograph of a toy she supposedly stole. Yet another prisoner was in jail for assault and robbery, despite the repeated insistence of the only witness that the convict was *not* the man who'd harmed him.

According to studies by the Centro de Investigación y Docencia Económicas (CIDE), one of Mexico City's most important research universities, only three out of ten people arrested have even been told with what crimes they have been charged, and a mere 33 percent were informed that they do not have to speak without a lawyer present. If you do not have the money for adequate legal representation, it is unlikely that you will receive anything resembling justice.

In late 2007, the Senate passed federal legislation to adopt an oral trial system in Mexico, in which the accused, the plaintiffs, and the witnesses would go before a judge and verbally present their arguments. This could be a giant step from the sixteenth to the twenty-first century. (Chile, which until recently had a system similar to Mexico's, adopted an oral judiciary in 2003, with positive results.) However, it will take eight years for the system to actually be put in place.

The Reclusorio Oriente, a jail on the east side of town, was built for fewer than two thousand prisoners and expanded to hold a couple thousand more. Nevertheless, about eleven thousand are incarcerated there. I only spent two afternoons in the *reclu,* principally as a guest at a writer's workshop in the prison's school, but my greatest intuition was that it is very much a microcosm of greater Mexico City, given its chaos, bureaucracy, corruption, and inequality.

The first time I arrived an armed guard told me I couldn't go inside because the black jeans I was wearing were the same color as his own trousers. In my faded-to-gray pants and green T-shirt, no one could have possibly mistaken me for one of the guards, who wear jet-black boots, shirts, and caps, and strap automatic weapons over their shoulders. Perhaps I was denied entry to help support a side business that accommodates visitors who make the mistake of arriving in black or beige (the color the prisoners wear). Outside, I paid a dollar to rent a pair of faded blue jeans; I had to wait in line as two other visitors changed clothes.

There are four visiting days per week; by ten in the morning, throngs wait outside to be let in. Aside from official visitors, each day more than a hundred people are allowed through a separate entrance, bearing two or three enormous market bags each, containing provisions that they pass on to prisoners, who heat, cook, and sell them at an enormous, ad hoc food court in an asphalt quad inside the prison. No one who isn't absolutely broke eats the official jail meals, for fear of becoming ill from the lack of hygiene in their preparation. From about two dollars upward, you can get filling (and very delicious) food from the vendors.

There is only a cursory examination of the bags. Prisoners in the workshop told me these people smuggle in drugs (widely available inside) and occasionally weapons, although the chief providers of illicit materials are the guards themselves.

To get to the school, I walked along a lengthy open-air passageway where hundreds of prisoners wandered back and forth. Some were gathering water in large plastic containers, and others wended their way to the gym or the school, but the majority had no apparent destination. They just strolled along purposefully, their eyes darting. There were no guards in sight, and the students assured me that in the majority of the jail there is no supervision whatsoever.

There is usually no response in cases of violence. The leader of the workshop noted how many men had broken noses or missing front teeth. This is because some of the tougher elements pop the unsuspecting newbies without warning, and then take whatever money they have in their pockets. "Conjugal visits" are allowed, and no one is particularly exacting about the visitor's relationship to the prisoner—indeed, prostitutes service the prisoners for between five and twenty dollars. Under the circumstances, sexual violence is far less prevalent than in many U.S. prisons.

The students told me that school was the only part of the jail available to them free. Everything else had a price—from the use of the gym to the rental of television sets in individual cells, to bedsheets, food, and drinking water. One even has to pay to sleep on the floor of a cell, rather than in the hallway or the bathroom.

Prisoners are divided among nine buildings according to their economic status. In the building inhabited by drug dealers, politicians, and white-collar criminals, some cells have Persian carpets, room service, Jacuzzis, and cable TV. However, most of the dwellings are populated by people sentenced for theft, robbery, or violent crimes. In their buildings as many as fifteen men are crowded into cells built for two.

After a lifetime of hearing about the violence of prisons in the United States, I asked the members of the workshop—some of whom admitted to being inside for homicide or rape—if they had any points of comparison. One of the prisoners said that he'd been in jail in Georgia on two separate occasions, and those penitentiaries, with their strict supervision at all times, were cakewalks in comparison.

The perception of danger in Mexico City has had significant consequences in terms of both architecture and urbanism. While it is frequently said that Mexico City lacks sufficient public space for its millions, it is rarely mentioned that the existent public space is seriously underutilized. There are many small and medium-size parks in the the D.F.'s four central delegations, but aside from the Alameda Central and Chapultepec Park, they are often deserted. I live near the Parque Hundido, one of the city's prettiest parks, and it is surprising how few people use it. Even on Sunday afternoons, I have rarely seen more than a dozen children playing there. After dark, few people walk in the city, except in certain districts (Polanco, Condesa, Roma, the *centro*) where there are many bars and restaurants.

The wealthy increasingly choose gated communities as their response to the perception of crime and danger. In the past ten years there has been something of a building boom in already established areas, while other communities—generally clusters of high-rise apartment buildings—are being created. Their centers, their "downtowns," are shopping malls, around which other businesses are established (Office Depot, Starbucks, McDonald's, a gym, a car dealership). There are no spaces where people can actually walk around or enjoy the sensation of living in a city.

About five years ago, "news"—alarmist and only vaguely substantiated—began to circulate about the supposedly skyrocketing number of kidnappings in Mexico. Some reports claimed it was on par with Colombia, while others suggested it had even surpassed its notorious South American counterpart.

Once again, the numbers were deceptive. Before 2000, express kidnappings—the joyrides that last only a couple of hours—were not included in the count; they were listed as robberies. Only the more complicated cases, that went on for days or weeks while a ransom was negotiated, were classified as kidnaps. Between 2000 and 2005, the number of reported kidnappings, both express and for ransom, held steady at about 140 per year. At the same time, the number of kidnappings in Colombia supposedly dropped. (In fact, many Colombians stopped reporting kidnappings to the police, due to legislation that made it illegal to negotiate with kidnappers.)

If other trends in Mexican victim statistics are an indication, there are perhaps three or four times as many kidnappings that go unreported. Five hundred and sixty a year is a deplorably high number. Still, it means that one's odds of being kidnapped are about one in thirty-six thousand, an acceptable risk for many.

The good news, according to police and criminology sources, is that since 2005 there are fewer kidnappings. This is because of the creation of the Agencia Federal de Investigación, known as AFI—Mexico's equivalent to the FBI, and according to all sources interviewed for this chapter, the only trustworthy police agency in the country—which had succeeded in disbanding the most important rings of kidnappers.

The bad news is that they left abductions in the hands of less professional, more haphazard cowboys. The bottom line is that it's hell if your number comes up.

On a chilly evening in November 2002, while stuck in traffic on the Viaducto, an inner-city throughway, Isaac Rubinski, manager of a textile shop in the *centro,* received a cell-phone call from his wife.

"What time will you get home?" she asked.

"Half an hour," he said. "Maybe forty-five minutes." Three weeks would pass before she would see him again.

As he arrived home, when Rubinski opened the door of his car, a man cracked him across the face with the butt of a gun. "This is a holdup," the man said, and he and a partner forced Rubinski to lie on the floor in the back of a white Suburban. "It'll be over in twenty minutes. Close your eyes or we'll kill you."

They transferred Rubinski to the trunk of the vehicle. When he was finally let out, his captors put a windbreaker over his head; all he could see was the floor of the apartment where they'd taken him. He was tied to a chair and beaten about the back, kidneys, legs, stomach, and head. The volume of a TV had been turned up high; he was warned that if he screamed they would kill him.

One of his captors—whom Rubinski would think of as *el gran jefe* (the big cheese)—said, "We know you have a lot of money. We want millions of pesos, not a handout. Who's going to negotiate for your life?"

His mind racing, Rubinski decided against his wife, who would have to take care of their daughters, three and seven at the time. He didn't want to involve his parents, fearful of putting them in danger. He decided on his eldest brother: "It would have to be someone who loved me enough, and was tough enough, to take care of business."

Unfortunately, the kidnappers were mistaken about Rubinski. They believed he was the son of the owner of the business where he worked. Although he lived well compared to the great majority of Mexico City—his own home and car, kids in private school, beach vacations a couple of times a year—he wasn't the millionaire his hostage-takers believed him to be.

During the first week of his captivity, he was periodically allowed to speak to his brother by phone (although not permitted to listen to the other side of the conversation). They would hit him beforehand so he'd sound agitated, and then make him follow a script: "I'm okay. Whatever you do, don't call the cops. Cooperate and do whatever they tell you."

According to the Mexico City scale of luck, Rubinski was "fortunate" that the kidnappers allowed him to speak to a relative on the phone. The director of the local branch of an international security firm told me that if he had to be abducted, he'd prefer it to happen in Colombia, where felons are more professional. "Mexican kidnappers are exceptionally violent and relatively stupid," he said. "For most of them, proof of life isn't a phone call. It's sending the family a finger or an ear of the victim."

For the first week, Rubinski had to ask permission to be untied so he could eat or use the bathroom. During the entire nightmare, he estimates he was blindfolded twenty-two hours a day, except at mealtimes. He slept four or five hours a night. To help pass the time, he exercised, walking in place six hours a day. He was given a substantial breakfast and lunch, and a light supper daily. At a certain point he realized that the man who cooked his meals—he thought of him as "the chef"—was subsisting on his leftovers. Rubinski began to eat less, so his captor wouldn't starve. "You make friends with the devil, hoping that God will help you," he explained.

Rubinski's brother, negotiating with the kidnappers, was being coached not only by AFI agents, but by a man who for about ten years was known as the "go-to guy" in the Jewish community during a kidnapping. Before he retired from this activity, he negotiated eighty-eight kidnaps, and in each the victim was returned alive. In seventy-six of the cases, at least some of the gang members were arrested and convicted. I'll call this man Jacobo. (Isaac Rubinski is also a pseudonym. He explained that some of the members of the gang who kidnapped him are still at large, and he feared for the safety of his daughters if his identity were exposed.)

Jacobo is about seventy, slim, bald-headed, and morbidly witty. I met him in his "office"—an elegant café off a hotel lobby. Jacobo blames the wave of kidnapping in Mexico to television coverage. He refers specifically to the news about the leader of a kidnapping ring named Daniel Arizmendi López, who before his capture was known as *el mochaorejas* (the ear chopper) because of his proclivity for sending the ears of his victims to accelerate ransom payments.

"Before him," said Jacobo, "a criminal would stick up a grocery store or rob people on the street, get five hundred or a thousand pesos and then, after a hard day's work, go home and watch TV. Thousands of these guys saw the reports about how much Arizmendi made and said to themselves, 'I'm in the wrong business.'"

Jacobo refused to offer any details about how a kidnap is negotiated, explaining that if a kidnapper read this book, he would be tipped off to the strategy. "How much is a life worth?" he asked. "Buying and selling shirts is an easy business. You know if you buy a shirt for ten pesos and sell it for twenty, you've made a ten-peso profit. If you sell it for nine, you've lost a peso. But how much a life is worth is the business of kidnap negotiation. They've got a person and they want to sell him. The family wants to buy him. It's all about money. It's not personal. They're just trying to move merchandise."

The father of another kidnap victim—whose son was returned to him for about twenty thousand dollars after the intervention of the AFI—was willing to go into more detail. He drew a triangle on a piece of paper. The line at the bottom represented the passage of time. The line on the left pointing upward symbolized the mounting pressure, both for the kidnappers and the victims' families. The line pointing downward on the right stood for the diminishing financial expectations of the kidnappers. At a certain point, a convergence is reached for a sum of money.

If the family of the victim agrees to pay the first amount requested by the kidnappers, then the criminals will decide that they've asked for too little and demand more. As painful as it may be when the life of a loved one is at stake, professionals urge the victims' families to start with an extremely low number, so the final price won't be usurious.

"Violence is always a part of it, verbal or physical," said Jacobo. "You can't be a polite kidnapper or no one will take you seriously." The longest period of captivity for one of the kidnaps he negotiated was one hundred days, and the shortest twenty-four hours. The smallest amount of money ever handed over was about five thousand dollars, and the greatest close to one hundred thousand dollars. "And three fingers," he added.

Isaac Rubinski wanted to live because the last time he saw his seven-year-old daughter, she had been crying on the way to the school bus. She'd begged to return home to get a teddy bear, but the bus was already parked at the corner. He insisted she board the bus, and could have her toy when she returned from school.

He wanted to live so he could tell his wife that he loved her, but that if he were killed she would have to get on with her life. "If she found another man that could be a father to my kids, that would be fine," he said. "I wanted to tell her life was for the living."

After twenty days he was released. His boss, who had been in touch with Rubinski's family throughout the ordeal, had offered a sufficient amount to satisfy the kidnappers. Rubinski wouldn't say how much, only that it was "a lot."

A kidnapping never ends with the release of its victim: the aftermath can drag on for a terribly long time. Rubinski is truly "lucky" in the sense that, rather than damaged from his experience, he seems more resilient. "Whatever doesn't kill you makes you stronger," he said. I realized there are many people who love me. You go about your life and you touch people. Many prayed for me, worried about me, stayed abreast of my situation."

María Elena Morera de Galindo, the wife of a kidnap victim who came home with only seven fingers, made crime and safety her cause after her husband's experience. She works with an NGO called Mexico United Against Delinquency that serves as a pressure group to coerce politicians and government to work harder against crime. Yet she says her husband has become more distant and less communicative. "He's a macho Mexican. He wouldn't go to therapy. He doesn't want to talk about it."

The father of the kidnapped teenager told me that the lives of his entire family are irrevocably changed. Four years after the fact, they continue to monitor their telephones and only take radio cabs. Everyone in the family has been to therapy. "I only carry one credit card. I don't wear a watch and my wife hardly wears jewelry. When I drive I'm always checking the mirrors to see if anyone is following."

Isaac Rubinski's brother is often depressed, and his elder daughter has had problems adjusting. Even he—the "lucky" one—occasionally wakes up in the night in a cold sweat.

The great majority of people in Mexico City not only haven't been kidnapped, but don't know anyone who has been, either.

How dangerous is it here? The bottom line is that it's not as dangerous as many of its residents believe. But it's still dangerous. It's worse in certain parts of town and during certain hours of the day. If anything happens to you on the street, it is most likely to be a robbery.

What makes residents most anxious is not so much our chances of being victimized at any given moment, but our vulnerability and lack of protection. *Si te toca*—if your number comes up—you cannot count on the police or the judicial system to support you.

The possibility of violence is also terrifying. If robbery is the most frequent crime, one often hears (or reads in the newspaper) of muggings in which victims put up no resistance but are beaten or even killed nonetheless. Years ago, another friend, hijacked in a taxi, was beaten so severely about the head that he suffered a brain hemorrhage. The director of another NGO told me about a young couple trapped by a gang as they were getting into a car. The mob beat the man to a pulp and stuffed him in the trunk, from which he had to listen to them repeatedly rape his girlfriend.

Still, in the past couple of years, the crime blotter in Mexico City has begun to be supplanted by even gorier news, principally from the northern states and the border cities. The struggle for territory among gangs of drug traffickers has resulted in wholesale murderers of dealers and the cops who go after (and sometimes conspire with) them. Notes are often attached to their corpses, along the lines of "So you'll learn respect." Sometimes their limbs, and even their heads, are severed from their bodies. Mexico City is beginning to look like Sunnybrook Farm in comparison.

Two more statistics: Surveyed by an NGO that researches crime and safety in the city about their experiences in the year 2004, 87 percent of Mexico City residents said they hadn't been victims of any sort of crime at all. According to the Department of Justice, in 2005, about 13 percent of people in the United States said they had.

The Crater

It was midafternoon, too early for rush hour, and as such I was able to choose between various available seats on the metro. I selected a place, but before sitting, glanced at the woman whom I would have been facing. Like many subway riders, her slumped posture indicated fatigue or even defeat. Her dyed curly hair and the slack skin on her exposed arms indicated middle age. She embraced and leaned into a huge market bag on her lap.

Her face was terrifying. On the left side, where her eye had once been, there was a huge crater. It looked as if someone had gouged it out with an ice-cream scoop. The cavity was surrounded by a thick crust of furrowed purple scar tissue, yet the gaping black hole in the middle was shockingly vacant.

A dozen stories came to mind about what could have happened to her, each more ghastly than the next. I couldn't look at her, let alone sit beside her, and moved to another place in the car. My hesitation and move lasted no more than a second, yet once seated I wondered how many times a day she must register people's repulsion, no matter how subtle we try to be.

That night I dreamt of a man whose left eye began to bleed until it fell out. It washed into a swimming pool with other people's eyes floating in it. A couple of fat pink pigs jumped into the water, swam over to the eyes, and began to eat them.

Mexican Lexicon, Part Three

No. A word most often avoided in Mexico City. If you offer a *chilango* a cigarette or a cup of coffee, and he doesn't want it, he will raise his hand, palm facing inward (a symbol of respect), and say *gracias*—thank you. He will not specify *no, thank you.*

The allergy to *no* is even more perplexing when attempting to work here. If you are looking for investors, if you are looking for a job, if you are looking for a permit to open a place of business, the *chilango* you solicit might be unwilling to help you, but he doesn't want to be the bad guy in the movie. His first promising phrases will be along the lines of *en principio me encanta la idea* (in principle I love the idea), but these will be supplemented with others that commence a war of attrition: *déjame ver* (let me see), *tendremos que investigarlo* (we'll have to look into that), *hay que hablar con mis socios* (I'll have to talk to my colleagues). He doesn't mind letting this go on for years, even generations; the story ends when you give up.

No sé (I don't know). When stopped and asked for directions on the street, many *chilangos* would be unbearably ashamed to confess their ignorance. Few will say "I don't know" flat out, but there is a pantomime that generally indicates this message. You ask a passerby how to get to Avenida Revolución. He stops, stands up straight, perhaps folds his arms. Then he contorts his face, as if he is trying to squeeze his eyes and his mouth as close to his nose as possible. Then he stares into the middle distance, his moue suggesting efforts toward a solution to the riddle of the Sphinx. This is as close as most *defeños* will come to "I don't know," and as they get there, it is advisable to head them off at the pass and say, "Thanks so much for your trouble; I believe I'll ask someone else." If you don't, they are liable to come up with a complicated set of instructions, probably invented on the spot. "Go straight for four blocks and make a left at the taco stand, until you get to the bakery with the red awning . . ."

Naco. Someone unlettered, ill-mannered, brutish. According to essayist Carlos Monsivais, the word is a derivation of Totonaco, the language of an indigenous group from northern Veracruz. When the word was popularized in the 1950s, it was a supremely insulting way to refer to the poor, the brown-skinned, the uneducated.

Through the years its definition has expanded to include any lout, regardless of socioeconomic background. Among younger generations of *chilangos,* the word has lost much of its bite, as well as its specificity. Almost anything or anyone can be judged *naco* if it doesn't please the beholder. A couple of years ago a company called Naco began to sell trendy clothing and accessories. Many *fresas*—literally strawberries, but colloquially yuppies—spent about twenty-five dollars on T-shirts that proudly displayed the Naco logo across the chest.

Cerca (near) and *lejos* (far). Even if you already live in a big city, increase your perspective of dimension by five times. A well-to-do *chilango* makes a date for lunch, and assures you the restaurant is nearby. He may be referring to a forty-five minute ride in his chauffeur-driven car. A less well-to-do *chilango* might say that something is "near" if it is only a two-day trip on a donkey. If the word "far" is invoked, be prepared for a long journey.

¿Cómo lo arreglamos? (How can we work this out?) You're behind the wheel and a traffic cop stops you for an infraction, real or
imagined. This phrase means you're willing to pay him a bribe so
he'll let you move on, but you're no sucker. You're going to bargain
over the price.

La Fondesa

Since 1958, Jesús Elizondo, known to his customers as Chucho, has cut hair in a beauty salon that overlooks a tiny plaza in a neighborhood called the Colonia Condesa. On the same block are a French bistro, a yoga studio, a combination boutique and CD store, a shop that sells aromatherapy products imported from Spain—and another, resolutely fancier, and more contemporary beauty salon.

Chucho doesn't care and refuses to even acknowledge the other business as competition. "They charge three hundred pesos for a haircut," he says. "I charge one hundred fifty, and only one hundred between Monday and Thursday. I don't think they're doing very well because they have to pay such high rent. I own this building." Chucho, seventy-five, never removes an old golf hat from his head, and the lenses in his eyewear look like they were fashioned from magnifying glasses. He claims to continue to work to keep from being idle.

The other shops have all opened within the last five years. Apart from Chucho's salon, the plaza's only holdouts from an earlier era are a tailor shop, a dry cleaner, and an Argentine steak house. The restaurant may survive because so many people come to the neighborhood to eat, but when their leases run out, the other two businesses are probably doomed.

If the story of gentrification is a familiar one in any sizable city, the Condesa is a unique neighborhood to Mexico City. Walk along its tree-lined streets, with Art Deco and neo-colonial buildings from the 1930s, and you can almost believe you're in a fairy-tale European town. You can rent a bicycle from Don Hilario's shop, eat exquisite *tacos de guisado* from a hole-in-the-wall run by a man called El Güero, and walk through two lovely parks.

Everything in the Condesa is in walking distance—the international restaurants that have recently emerged, the bars and gourmet shops, the market, branches of every bank, the gym administered by Chucho's son (as well as a more upmarket fitness center frequented by South American models and every imaginable species of yuppie). In Mexico City, walking distance is a true luxury in well-to-do quarters, which are mostly designed for people who go everywhere in cars.

Rents have become so high in the Condesa that few Mexicans can afford to live there. Those who do (such as Mayor Marcelo Ebrard) are distinctly well-to-do. On the street, most people appear to be foreign. The Mexicans who live here are white and of European descent; indeed, the only people of a more indigenous aspect are the valet parking attendants, the employees in the kitchens, the police, and the cleaning women.

Wags have dubbed the neighborhood La Fondesa, a play on the word *fonda*, which means restaurant. This is because in the past decade, more than two hundred restaurants, bars, and cafés have opened here. While some trendy shops and boutiques have appeared, most of them open and close quickly, and those that survive tend to have so few customers that one wonders if they are money-laundering operations. Still, most of the restaurants—even the ones with the most tepid kitchens—are always full. The customers still include some artists, writers, fashionistas, and advertising types who live in the neighborhood, but the restaurants are mostly thronged by people who live elsewhere and come here to eat.

In Spanish, *condesa* means "countess." It was once part of an enormous swath of the hacienda of the third Countess of Miravalle, wife of a Spanish grandee. But it remained a *rancho* until its development in the early twentieth century. During the first decades it housed the Jockey Club, a race track and recreational facility for the city's wealthiest residents. In the early 1920s, the club closed and the land began to be developed for residences—with a decree that a large section would be maintained as green space (a lovely anomaly today).

Architects call it Mexico City's first modern neighborhood; before it was built, homes and public buildings were constructed with heavy stone in a Frenchified nineteenth-century style. Its new residents were the Bohemian elite, as well as Jewish immigrants, primarily Ashkenazis from Eastern Europe. In addition to synagogues and community centers, they opened kosher butcher shops and European-style bakeries.

The Condesa prospered as such for close to sixty years, until the disastrous earthquake of 1985. Although the neighborhood wasn't very hard hit, it was next door to the Colonia Roma, large sections of which were destroyed. Services deteriorated and many of the neighborhood's most notable citizens fled to other areas.

One person's disaster is another's opportunity. A group of painters moved into the neighborhood, taking advantage of plummeting rents to set up studios and living spaces in the spacious apartments. After the peso crash of 1994, many took advantage of low prices and bought their apartments. The Condesa is in an enviably central location between two metro stations, easily accessible to the rest of the city.

In 1993, an Argentine restaurant called Fonda La Garufa opened on Calle Michoacán. What made La Garufa stand out was not its menu of empanadas, steaks, and pastas, but that tables were set on the sidewalk, a custom nearly nonexistent in Mexico City in those days.

"The first day we put the tables outside, the restaurant filled up," says Ernesto Zeivy, who briefly managed La Garufa. Zeivy had spent several *wanderjahre* in London and New York, and sought to imitate the kind of restaurant in whose kitchens he had labored. "From that moment on, we were full every day. People waited on line for as much as two hours to get in."

The law of supply and demand spurred the exponential multiplication of the restaurants. Today in the Condesa you can have a French, Italian, Japanese, Spanish, Vietnamese, Polish, or Argentine meal. A few places are standouts, but most of their kitchens turn out unremarkable fare at high prices, and their main selling points are their pleasant decoration and fashionable location. Most have tables on the sidewalk.

For a brief window of time, roughly between 1995 and 2000, the Condesa had all the elements of a vital neighborhood as described by Jane Jacobs in her classic of urban planning, *The Death and Life of Great American Cities*. It was of mixed use (people who lived there rubbed elbows with others who came to work during the day; while still more came to visit the restaurants at night), which made it a lively center nearly twenty-four hours a day. Small blocks made it pleasant and easy to get around, and a combination of old and newer buildings, with varying rents, made it accessible to people of different economic levels. A mixed-class population, very rare in Mexico City, made it possible for a plumber, a locksmith, or a tradesman to live within a few blocks of a doctor or an architect, and to keep his business alive.

With the rise of the restaurants, a vehemently vocal minority of neighbors, principally elderly, began to complain to the local authorities: the noise levels were intolerable; it was impossible to find a parking space any longer; drugs and prostitution were rampant.

Most of their complaints were exaggerated. If you had the bad luck to live above a bar or restaurant, your life inevitably changed. Condesa crime rates are far lower than in much of the city. In a corner of the area a handful of transvestite hookers ply their trade with as much discretion as possible (admittedly not much, given that they tend to wear bustiers and hot pants even on frigid January nights).

The true explosion of the area was not in restaurants but in real estate. Since the first years of the new millennium, crummy Condesa apartments with tiny, boxy rooms and plasterboard walls suddenly became subject to sky-high rents. Each spindly, dilapidated building, every patch of ground on even the least prepossessing blocks, was the object of massive speculation. A building boom ensued, and on almost every block one or two of the old private houses or buildings were razed to be replaced by new five- or six-story apartment buildings in a cookie-cutter design of white-painted metal with floor-to-ceiling windows and ample balconies.

There are two reasons for the heady climate in the real estate industry, which is happening not only in the Condesa but also all over the four central delegations of the Federal District, and beyond. The 1985 earthquake most strongly affected those four areas, and as a consequence lost significant numbers of their populations to the outskirts. Andrés Manuel López Obrador, after being elected mayor in 2000, changed zoning laws to allow for new construction in those delegations, which included four or five added stories to buildings that had previously been zoned for one or two. The real-estate boom is also a reflection of Mexico's improved economy in the last few years; today home loans, previously difficult to acquire, are more easily obtained.

When people talk about the Condesa, they tend to paint dooms-day scenarios in which the neighborhood will become impossibly unlivable. They compare it to the Zona Rosa, which in the 1960s was similarly trendy and Bohemian, but is today full of drug dealers, table-dance bars, and underage prostitution.

There are, however, significant differences between the two areas. The Zona Rosa changed drastically in the 1970s with a couple of huge obstructions, including the construction of an enormous traffic circle and plaza to make way for a metro station, as well as the building of the city's central police headquarters there. Most people point to these additions as the beginning of the Zona Rosa's fall.

If the comparison to the Condesa is alarmist, the truth is that the neighborhood has already flattened and become less colorful than it was a decade ago. There is a chapter in Jacobs's book about how vital neighborhoods with mixed activities and populations self-destruct, victims of their own success. "The winners in the competition for space will represent only a narrow segment of the many uses that to-gether created success," she wrote. "Whichever one or few uses have emerged as the most profitable in the locality will be repeated and re-peated, crowding out and overwhelming less profitable forms of use."

Predictably, it has become ever more difficult to find the shoe-repair shop, the locksmith, the stationery store, and such businesses that made the Condesa feel like a neighborhood in the first place. Fewer families live here, having been displaced by singles with lots of disposable income.

Various restaurants open or change hands every month. The new-est have European names and serve generic high-end fast food: ba-guette sandwiches, salads, soups, a few hot plates. The U.S. franchises certainly stand out; as of this writing there are three Starbucks, a Krispy Kreme doughnut outlet, and a Subway sandwich branch.

These manifestations, and the new buildings of identical design, conspire to denude the neighborhood of its character. Chucho the hairdresser will no doubt keep styling old ladies' heads until he can no longer stand, but once that inevitability occurs, his locale will certainly be replaced by a business infinitely trendier and triter. While he remains, he is impervious to fashion. "Just because the neighborhood is *de moda*," he says, "doesn't mean I'm going to change the name of my shop to Les Chuchés."

Making a Scene

Phil Kelly's studio is similar to those of many painters—after a hurricane. It reeks of oil and turpentine. All over the floor and atop every surface are heaping piles of squeezed-dry paint tubes, the boxes from which they were extracted, old newspapers, empty wine and beer bottles. In the middle of the floor there is also a mound of more than one hundred CDs, mostly tinny jazz from the 1930s, but also the odd Bob Dylan or Italian opera. Novels in English, magazines in French, newspapers in Spanish, and exhibition catalogs in various languages are sprinkled all over.

On a recent Wednesday, a little after high noon, he opened his second bottle of wine of the day. The first had been his breakfast, consumed while he prepared a more orthodox meal—oatmeal, milk, and toast—for his wife and daughters. He never bothers with coffee or tea. "A long time ago I tried to have tequila for breakfast. But that's dangerous," he says.

Kelly is an Irishman raised in England who became a Mexican national in 1994. The walls of his studio are covered with his work, primarily impressionist panoramas of Mexico City. Full of emotion and movement, his canvases absorb the chaos of the city and make it somehow attractive—huge skies of toxic beige (or pink or orange), the crowds, the speeding traffic around boulevards and monuments like the Angel of Independence, Avenida Reforma, or the Torre Mayor. Here and there will appear a Volkswagen taxi or a tree asphyxiated by smog.

Art historians, curators, and critics in Mexico City have compared Kelly to De Kooning, Matisse, Van Gogh, Cézanne, Dufy, Pollock, and Soutine. They've called him figurative, Fauvist, Expressionist, neo-Expressionist, and, in one case, claimed that he represents "the Fauvist frontier between Impressionism and Expressionism." While Kelly cites the postwar British painters as influences, he hates labels. "I just want to paint," he says.

In his late fifties, Kelly is heavyset and sturdy. Bald, his face and pate are the color of raw veal. His denim shirt and khaki pants are stained with the entire rainbow of primary and secondary colors. He wears heavy black shoes, one yellow and one green sock.

A clanging bell is heard from the street: the signal that the garbage truck has arrived, and for residents to go downstairs to deliver their refuse to the trashmen. "Come and take a look," says Kelly. He grabs his wine, in a highball glass mixed with club soda, and goes to the balcony to watch the spectacle.

In the entire history of Mexico City, no one has ever watched the vista of garbage collection with such a discerning eye. "See the guy folding the cardboard boxes? He's dividing it into the 'good' and the 'bad' cardboard. Then they piss on top of it so it'll be heavier: they pay according to how much it weighs. That guy who just got out of the truck, he's the driver, the boss of the group. But the guy with the clipboard, he's new, he's like the cop among the garbagemen. You see how they're talking? The boss is so scared he's shitting his pants. And look at the guy tying up the sack of empty cans, and how he fastens it to the truck. And coming out of nowhere, look, a mysterious yellow butterfly."

Kelly arrived in Mexico City in the 1980s, already well into his thirties, his last fifty dollars in his pocket. Here, among the chaos and disorder, he found a home as well as a theme, a public that responds to his work, a wife, a family—in sum, a life. "I can't imagine living anywhere else," Kelly says. "They wanted to give me a grant to live in Ireland for a year, but I didn't want to go. It's too cold there."

Kelly paints every day, and sells as much as he can produce. His canvases usually measure about three by four feet, and fetch around forty-five hundred dollars in Mexico and forty-five hundred euros when sold through the Panther & Hall Gallery in London or the Frederick in Dublin. Although he has had solo exhibitions in some of the most important museums here, including the Museum of Modern Art and the Museum of Mexico City, tellingly, he is not represented by any gallery in the city. His wife, Ruth Munguía, handles his sales.

Despite his success, Kelly doesn't even figure on the hipness map of contemporary art in Mexico City. It is a world in which he exists, at best, on the margins.

In the mid-1990s, a group of young artists—a mixture of locals and foreigners—began to emerge in Mexico City. Ignored by the establishment, they exhibited in fringe galleries, many of which lasted only a year or two. Yet by the first years of the new millennium, their shot had been heard around the world. Their work had moved from those minor Mexican galleries to many of the most important museums of New York, Berlin, Los Angeles, Madrid, and Paris, as well as virtually any city that has a biennale or an art fair, from Venice and São Paulo to Seoul and Sharjah.

Although their art bears no similarity to Kelly's, Mexico City had also clearly gotten under their skins. Their efforts, like the Irishman's, were also an interpretation of the city, a challenging urban narrative based on their observations.

In many ways the rise of the Mexico City art scene is representative of contemporary art in general. Young artists need to find a way of distinguishing themselves from the multitudes who exhibit in the innumerable art fairs, biennales, and galleries around the world. Aesthetic considerations rarely come into play. Political messages, however facile, are more likely to make noise. For instance, Gabriel Orozco, the first Mexican artist to emerge in the 1990s, is to this day most famous for sending an empty shoe box to the Venice biennale of 1993. Meanwhile, his Mexico City counterparts, only marginally interested in such Duchamp-inspired considerations about what constitutes art, found their métier and meaning through the violence and lawlessness of the city.

At this point Mexico City has been consecrated as an official stop on the art-world tour. Articles, often gushy in tone, about its artists, galleries, museums, and collectors have appeared in international art and travel magazines, and it has become an obligatory location for many global dealers and collectors, critics, and curators. Yet at the same time the work of those artists who turned the place into a scene has evolved away from Mexico City. Recent exhibitions indicate that the detour from the city's inspiration has diluted their creations, and taken away much of their bite. Nonetheless, few new artists have emerged to challenge their place.

Much of what the nineties artists produced was determined to have a visceral effect on the viewer at any cost. Their medium is the installation. They filled gallery space with photographs, video, and film, handbills filched from lampposts, stolen car stereos, half-eaten corn cobs, wet cement, or—in one instance, mounted on a small stand—a human tongue pierced with a silver stud. The tongue was once attached to the cadaver of an impoverished junkie. After his violent death, the artist, Teresa Margolles, made a deal with his family: if they gave her either his tongue or his penis, she would give them a casket. The relatives, too broke to pay for a funeral, conceded the former organ. It was exhibited in a small gallery here, then later at the ACE Gallery in Los Angeles, and finally in Mexico City's Palace of Fine Arts.

Margolles's work consistently invites the spectator to reflect upon death. Although neither a doctor nor a medical student, she studied forensic medicine in the Mexico City morgue. There she found the inspiration and materials for much of her efforts. Among her most talked about and widely exhibited works was a series of sheets that had been pressed against gory cadavers; the Rorschach prints of their blood, often outlining their bodies, were hung on museum and gallery walls. For the installation *Vaporización,* an empty space was humidified by water obtained from the morgue that had been previously used to wash corpses during autopsies.

Santiago Sierra also magnifies a tension between the sedate and supposedly civilized art world with the most violent realities of Mexico City. He has principally lived and worked here since his arrival from Madrid in 1995. Apparently, upon getting here, he was astounded to find rampant injustice and inequality. He has made a brilliant career from this unearthing. Like an advertising man, he established his "brand," stayed on point, and repeated his message over and over, industriously coming up with infinite ways to plant the same argument.

He began with projects that exposed the gaping vacuum where authority ought to exist in the city. One of his first works—he calls them "actions"—was to attach masking tape to the stairway of an overpass on top of a highly trafficked avenue, thus preventing pedestrian use of it. On the marginal street where he lived in the *centro histórico,* he tied plastic ropes from inside the building to a parked car, tilting the vehicle two feet off the ground. In his most dramatic impediment, he paid a truck driver to block traffic on one of the inner-city highways for five minutes.

But the inspiration that made Sierra's name was to move from inanimate objects to human subjects, a formula he repeats to this day. He tended to hire the most vulnerable elements of society—soldiers in the army of the underemployed, beggars, or even desperate junkies and prostitutes—to illuminate the savagery of inequality in Mexico City. In his first work of this kind, he paid a man about five dollars to tattoo a foot-long straight line on his back. (Apparently Cubans are even more desperate than Mexicans. During a Havana biennale, Sierra paid six islanders to similarly tattoo their backs, although he gave them the princely sum of thirty dollars apiece.)

In Mexico City art galleries, Sierra has dislodged a wall and paid people to hold it up, or to sit in corners facing the wall as if they were punished children. For a month, he hired two blind indigents to play the maracas for four hours a day in the Enrique Guerrero Gallery.

In time, Sierra would figure out that injustice, exploitation, and lawlessness are not exclusive to his adopted metropolis. He began to expand his product geographically, at first finding ways to milk his formula in other parts of Latin America. Returning to Europe, he unearthed an unlimited number of willing participants for his interventions among the immigrant populations from Turkey, North and Central Africa, or the Middle East. He has paid them to be stuck in a ship's hold for several days, to have their backs painted with polyurethane, or to have their hair dyed blond. On his website, almost as a point of pride, Sierra lists how little he paid his subjects in his first "actions" in Mexico and Latin America. He no longer includes such data; one can assume that, given the strength of the euro, even an Iraqi immigrant in Germany can command a greater sum than a Mexican on his home turf.

Sierra is represented by galleries in London, Madrid, and Zurich. According to his Spanish dealer, photographs of his interventions fetch between twenty-five hundred and thirty-five hundred euros. When complaints are registered about his exploitation of his subjects, his answers run along the lines of, "I don't break any rules. My limits are those of the capitalist system."

Other Mexico City artists explore similarly subversive themes with less violence and more subtlety. For example, Francis Alÿs came here from Antwerp in 1987, apparently to practice architecture, which he'd studied in Belgium. Instead, he began to produce a series of works based on his walks around the city, principally the *centro histórico,* where (unlike most successful artists) he still has a studio. One series of photographs is called *Sleepers,* and portrays homeless men and dogs taking their siestas on the sidewalks. In another series, *Ambulantes,* Alÿs showcased the magnitude of the informal economy on the streets here. He recorded workers pushing and pulling handcarts through the streets, moving wares from ice cream and cactus plants, mattresses and balloons, to plastic tubes and boxes—in the latter case, heaped three times as high as the man pulling the cart. One night, Alÿs contracted various street sweepers to push their brooms until they had accumulated a pile of garbage too large and dense for them to move.

Tall, skinny, with a long, pointy nose, Alÿs frequently appears in his videos as a kind of Buster Keaton figure, wearing sneakers and pants too short for his legs. He'll kick a block of ice or an empty plastic bottle through the streets, and even take the occasional pratfall. In *The Collector,* the artist walked a magnetized toy dog that picked up every metallic object on the sidewalk. In his most controversial work, *Re-Enactments*, he walked the streets carrying a 9mm Beretta at his side for twelve minutes before a patrol car stopped and arrested him. He managed to convince the police that he was an artist and not a criminal, and they participated in the video restaging of the event.

Yoshua Okon also solicited the involvement of the police for a video called *Oríllese a la orilla* (which is what patrolmen say to drivers when they want them to pull over, their droning voices magnified through walkie-talkies). In the work, three street cops "perform" for Okon's camera. The first faces the lens and verbally abuses and threatens its operator, as if he were a criminal he'd picked off the street on unstated charges. The second carries out a vaguely disturbing erotic dance with his nightstick, while the third boogies awkwardly alongside a boom box playing a Mexican country tune. The work is disarming on two levels: it underscores how nakedly the police are for sale in Mexico City (Okon paid them about thirty dollars apiece for their efforts), but at the same time, seeing them in a comic light disarms their ordinarily intimidating, even frightening, presence.

Okon collaborated with Miguel Calderón (with whom he opened an art gallery called La Panadería in 1994) on a piece called *A propósito* (*On Purpose*). The installation consisted of a repeating video loop of Calderón breaking into a car and stealing its stereo, while in the center of the gallery 120 stolen car stereos were piled on the floor. (The artists bought them from more dedicated thieves.) A decisive work of this generation of Mexico City artists, *A propósito* was also shown in New York, Berlin, Cologne, and Madrid.

Few artists have shown in as many places internationally as Calderón, who is represented by the Andrea Rosen Gallery in New York.

The majority of his most talked-about pieces were produced before he turned thirty in 2001, and many of these first works called attention to the institutional aspects of the art world and its inherent elitism—although always within a Mexico City context.

For instance, in *Ridículum vitae,* he reproduced his resumé on a white carpet laid over the gallery floor, which a maid in uniform dutifully vacuumed as spectators stepped over it. (The piece at least covertly calls attention to the fact that virtually all artists here come from privileged backgrounds—the kind of families that might even employ a uniformed maid.) *Historia artificial* (*Artificial History*) is a series of photographs taken in Mexico City's Museum of Natural History, in which the artist, clad in dark glasses, an Afro wig, and fake teeth, brandishes a handgun at the stuffed animals. For *Empleados del mes* (*Employees of the Month*), Calderón had members of the maintenance staff of the National Museum of Art sit for photographs in poses reminiscent of some of the institution's most famous paintings. These pieces showed how easy it is in Mexico City to subvert the art establishment.

One of the most ambiguous art-world figures is Daniela Rossell, a former drama student who in 1994 began a series of theatrical, viciously witty photographs that would be published in a 2002 book titled *Ricas y famosas* (*Rich and Famous*). The jarring images depict, in all their garish glory, young women who clearly belong to the most opulent sector of Mexico City society.

Rossell framed her subjects with a pointillistic, attractive-repulsive exactitude. Most of them are bottle-blondes in provocative outfits, shot under chandeliers, among Chippendale dining sets or around various stuffed lions or jaguars. In one shot, a resolutely slutty platinum blonde, in a white fake fur and a red dress with two high slits, sits with her legs spread on an Empire sofa flanked by antique dolls, colonial-era paintings on the wall behind her. In another, a woman in a cowboy hat and pink hot pants, splayed in a saddle mounted on a table, is about to flick her cigarette ash on a stuffed crocodile. (In the background of this image is a portrait of Emiliano Zapata, a hero of the Mexican Revolution, whose program of "land and liberty" was meant to free the peasant class from the bondage of serfdom.)

The juxtaposition of these women next to familiar Mexican iconography is a hallmark of *Ricas y famosas*. A slender blonde whose breasts are almost falling out of her shiny black shirt, fastened by only one button, is shot next to a portrait of the Virgin of Guadalupe. In many of the photos, brown-skinned maids and servants hover in the background, either dusting, with trays in hand, or attentively waiting their charges' next commands.

In the book, the photographs are untitled, and there is only a brief and bland text accompanying the images. Yet soon after it came out, a huge polemic ensued in the press when the identities of many of Rossell's subjects were revealed. They included Paulina Díaz Ordaz, the granddaughter of one of Mexico's most reviled presidents, and various other scions of the PRI, the political party that ruled Mexico for seventy-one years. Dozens of searing articles about *Ricas y famosas* appeared in Mexican magazines and newspapers. As Rubén Gallo points out in his book *New Tendencies in Mexican Art,* these critiques excoriated the people depicted in the photographs and the political corruption that generated their wealth, but almost never mentioned the artistry inherent in Rossell's work.

Rossell had access to her subjects because of her own family connections. Both of her grandfathers were politicians, and their collective résumé includes stints as senators, cabinet ministers, and governors of two states. Apparently her models believed that they had posed for flattering portraits, and were delighted while Rossell's work was exhibited across the United States and Europe. But after the indignant articles were published in Mexico, a line was crossed. Among the press clippings for *Ricas y famosas* was a tearful testimony by Díaz Ordaz, stating that she felt betrayed and defrauded by the photographer, and was considering a lawsuit.

Publicly, Rossell has only taken an ambiguous position about the meaning of her work. Indeed, after a few panicky interviews, the artist virtually disappeared from public view in Mexico City, and has lived for the past few years in New York.

The Mexico City artists' work from the 1990s spoke to an audience far beyond the city limits. The creators—and international curators—managed to tap into the collective guilt that people who live without deprivations feel about the indecent distribution of wealth in the world. Visitors to museums and galleries in New York, Berlin, or Paris have read about the slavery in Nike sneaker factories, and perhaps have seen movies like *Amores perros* with a subtext of social injustice. The art-world audience is hip enough to know that there is at least some correspondence between the advantages they enjoy and the suffering of the majority.

Today, those nineties artists—who couldn't find space in the established Mexico City galleries when they were emerging—have become the establishment. The cream of the crop of art galleries show their work on a standard basis. Most of the conventional museums that ignored them when they were coming up now bend over backward to exhibit them.

However, now that the scene has not only been established, but also internationally consecrated, it's not quite clear where it, and the nineties artists, are going. Teresa Margolles is still sticking to her theme of death, but she seems to be running out of gas. Researching on the Internet, I found that most of her exhibitions in the last few years have been in Europe, and featured pieces that had already been exhibited elsewhere.

At the end of 2007, in a small Mexico City gallery, she covered a wall with phrases supposedly uttered by drug traffickers when they murdered people who have crossed them, such as, "This is how rats end up," and, "So you'll learn how to show respect." While its effect was jarring, reports about murders among narcos in any Mexican daily have at least as much impact, if not more.

In cities all over the world, Santiago Sierra has hammered home his statement about how cheap it is to buy off the poor. An irony of the current stage of capitalism is that the only result of his efforts is his becoming rich and famous. Hordes may have seen his work by now, but his message, far from being strengthened by the obsessive repetition, is weakened. Viewers become inured, and no longer experience the shock of recognition they had the first time—or the first ten times—they were told.

Sierra seems increasingly desperate to re-create the shock value of his earlier pieces. In 2006, for example, in Pulheim-Stommeln, Germany, he installed a gas chamber in a building that was formerly a synagogue. Filled with noxious carbon monoxide, visitors were encouraged to go inside wearing gas masks, after signing disclaimers releasing the artist of any responsibility. He explained that his piece was a complaint against "the banalization of the Holocaust." Local authorities closed down the exhibition after a couple of days.

With varying results, other artists, such as Francis Alÿs and Miguel Calderón, have tried to internationalize the sort of work they previously based in Mexico City. Alÿs, for example, set loose a fox in the National Portrait Gallery in London, an escapade recorded by the museum's video cameras. At an enormous dune outside the Lima city limits, Alÿs found five hundred volunteers willing to prove that faith could actually "move a mountain" (or at least a few shovels full of its sand). In 2007 he showed three hundred found images of St. Fabiola at the Hispanic Society of America in New York.

In a show in Mexico City in 2006, Miguel Calderón set up a darkroom, and with light and sound simulated the presence of a panther inside it. This was quite amusing, but the rest of the exhibit—photographs of the artist with a worried expression at a highway rest stop (redolent of Cindy Sherman, whom he professes to admire), or images from the bathroom mirror of a hotel room—was anemic in comparison.

Alÿs's whimsy almost always charms, and Calderón can still find ways to provoke. But it seems clear that their work, and the messages it sends, undergo a process of neutralization once Mexico City is no longer its backdrop or its detonator. The shock, the bang, the collision with which they connected with the viewer in the Mexico work is missing.

If today there are more galleries in Mexico City than anyone can possibly keep up with, only a handful are important. In those—among them Kurimanzutto, OMR, Nina Menocal, and Enrique Guerrero—the aggressive, provocative elements that marked Mexico City work just a few years ago are rarely evident.

If the scene has been officially sanctified, institutions and collectors have become as important as the art, if not more so. The Mexico City art story that most recently, and most incessantly, has made the international press is that of the Jumex Collection, which is located inconveniently in the industrial corridor of Ecatepec, in the back of the factories of the largest juice manufacturer in Latin America.

Functioning since 2001, it is the baby of Eugenio López Alonso, the only child of the juice-producing family. An *L.A. Times* profile of López from June 2006 referred to the unmarried heir as a "jet-set playboy" and a "swingin' bachelor." In the late 1990s, he opened the Chac Mool Gallery in Los Angeles, which exhibited Mexican art. López described that project as a "mess" and closed its doors in 2004. He has reportedly invested between $50 million and $80 million of his family's money in a collection that includes work by the important young Mexican artists, as well as pieces by Sol Lewitt, Donald Judd, John Baldassari, Cy Twombly, Jeff Koons, and Ed Ruscha. However, the foundation behind the Jumex Collection has been extremely important for reasons besides the work it has acquired.

It doles out enormous sums of money to other, less wealthy institutions, including galleries, museums, and libraries. It has also given out numerous grants to individual artists. It has helped to produce books, magazines, catalogs, films, and videos. It has funded international residency programs. It has given grants to artists and curators for both work and study. It has loaned pieces to museums around the world. It has a substantial library about contemporary art in general and, perhaps more important, what is surely the most comprehensive archive of written material about Mexican contemporary art in the world.

The value of the public relations it has generated has been immeasurable for Mexican art. Seeing the works of emerging or unknown Mexican artists along with those of the internationally famous not only improves their individual profiles but that of Mexican art in general. The *L.A. Times* article referred to López as a "world-class shmoozer," and no doubt his aptitude and dexterity in the shmooze sphere has helped to make the collection a necessary stop for any gallery owner, collector, or curator who passes through Mexico City. During the first few years of the collection's existence, López opened its doors for a semiannual blowout party with limitless food and drink, attended by a thousand-odd souls, divided fairly evenly between weedy art-world types and the socialites that guaranteed the event's coverage in glossy magazines and the society pages of the newspapers.

Still, when I visited the collection, what I found most striking about the exhibition was its utter lack of provocation or political content. Given the Mexico City art that had made an impact in the previous decade, Mexico City itself was conspicuously absent, explicitly or implicitly, in the work.

There were around two hundred pieces on display, including Brandon Lattu's photo collage of the street signs at night on Los Angeles's Miracle Mile, a collage of pencil shavings by Piotr Uklanski, and an entire room in which Jorge Méndez Blake had placed each page of *Moby-Dick* in an individual frame. Other pieces included Mungo Thomson's installation of candles in beer bottles, Gabriel Kuri's shirts wrapped in dry cleaners' plastic hanging in a refrigerator, and a careless sketch of an orb, some doodles, and the words "FUCK OFFICE" by Mindy Shapero.

The commentary of most of these pieces, about what constitutes art and what doesn't—pencil shavings, candles in bottles, or the artist's laundry—might have tweaked a couple of nipples in the 1970s, but today? Nothing took your breath away, or hit you in the stomach. Indeed, the most arresting part of the show was a series of erotic drawings from Germany, made in 1923 (which didn't even appear in the catalog because, according to one insider, it was part of the curator's family collection and not Jumex's).

Many eyes in Mexico City will be on the Jumex Collection in the next couple of years. As I write these lines, the semiannual parties have been suspended and they are negotiating for a space closer to the city's center, which they hope to open in 2008.

Predictably, Phil Kelly is entirely dismissive of conceptual art. "It's too easy," he says. "You can go into my kitchen and set down the bottles and a chair and call it an installation. These people studied art for five or six years and think they have something special to say. Their way of seeing is asinine. You need to be more concrete, more tactile."

The absolute contempt held for painting by the Mexico City art establishment provokes Kelly's laughter. "Absolute contempt makes me feel marvelous," he says. Then he becomes thoughtful: "I think painting is terribly important, and I'd love to see more people painting instead of posing."

Kelly's romantic Bohemianism has its price. On several occasions, he has vomited blood, and Ruth, his wife, has had to take him to the hospital. "I'm amazed that my body has survived its general decomposition after so many years," he confesses. He has tried to give up alcohol, but abstinence was even less agreeable than continuing to drink. He sticks to wine and beer, although once in a while in a cantina he will order a scary cocktail that contains vodka, red wine, 7-Up, and lemon juice.

Ruth tried taking him to an acupuncturist. Kelly describes the experience with elegant contempt: "The walls were painted the color of toothpaste. They stick you with needles and there's esoteric music mixed with the murmuring of whales. Everyone in the waiting room loves their guru-doctor and they all read Deepak Chopra. I don't want to be healthy. I want to paint."

On his balcony overlooking the garbage truck, he says, "Really, I keep doing the same shit. Sometimes there are surprises, stupid things that come up. For example, after they built that horrendous tower"— he's referring to the Torre Mayor, the city's tallest building, which went up in 2003—"I began a series of paintings about towers. And when they built the second level of the Periférico [an inner-city throughway], it occurred to me that no one else was painting that, so I began. It's all iconoclastic observation."

Kelly can serve as a metaphor for Mexico City: a walking disaster that should have crumpled years ago, but somehow keeps functioning, despite the odds. On the street, the neighbors have all deposited their garbage and left. The garbagemen are smoking cigarettes, a couple of them sitting in the back of the truck. Kelly, fascinated, says, "I'm still trying to figure out how to paint all that."

Alternative Art

Apart from the Jumex Collection, there are more than 150 museums in Mexico City—from the most splendid and well known (the Museum of Anthropology, Frida Kahlo's house, the Museum of Modern Art) to the decidedly quirky (the Museum of Foreign Interventions, the Museum of Cowboys, the Footwear Museum).

Yet there are other spaces in the middle of the city that, while not strictly museums, are characteristic of the city's eccentricity. For instance there is the Pastelería Ideal, a century-old bakery in the *centro*. On the enormous ground floor, there's an overwhelming selection of everything sweet that could possibly emerge from an oven: cakes, breads, cookies, doughnuts, pastries, and muffins. The smell of sugar is so strong that it alone could send a diabetic to the hospital. But up on the first floor, there is a veritable museum of cake.

Six- and seven-tier wedding cakes, with green, blue, or peach-colored icing. Cakes that weigh 240 pounds, can be divided into eleven hundred portions, and cost over a thousand dollars. Cakes that sport spurting, functioning fountains. Cakes with immense platforms, atop of which are staircases composed of six progressively smaller cakes.

There's a section of white wedding cakes, in the midst of which you feel as if you were in front of the Winter Palace in St. Petersburg after a snowstorm. There's also a section of cakes for children, with football or soccer fields on top, or with icing illustrations of well-known characters. Today, there's a greater offering of Harry Potter, SpongeBob SquarePants, or Hello Kitty than of Mickey Mouse and Donald Duck. (There used to be a cake that depicted Pluto, but a devilish child or his ward scooped out the *L,* changing the name of Disney's dog to the most degrading Mexican slang word for homosexual.) A few days after a notable earthquake in 1999, I visited the Ideal and asked if any of the cakes had fallen. "No," the woman who attended the cash register said. "They just danced a little."

Then there is a store in the Colonia Roma that sells institutional attire called Uniformes Oskar. The mannequins in the front windows are fascinating. There's a nurse, wearing a green uniform, with an expression of unbridled ecstasy, her eyes shut tight, her lips open. The chambermaid, in a striped uniform, has a sad face, long lashes, and only one hand. A black waitress, her blond wig askew, has green-painted lips. Beside her, a sign: "Hiring seamstresses, pressers, and textile workers." At Oskar, the entire cast of characters of the institutional world is represented—doctors with white jackets, French maids in short black dresses, laborers wearing green overalls.

All the mannequins appear to be between thirty and forty years old and wear wigs with the corresponding decades of neglect. They look like shipwreck survivors, or people who've had their hair cut with a lawn mower. Their hands—those that still have them—tend to make expressive or even extravagant gestures, sometimes bent into positions impossible to duplicate in real life. Some are in disturbingly suggestive poses, like the two on top of the showcases inside, who wear nothing more than abbreviated smocks. One, handless and reclining, her arms open in an invitation, shows a lot of modestly crossed leg. The other is bald, openmouthed, and on her knees.

If you come here tired or hung over, it's almost possible to imagine the mannequins as human beings. It would be a great setting for a horror movie, with the protagonists trapped inside and the mannequins coming to life.

Many cantinas are decorated to reflect a passion for bullfighting, with posters of promising corridas and stuffed heads of defeated animals adorning the walls. Although in deep decadence, La Faena in the *centro* is a bullfight cantina *por excelencia*. One night the manager told me it has been around for about forty years, but even the glasses seem older than that. There are mosaic tiles, clay molding, and the coats of arms of various Mexican states in relief. Given its enormity, and its utter lack of clientele, it has a solemn, almost funereal, air—a good option to meet someone with whom you'd prefer not to be seen, or to invite forty or fifty of your closest friends.

What is most fascinating about La Faena is its series of showcases, inside of which are an exhibition of bullfighters' costumes. Some belonged to well-known matadors, like Juan Belmonte and El Soldado, while the rest belonged to forgotten novices. The suits are so decrepit that they seem to be crumbling into dust before your eyes. Some hang by themselves, while others take on the form of the mannequins that wear them (such as the *banderillero* with the grotesque expression who stands guard on top of the men's room). Connoisseurs of homoerotic art will note that the figures of Carlos Arruza and Manolo Dos Santos appear to be on the brink of a passionate kiss, while a couple of *toreros* are in what may be suggestive situations with their boyish dressers.

High and Low

In Mexico City, the cultural offerings are vast and varied. There is not a single city in Latin America whose list of possibilities can even compete with those available here. A glance at this week's *Tiempo libre,* the listings magazine, reveals the opening of new films from Hollywood, Spain, France, and Germany. In the Cineteca Nacional (the national film library) and various cinema clubs around town, there were also offerings from Brazil, China, Korea, and Cuba, from Bergman, Fassbinder, Kieslowski, and Almodóvar.

In the theater, apart from commercial shows like *Beauty and the Beast* and *The Vagina Monologues* (approaching its 5,000th performance here), there were plays by Shakespeare, Buchner, Lope de Vega, Martin McDonagh, and Wajdi Mouawad. The José Limón Dance Company was in town, and the Bellas Artes Chamber Orchestra and the National Autonomous University's Philharmonica Orchestra were in season. Although few in number there are bars with theater-cabaret, jazz joints, a blues club, and a place called the Foro Alicia, where, depending on the night, you could hear ska, metal, surf music, or indie rock. On several nights of the week, different books, just published, were given public presentations.

Although there are arts scenes in various places in Mexico, by far the greatest concentration of cultural production is in Mexico City. Still, in culture high and low, the city is often absent in its artistic offerings, even when they're made by local artists.

Given how much raw material there is on the streets of Mexico City, and how many novelists make it their home, it is surprising how few of them use the place as content, backdrop, or subtext to their narratives. A lot of them, such as Jorge Volpi, Mario Bellatín, and Javier García Galiano, set their books in real or imagined versions of Asian or European countries, while numerous others—Mónica Lavin, Mauricio Montiel, and Ana García Bergua, among them—write stories and novels that take place in cities which, whether or not they are named, remain generic and for the most part unde-scribed. In an interview, Cristina Rivera Garza (born in Matamoros, but a sometime Mexico City resident) assayed this explanation as to why the stories in one of her collections took place in imaginary spaces: "The production of a non-place from a non-place is complete exile, or complete not-being-there, not to be too specific."

Hoping for a little more clarity, I asked several Mexico City writ-ers why so little literature is set here. They had various explanations. One said his work was a reaction against the kind of novels that Carlos Fuentes and others of his generation produced, so intent on defining Mexico. Another said that he was much more influenced by the metaphysical Borges-Cortazar camp of Latin American litera-ture than the more realistic, place-defined faction of García Márquez and Vargas Llosa. One more confessed that she felt the city was so large and overwhelming that it would defy any of her attempts to de-fine it. It is worth mentioning that most of the city's authors are from privileged backgrounds and few have explored the city, outside of the predictable academic-literary circles, with much dedication.

There are a couple of notable exceptions. The most celebrated, or in any case notorious, is Guillermo Fadanelli, whose novels and stories have been described by critics here as dirty realism. (He tends to respond to that designation by claiming he only practices it in bed, not in literature.) Akin to a Bukowski-type figure, noted for the posses of teenybopper fans who accompany him to cantinas, Fadanelli's highly readable novels are set in an instantly recognizable Mexico City, mostly in neighborhoods of dingy housing projects, cheap hotel rooms, and Chinese-Mexican cafeterias whose patrons linger forever over a single cup of coffee. His books are populated by pedantic professors and petty bureaucrats, unloved prostitutes, submissive garbagemen, and drug-addled girls from well-to-do families who get their kicks from going to bed with strangers for money.

Fadanelli's books are now distributed by Anagrama, a prestigious publisher in Spain. This is akin to arrival in Mecca for Mexican writers, as most of their books are only printed and circulated in small editions here. His most successful novel—it's been translated into French, Italian, Portuguese, and German—is called *La otra cara de Rock Hudson* (*The Other Side of Rock Hudson*), and is mostly set in the *centro histórico*. The story of a teenager's relationship with a petty gangster, the texture of the prose demonstrates Fadanelli's innate romanticism and the influence of the nineteenth-century *poètes maudits*.

The young protagonist likes to sit on a street with a view of Calle Bolivar, described as "full of craters and tumors, spitting acid odors from the sewers, inside of which stewed the dozens of dogs run over by cars every day." In the same panorama are "hunchbacked buildings, tattooed with religious imagery, painted with shrieking colors that the passage of time turned into a gray like lead, like the cement of the sidewalks, like the skin of rats." As with Henry Miller's Paris or Paul Bowles's Morocco, these are the sort of descriptions that can be appreciated equally by people who know those streets intimately and by others who have never seen them.

J. M. Servín also takes a gritty view-from-the-sidewalk approach in his fiction. His novel *Cuartos para gente sola* (*Rooms for Singles*) culminates in a street brawl between a desperate man and a dog that has been trained to battle other canines. (The book was published in 1999, two years before the release of the film *Amores perros* (*Love Is a Bitch*), parts of which were also set in a dogfighting milieu.) In 2007, Servín published *Al final del vacío* (*At the End of the Void*), a postapocalyptic novel set in a near-future Mexico City where the streets are full of demolished buildings, citizens can go to the bathroom only in public conveyances where waste products are supposedly processed, and the streets are controlled by adolescent delinquents known as Dingos. Many of his readers believe that Servín's best book is *Por amor al dólar* (*For Love of the Dollar*), his memoir of the years he spent as an illegal immigrant working in gas stations and restaurant kitchens in the New York tristate area.

Most local writers concur that the late Chilean novelist Roberto Bolaño ran rings around his Mexican counterparts when he conveyed Mexico City in his award-winning novel *Los detectives salvajes* (*The Savage Detectives*, translated into English in 2007). Bolaño lived in Mexico City in his late teens and early twenties, and much of his book is an autobiographical recollection of his youth here, as part of a group of poets called "visceral realists" in the novel (and "infrarealists" in real life). By the time *Los detectives salvajes* was published in 1998, Bolaño had not set foot here in more than two decades.

However, apart from self-help books and adult comics, this is not a city of readers. While novels are published all year round in Mexico City, it is a struggle to sell out a print run of one or two thousand copies, no matter how well a book has been received by local literary critics. It has long been a commonplace that Mexicans read a half a book a year (although a professor told me that the number had recently been updated to 1.9 books annually). This is perhaps unsurprising in a city where the daily minimum wage is five dollars and books are as expensive as in the United States and Europe. Despite this inauspicious set of circumstances, it will be interesting to see if a Mexican comes along to contest Bolaño's supremacy, or if they will continue to avoid the capital.

What little there is of a Mexican film industry is based in Mexico City. That Mexican directors made three films (*Babel, Pan's Labyrinth,* and *Children of Men*) that were nominated for various Academy Awards in 2007 was not only a source of national pride but, less cheerfully, evidence that a Mexican filmmaker's best chance is to find work funded and filmed outside of the country.

Some films set in the capital have had not only film-festival and art-house distribution in recent years, but have won numerous prizes. The most successful, *Amores perros,* was released commercially in 2001. Jarring, shocking, violent, at times acidly funny, it depicted the inhabitants of a lawless metropolis careened off its bearings, a city of petty crime, corrupt cops, rich brothers who hire hit men to kill each other, and ex-revolutionaries walking the streets with their belongings (including firearms) in shopping carts.

Although its milieu is very particular to Mexico City, the film, directed by Alejandro González Iñárritu from a script by Guillermo Arriaga, was one of those miracles in which the local became global. Shown in more than fifty countries, it won or was nominated for awards in about two dozen. Moviegoers in developed countries clearly identified with it, or it at least tapped into their collective guilty conscience about "the Third World." The film grossed nearly

$21 million. Later the same year, Alfonso Cuarón's *Y tu mamá también* (*And Your Mother Too*) was released. A coming-of-age story about two young men from Mexico City and their road trip to the beach with a Spanish woman in her thirties, it dealt surreptitiously with both inequality and sexuality in Mexico, and also won multiple awards, grossing $33 million.

Other films have made less noise. Fernando Eimbcke's *Temporada de patos* (*Duck Season,* 2004) was certainly the most surprising. Since *Amores perros,* anyone who has seen movies set in Mexico City has come to expect crime, violence on the part of the government, melodrama, or at the very least some lurid story elements. *Temporada de patos* has none of those specialties. Set in the middle-class Tlatelolco housing projects (noted for antistudent violence in 1968), it's about two adolescent boys who spend a Saturday afternoon alone together without parental supervision, drinking Coca-Cola and playing video games. Their idyll is interrupted by their lonely next-door neighbor, who wants to bake herself a birthday cake (her oven is on the fritz), and a petulant pizza-delivery man.

A kind of a cross between Ozu and Jarmusch, shot in black and white, it's a bittersweet reflection on the joy and pain of adolescence, and the tempting possibilities of freedom. *Temporada de patos* won awards in Los Angeles, Salonica, and Paris. Distribution rights were sold to more than thirty countries. Still, it has yet to earn back the $900,000 it cost to produce, let alone realize a profit.

The Mexican film industry is constantly struggling because it is virtually impossible to make money in movies here. Two movie-theater chains, Cinemex and Cinepolis, own more than 70 percent of all the screens in the country. At any given moment, most of them show Hollywood blockbusters; at multiplexes with ten or fifteen screens there will be perhaps one Mexican film on display. According to Christian Valdelievre, producer of *Temporada de patos,* Cinemex

and Cinepolis are among the most profitable chains in the world because they pay less for product. In the United States, the producer
tends to get 50 percent of the ticket sales, but for *Temporada de patos,* the chains are only paid 38 percent.

The producers don't make money from DVD sales, because the
piracy problem is so endemic here. (The Motion Picture Association
of America estimated that nearly a million pirated DVDs of Mel
Gibson's *The Passion of the Christ* were sold on the street in this
country, more than half in Mexico City, many of them before the
film actually opened in cinemas.) Nor are TV sales a viable way for
them to recoup their investments. As so few Mexican films are released in any given year, they are of little interest to TV program-
mers or advertisers.

In addition to the directors of the three Oscar-nominated films in
2007 (Guillermo del Toro, Cuarón, and González Iñárritu, known
in the United States press as "the three amigos"), most movie actors
who have learned their craft in Mexico City in recent years (among
them Diego Luna, Gael García Bernal, Ana Claudia Talancón, Kate
del Castillo, and Ana de la Reguera) have tried their luck either across
the border, in Europe, or the United Kingdom. Even screenwriter Arriaga went Hollywood after *Amores perros.* He writes his scripts in
Spanish and says he works with a New York poet named Alan Page
on their English translations. This method didn't stop him from winning the 2005 screenwriting award at Cannes for his second English-
language script, *The Three Burials of Melquiades Estrada.* As of this
writing, he had begun filming his first effort as a director, *The Burning Plain*—in Oregon, in English, with a U.S. cast.

It seems likely that Mexico City's most talented filmmakers will
continue to use their home as a launching pad for their talents abroad.
Some, like Arriaga, are trying to divide their efforts. Recently, actors
García and Luna, along with producer Pablo Cruz, started a produc-

tion company in Mexico City called Canana, which has committed to make films here.

Through most of the 1980s and 1990s, the principal pop-culture export from Mexico City was the *telenovela,* as soap operas are called here. Produced by Televisa, which until the mid-1990s had a monopoly of Mexican television production, *telenovelas* were shown in more than one hundred countries in dubbed versions, their stars mobbed by fans when they visited Russia, Japan, Croatia, or any number of the dozens of other countries where they were televised.

In a few quick years, however, other countries got wise, and today *telenovelas* have become a globalized industry. The two most popular soap operas recently shown in Mexico have been adaptations of *telenovelas* originally shown in other countries. *La fea más bella (The Most Beautiful Ugly Girl),* the story of an unattractive woman who works as a secretary in a fashion company (and is of course terribly beautiful inside), aired in Mexico between 2006 and 2007. However, it actually began life in Colombia as *Yo soy Betty la fea (I'm Ugly Betty)* in 2001. By the time it aired in Mexico, it was playing catch-up and its version was aired in few other countries. The U.S. version, *Ugly Betty,* produced by Salma Hayek, was already being broadcast at the same time.

Rebelde, a *telenovela* about teenagers at an elite prep school who form a pop band, had better luck, even though it was an adaptation of an Argentine soap called *Rebelde Way.* While the South American version aired in a dozen countries, including Bosnia, Cyprus, and Russia, the Mexican rendering far outpaced it and was aired in sixty-five countries. (India made its own version, perhaps appropriately called *Remix.*) Just as the actors who portrayed the group in Argentina went on to form a successful pop band (called Erreway), so the Mexican youths became RBD to perform in concert halls. Their first CD sold four hundred thousand copies. RBD began to tour not only in Latin America, but in the United States, Canada, Europe, and Asia, and by 2006 had sold five million CDs. On the streets of Mexico City you can buy RBD magazines, comic books, chewing gum, knapsacks, perfume, and cologne.

In a country whose politics were dominated by the "Institutional Revolutionary Party" for more than seventy years, it is not surprising that a group whose name means "rebel" has become so establishment. Clearly alluding to the Zapatista uprising, one of the show's producers told the *New York Times,* "To be *rebelde* used to mean you had to have a mask and a gun and come out of the jungle. Now you have to have a short skirt and a red tie and be very cute and very nice. It's rebellion as a lifestyle and an aesthetic."

Today, Televisa is a duopoly along with TV Azteca. Their rivalry is most notable as a contest for which network produces the tackiest shows. For both, the most successful programming of recent years has been inspired by another brilliant idea from economically advanced countries—the reality show. Even in popular bars in the most trendy Mexico City neighborhoods I have overheard customers arguing over the chances of survival of their contestants.

Emblematic of the trend are two shows that were repeated ad infinitum from the early to the mid-2000s, constantly renovating their dramatis personae with new faces. The first was *La academia* (inspired by the British show that morphed into *American Idol*), in which a handful of youths who aspired to be entertainers were trapped in a house together, as well as treated to singing and dancing lessons courtesy of the network that produced the show. The other, even more riotously successful, was *Big Brother,* a sensation around the world (Holland can be thanked for the first version of this opus).

Perhaps everyone around the globe, except the Bemba tribesmen of Zambia, knows that in *Big Brother* a number of people are enclosed in a house with cameras in every nook and cranny, allowing for no privacy, not even in the bathroom. On a weekly basis viewers are encouraged to telephone a "900" number (paying for the call themselves) to vote for which of the housemates should be expunged from their screens. The last one standing wins a cash prize.

To avert the boredom of the audience, the format requires the denizens of the house to be not only reasonably telegenic, but also moderately at ease with their bodies and their sexuality; temperamental, narcissistic, provocative, or even contemptible. When these fundamentals turned out to be beyond the pale of ordinary Mexican citizens, the show metamorphosed into a rendering called *Big Brother VIP,* in which those ensnared in the house were "celebrities."

Only luminaries of a certain stripe were willing to engage in this kind of enterprise, and they didn't tend to be noted for their interpretations of Shakespeare or bel canto. Among the "VIPs" were has-been eye-candy actresses hoping to rejuvenate their careers, boyfriends or girlfriends of the moderately well-known eager to cause headlines by flirting outrageously with other residents, and entertainment reporters of indeterminate sexuality. *Big Brother* ran for three seasons here, while *Big Brother VIP* endured five.

Most of the Mexican media treat show business with a strange, even absurd, reverence. When a Cuban *vedette* called Niurka, who lives in Mexico City, married an "actor" with a dubious background named Bobby Larios, the magazine *TVnotas* treated its readers to twenty-five pages covering the event, as if it were a royal wedding. (Niurka—who sings and dances a little, and has an exceptional body which she is not at all hesitant about displaying—had made her biggest headlines previous to the wedding for complaining to the press about how infrequently and ineptly her ex-husband, a Televisa soap-opera producer named Juan Osorio, made love to her.)

The brightest light in this depressing panorama is a weekly magazine, published from a tiny house in Mexico City, called *Ooorale!*, which debuted in 2000. It has a circulation of 160,000, half of which is the capital. (Its editor told me that it is also popular among the incarcerated Mexican population of U.S. jails.) It is the only magazine that treats Mexican show business with the respect it deserves. Some recent headlines tell much of the story:

> *"Chabela Madow Got Married with Her Ass Exposed!"*
> *"Lorena Herrera: 'I'm Dirty in Bed!'"*
> *"Sergio Andrade Has a Tiny One!"*
> *"Nacha Plus: 'I Sing with a Voice Like a Whistle—They're Only Looking at My Ass!'"*
> *"Lyn May Froze Sperm in Her Fridge—But It Spoiled When the Lights Went Out!"*
> *"Paty Muñoz's New Face! [accompanied by a photo of her bare behind] 'I Pose Naked but I'm No Prostitute!'"*

The weekly's reporters, a team of four young women, set up interviews or arrive at events such as movie premieres, concerts, or the recording of TV shows, and ambush their subjects with a list of questions along the lines of *How do you like to make love? Is it true that you're an alcoholic? What do you do with your girlfriend in bed? Does size matter? Have you ever given up your ass to get a role on television? What do you scream when you have an orgasm?*

"The difference between us and the rest of them is in the language," David Estrada, the jovial editor of *Ooorale!,* says. "The others write as if their magazines were made for Spaniards, or maybe Germans. Their editors see themselves as a part of show business. We're with the people—we're on the readers' side."

The entire magazine is written in street language, with choice elements of Mexico City slang. (Including its name: *Óoorale* is a chameleonic, all-purpose exclamation that in this context connotes admiration, frequently for a dubious success. If it is mentioned in a cantina that the brother of a former president was found to have $130 million nestled in a Swiss bank account, stolen from the public trough, the response might well be "*Óorale!*" The same word might be emitted after a boast of how many women someone has slept with, how much someone drank the previous night, and so on.)

Estrada, a roly-poly man in his late twenties, reeks of the sidewalks of Mexico City. Indeed, his first job, while barely in his teens, was on the street shouting the routes of the *peseros* that stopped in his neighborhood, in an effort to attract passengers. Most of the drivers would give him half a peso for his efforts.

"The world of show business is a show itself," he continues. "People look at the stars as if they were heroes, beautiful people who can do anything, the antithesis of ugliness. People look up to them in the clouds, far away. We bring them down and put them in their place, here with us. If Verónica Castro [the hostess of *Big Brother*] breaks wind, I'm going to publish it, and we'll use the language of the people. We won't say she was flatulent. We'll write that she cut a fart."

Despite its repetitive nature, the magazine can be addictive. The bodily functions of the cast of *Big Brother* was a recurring theme in *Ooorale!* as was its showering techniques, and the bitter comments of the people who had been banished from the program. The issues of the magazine with stories about the show sold so briskly that sometimes the reporters had to apply themselves to thinking of new angles to cover it.

For example, when correspondent Xiomara Santana saw cultural critic Carlos Monsiváis at a memorial service, she approached him and asked his opinion about the show. The result was a story titled "Wise Man Monsiváis Says *Big Brother* Is Just Tits and Ass!" The article was accompanied by photos of some of the show's participants, with helpful red arrows provided by the art director, locating the "tits" and "ass" for the unfortunate readers who otherwise couldn't find them. In the story, the "writer and intellectual" offered the opinion that the stars of the show have neither "a basic level of neurons" nor "more than a peanut in their heads."

An assiduous reader of *Ooorale!* realizes that in addition to *Big Brother,* other themes are repeated ad infinitum. A study of recent issues revealed some of the obsessions:

- *Feminine alcoholism.* A few nearly identical stories ran in successive issues:

    "The Cops Booked Carmen Campuzano for Public Drunkenness!"

    "Adriana Fonseca: I'm Not an Alcoholic, I've Just Gone Out and Got Drunk!"

    "Kenya Gascón: I'd Rather They Say I'm Gay Than Alcoholic!"

    With an impressive show of compassion, the magazine reported that "Itati's Alcoholism Finished Off Her Marriage!" while "Laura León Likes to Drink Beer on the Street!" The source of that last story was a saleswoman in the Lomas Verdes outdoor market, who saw the singer eating at a taco stand, accompanying her meal with a beer. Perhaps to the editors' disappointment, León was not drunk, but she "drank as if she were reaching the bottom of the barrel."

There isn't much one can add to "Barbie Has Become an Alcoholic and Is Depressed!"

• *The gay and lesbian universe.* The headline "Salma Hayek Is a Big Lesbian!" ran next to, in much smaller type, *"in her role in the movie* Frida!" In the same issue, the magazine published the two stories "Raquel Has the Face of a Lesbian!" and "Ricky Martin Seems Gay!" Former boxer *El Púas* Olivares confessed to *Ooorale!* that "I've Had a Lot of Women, and Men Too!"

The story "The Big Kiss Between Bosé and Alejandro Fernández" was illustrated with a shot of the two singers in a passionate clinch, with the Spaniard Miguel Bosé dressed as a woman. It was produced with Photoshop, and dealt with an alleged fantasy of Bosé who, according to an anonymous source, is infatuated with Fernández.

• *God's mercy.* Although *Ooorale!* is not a religious magazine, its pages are graced by various people who are pious. In a story that appeared the week before the one about the connections between Itatí Cantoral's alcoholism and her divorce, the actress was asked if she predicted a new romance in her future. "God knows what will happen," she said.

After an affair with Arlett Pacheco, Gerardo Peirano explained that he had gone back to his wife because, "God spoke to me and said I'd been bad." Lorena Tassinara was shot by a mugger and supposedly died, but claimed she "talked with God, who said I had to come back to complete my mission." In the same story in which he confessed to his bisexuality, *El Púas* assured readers that this element of his life was over, and that, "Now all I want is to personally meet Jesus Christ."

Meanwhile, magician David Copperfield told the magazine, "I haven't made a pact with the devil."

In what is either the most ingenuous or the most shameless argument in the history of journalism, Estrada explains, "*Ooorale!* is not a morbid magazine. The people who read it are." The truth is that many in Mexico City have a limitless tolerance for morbidity. *Ooorale!* is our scandal sheet. It is surely the most fun a *chilango* can have for ten pesos.

Island of the Dolls

Within the Mexico City limits, you can trawl along a network of canals, in a landscape of evergreens, spruces, cypresses, and willows ringed by richly green mountain ranges. It is a site so picturesque and, above all, so tranquil that it is hard to fathom that you are still in one of the most chaotic cities in the world.

This enclave in the south of the city is known as Xochimilco, "the place where flowers grow," in Náhuatl. It is the closest approximation to what Mexico City was like before the Spaniards arrived. Tenochtitlán was a lake city, with a network of man-made islands known as *chinampas*. Some *chinampas* were big enough to support entire villages and towns. Broad canals were the "avenues," while narrower waterways served as "streets." They were traversed by canoe.

Xochimilco, one of the Federal District's sixteen delegations, still has a system of some ninety miles of canals. There are several wharves from which *trajineras*—Mexico City gondolas, large launches with roofs—slowly ply the brackish waters. The boatmen, known as *lancheros,* glide along by pressing wooden poles to the bottom of the canal, about ten feet deep, and pushing off.

The canals nearest to the docks are heavily trafficked, primarily with *chilangos* and Mexican tourists, who tend to drink heavily and attach their big *trajineras* to tiny ones where trumpet-blasting mariachis or marimba bands entertain them. On weekends and holidays, this part of Xochimilco is so crowded that it resembles the Viaducto at rush hour. This is the prosperous part of the area, where the houses lining the *chinampas* cater to tourists as restaurants or snack shops.

A little farther away, the canals of Xochimilco become both greener and grittier. It is not called "the place where flowers grow" for nothing. There are large plant nurseries, and many of the residents sell what they grow from greenhouses. Here, there are no more mariachis. You can read graffiti on some of the walls and hear rap music emanating from some of the houses.

If you ask the *lanchero* for the four-hour ecological tour, you will soon be in an area of canals that is barely trafficked at all. Hardly a soul is visible, although ducks, herons, and gulls swim and squawk, and an occasional cow sleeps or grazes on the pasture of someone's *chinampa*. Although hardly impoverished, Xochimilco is one of the cash-poorest areas of the city. Most who live there have inherited their property. They shower with hoses and rig an elaborate system of cables to get electricity without paying for it. Garbage is collected in motorized canoes. Sewage is treated with septic tanks. Residents fish for carp and bream in the canals' murky waters.

The culmination of the ecological tour is a *chinampa* where, as you approach, you see an image that might have appeared from a dream, or one of those low-budget horror films that haunt you for ages. A couple of hundred dolls are suspended from metal wires hanging between trees, and on the walls both inside and outside a couple of dilapidated shacks. As you step off the boat and onto the island, you get a closer look and see that most are headless, limbless, or hairless. Some are green with verdigris. Many are naked, and most of the remaining clothes are tattered rags. The enduring hair is matted, windswept, or blue.

The dolls are disquieting. A couple have the demonic look of Chucky. A baby sits in a carriage with a tinier baby in her arms. There is a headless torso on roller skates, its pants pulled down to its ankles. Most simply appear wasted, dead, or half-dead.

If you ask the *lancheros,* they will tell a hard-to-believe story about the island of the dolls. An inconsolable man remembered as Don Julián came to live here, alone after his entire family died. One day, he heard the cries of a woman drowning in the canal next to his property. He dived in the water and saved her life. Despite his efforts, not long after, the woman died. On a nightly basis Don Julián began to hear her voice. Frightened, he began to collect the old dolls and hang them from the trees to ward off her spirit. Through the decades, he became a Xochimilco legend, and people from far and wide began to bring him dolls to expand his collection. He died in 2005 at age eighty-six. He had fallen into the water but the coroner said it was heart failure.

Before returning to your *trajinera* for the trip back, you ponder the story as you walk around the property. Can any of it be true? Can Don Julián even have existed? And suddenly, inside the last of the shacks, there he is, smiling from a poster-sized photo. A wrinkled ancient with a Pancho Villa mustache, he wears a merry smile. Yet it is belied by the imploring eyes with their network of lines, which suggest intense pain and sadness.

Globalization and *Malinchismo*

S ince the early 1990s, Mexico City has gradually acquired a more international flavor. It isn't London or New York, but in certain sections of town it is common to hear foreign languages and accents, particularly from South America, Europe, and the United States. The Chinese are growing in numbers, there is a small but visible Korean population, and one can even see a smattering of Haitians and Africans on the street.

Their presence is making it a more dynamic city, with greater cultural offerings and international products (albeit only available to the fraction of residents who can afford them). In the trendy neighborhoods, restaurants that offer foreign cuisines far outnumber Mexican eating places. Live music and dance clubs boast performers and deejays from all over the world.

In a city this size there isn't a single "scene" where foreigners congregate; rather there are several. The international art-world crowd (along with its Mexican peers) gathers at the cantina on the ground floor of a restaurant called Covadonga on Thursday nights, while English-speaking foreign correspondents meet at the Bar Nuevo León on Fridays. The restaurant La Hacienda de los Morales sometimes feels like an outpost of the U.S. Embassy, and on the last Wednesday of each month foreigners of all stripes gather to network at the Polanco bistro Le Bouchon. Intercontinental bankers can be found at the expensive restaurants on any afternoon. Some foreigners eschew these milieus altogether, preferring the company of Mexicans to that of their own tribes.

The stories of the immigrants vary. Most of the Europeans and people from the United States are either looking for adventure or opportunities for professional advancement that might not be so easily available in their own countries. The South Americans are principally Argentines who came here looking for brighter prospects after their peso collapsed in 2002, but there are also Colombians unhappy with the guerilla warfare and drug traffic in their country. Some Venezuelans who can't stand Hugo Chávez are here, too. The Caribbean is represented by a large number of Cubans (many of them involved in the arts) who have found their way here from the island.

Mexico City does not attract the tired, poor, and huddled masses of other climes. Sometimes it serves as a trampoline for Central Americans illegally en route to the United States, but they don't stay. They wouldn't be welcome, either. The city doesn't open its arms to unskilled laborers with brown skin; plenty of them already live here.

What most foreigners in Mexico City have in common is the education, talent, or savvy to find a decent job or a business possibility fairly quickly. The majority of people from other countries have privileges that most Mexicans don't even dream about. One is almost always luckier to be a foreigner here than a Mexican.

Working in our favor is not only the world's tendency toward globalization, but a Mexican phenomenon known as *malinchismo*. The word refers to Mexicans who favor other cultures over their own. Although it was first coined in the 1930s, its context stems from the first days of the conquest. *Malinchismo* refers to La Malinche, an indigenous slave who, after the Spaniards arrived, became the official interpreter, as well as the lover, of their captain, Hernán Cortés.

The corporate offices of Procter & Gamble are in Bosques de las Lomas, a high-rent enclave west of the city center. The main building is of an indefinable, institutional color, a lulling blend of gray, green, and beige. In the lobby, some of the company's top-selling brands are displayed behind glass: Dawn, Secret, Tampax, Pampers, Mr. Clean. An award from *Expansión,* Mexico's leading business magazine, identifies P&G as one of the best companies to work for in the country.

The offices are constructed with sets of cubicles that allow colleagues easy access to the members of their teams: low walls, no doors, and, above all, no privacy. For a confidential chat, Silvia Herranz takes me to the "Hair Care Huddle Room."

Slender, stylish, and bucktoothed, Silvia is a native of Madrid. By the time she arrived in Mexico City, at thirty-two years old, she had already devoted seven to P&G. She started with an internship in her home city, and then was offered a job in Paris, where she worked for close to five years. Only months after she married, Procter transferred her to Geneva, giving her a "split family" travel allowance that let her visit her husband back in Paris nearly every weekend. Still, the arrangement was cumbersome, and within a couple of years she was looking for her next posting.

Mexico City had never appeared on Silvia's dream map of where she might be transferred. She and her husband, a Frenchman named Alexandre de Saint-León, had mused about living in South America, but P&G's corporate offices in the region are in Caracas, where the high crime rate and political instability were disincentives for the couple. When the job of "hair care brand manager"—Silvia's specific area of expertise—became available here, it was tempting. Mexico represents 55 percent of the company's sales in Latin America, and 60 percent of its profit in the region. It is one of Procter's six most important countries in sales volume.

P&G sent them here for two weeks to get the lay of the land, putting them up in the Four Seasons. Procter's security guidelines were written in such alarmist tones that Silvia said it was as if they were going to Baghdad. Once here, the couple traveled by metro and the *peseros* to explore different neighborhoods. Not only did they feel safe, they left with a positive impression.

"We weren't naïve about Mexico," she says. "We didn't imagine we'd be sitting under palm trees on the beach. It isn't very exotic. But it was a good career move."

Silvia earns a 75,000-euro salary (of which she is taxed at the European rate of 45 percent). She and Alexandre live in an almost comically huge three-bedroom apartment with floor-to-ceiling windows near her office. (Like many young European couples, despite their dual incomes, they had lived in Paris in an apartment the size of a cracker box.) The rent is higher than what they paid in Paris, but P&G picks up the difference. Procter also paid for the move of their furniture, dishes and cookware, paintings and decorations, and covers the rack-rate air fares for their annual trip home. (If they find bargain fares, this money can be stretched to two visits a year.) P&G also provides each with no-interest car loans. A cleaning lady comes twice a week.

Silvia and Alexandre are representative of a generation that came of age with the European Union. Promising employment isn't easy to find in the new Europe, and once a job is secured, many people stay with the same company indefinitely. While they are not as unbendingly loyal as the postwar Japanese, young Europeans think long and hard before leaving a paternalistic corporation.

"Procter & Gamble is an up-or-out company," explains Silvia. "No one at the executive level is recruited from the outside. You start as a junior assistant brand manager, then go to senior assistant brand manager, then brand manager. There are official evaluations each year, with clear, fact-based criteria to judge how you have built your business and what your skills, strengths, and weaknesses are."

Many of Silvia's junior colleagues at P&G here are Mexican. But the further up the ladder you go, the fewer Mexicans there are, and the top executives are almost all foreigners. Does this qualify Procter as a *malinchista*? Not according to Silvia, who says that the lack of Mexicans in senior management positions has to do with the "up or out" policy that involves relocation. Mexican executives, she says, are reluctant to go to another country to further their careers.

"The Mexicans who work at P&G tend to come from wealthy families. They've been to private schools, they've lived or studied in the United States, and money isn't an issue for them. They stay for a couple of years and then go to work in the family business, or open their own with family money. Or else they go to get an MBA, which is still fashionable here." She also believes that Procter doesn't fulfill the expectations of Mexicans from the upper echelons. "If you have money here, you live well. While there are hierarchies in Procter & Gamble, the treatment is egalitarian. The Mexican at the executive level expects to have a chauffeur, a private secretary answering his phone, and all sorts of perks you won't find in the company."

Most of Silvia and Alexandre's friends are other Europeans. During their first year in Mexico, they got to know the city little by little, exploring only on weekends and enjoying "domesticity" during the week, cooking dinners and watching DVDs. Friends who visited brought them chocolate, cheese, and champagne from Europe. When such friends visit, the couple sometimes travels with them on weekends to beaches or colonial cities.

If her home life is like a corner of Europe, Silvia's job brings her closest to Mexico, including its economic and social realities. To elicit information about her customer base, Silvia spends entire days with families who live in tiny houses with tin roofs, concrete floors, and once in a while no running water.

"Sixty percent of Mexican families earn less than eight hundred dollars a month," she says. "We need the women in those families to dominate the market. They look at some of our products as a splurge. They use our normal shampoo, Caprice, which costs about two and a half dollars a quart. But they keep a bottle of Pantene, our premium brand, under lock and key as a luxury, the same way I might splurge on clothes, perfume, or travel."

Procter & Gamble requires its managers to stay a couple of years after it has invested in moving them to a foreign country. Even before that, Silvia and Alexandre were musing about the next move. Perhaps they'd return to Europe, where both have aging parents. Other possibilities tempted within the P&G universe—Brazil, or even China. Unexpectedly, however, Ipsos-Bimsa, the French-owned multinational market-research agency where Alexandre works, offered him a promotion he couldn't refuse. The couple had moved to Mexico to promote Silvia's career, but decided to stay to further Alexandre's.

Soon after the promotion, Silvia became pregnant. Continuing in Mexico and taking maternity leave mean that Silvia may not rise as rapidly in P&G as she would if she'd been more flexible. "Both members of a couple have to be adaptable," she says. "We're extremely happy." As of this writing, Silvia just turned thirty-four and their daughter, Anouk, is a nearly a year old. They haven't set a firm date to return to Europe, but are sure they will leave before the child begins grade school.

Analía Lorenzo came to Mexico City with only one book, the *I Ching,* which had counseled her encouragingly about the possibilities of moving. In a few months she managed to accumulate a few more—novels by Juan Villoro and Cesar Aira, the Spanish translation of Virginia Woolf's *A Room of One's Own,* and some that she confesses left her cold before finishing the first paragraph (stories by Raymond Carver, *Fateless* by Imre Kertesz, and an essay collection by Carlos Fuentes called *This I Believe*).

Accumulation is an obstacle for the thirty-one-year-old Argentine. When Virginia Woolf wrote her manifesto, she surely wasn't thinking of the kind of room where Analía lives—a 12×12-foot box on a roof overlooking one of the most heavily trafficked thoroughfares of the Colonia Roma. A friend from Córdoba, Argentina, her hometown, rents an apartment in the building; Analía's quarters are the storage space that came with his lease.

So she must keep possessions to a minimum. Her walls are decorated with a few drawings she cut out of a desk calendar, a handbill for a local oracle called "Profesor Córdoba," and a photo of Prince. She has perhaps fifty CDs and a small suitcase, splayed open on the floor, in which her clothes are heaped in a magic mountain: four dresses, five skirts, two pairs of trousers, and five plain white panties. "My mother gets them for me," she says. "I can't be bothered. I'd rather get myself something nice like a new dress or a pair of shoes."

She is diminutive, with pale skin, wavy jet-black hair, and a bright smile that's reflected not only in her full lips but in her dark eyes. In Córdoba, Analía wrote freelance articles about poverty, the homeless, and street children. She also worked for the city government organizing workshops for those children, in drawing, photography, theater, and music. Additionally, she taught film and journalism at a technical college, for a combined salary of about $230 a month. She insists that while her country's economic crisis might have influenced her decision to come to Mexico there were other, more important, reasons.

"I always wanted to experience another country and another capital," she says. A network of four friends from Córdoba in Mexico City assured her she could earn a minimum of eight hundred dollars a month here. One offered her a place to stay, and another, who taught Spanish grammar at the University of Anáhuac, was planning to leave the job. He was certain she could take over his classes.

Once she arrived, apart from teaching, she was offered freelance work from Deutsche Presse Agentur, a German wire service that publishes in four languages. The prospect of earning eight hundred dollars, plus more from journalism, dazzled her: "I thought, *¡Soy Gardel!*" she says, referring to the most famous tango singer in history.

Reality fell short of her expectations. During her first few months, she had a tourist visa and no work permit; as such, the university never paid her salary. Deutsche Presse Agentur only offered a dollar per line and never commissioned stories longer than fifty lines. She sent her résumé to fifteen magazines and only one responded. For two months, she only spent money on the metro and cigarettes, and then was offered a job at the Mexican edition of *Playboy*. The editor in chief who hired her, not coincidentally, is another Argentine. There are hundreds of Argentines in Mexico City with executive jobs in media, public relations, and market research firms.

Analía's post at *Playboy* involves a minimum of eight hours per day and includes line editing, rewriting, and crafting the sort of articles that inspire little enthusiasm among journalists—say, a roundup of Father's Day gifts, or interviews with celebrities about their pets. She earns nine hundred dollars a month. Editors in similar jobs who are Mexican would tend to ask for a minimum of $1,350 for such employment. A frequent chant about Argentines here is that "they work more efficiently for less money."

"I'm happy but I desperately want my own place," says Analía. "I want my own kitchen, bathroom, and a TV." In a safe, central neighborhood, it is hard to find rentals for less than five hundred a month; paying that much on her salary would be a tight squeeze. She wonders whether her room will be dry in the rainy season or too cold in the winter. Year round, the noises of traffic permeate day and night. She also hears the shouts from a basketball court a half block away and the drilling from a construction site across the street.

"I'll be here at least a year," she guesses. She is in no hurry to return to Argentina but doesn't think Mexico City could ever be her home. "It's violent, it's noisy. I don't like the obsequious treatment I get because I'm white. If I lived here thirty years, I don't think I would have more than five friends." Could that possibly have more to do with her own character than with Mexico? "I think maybe in Spain they are more open to friendships," she says. "Can we talk about something else?"

The Argentines are the most notable group of recent immigrants here. They are evident for their skin color, their European physiognomy, their fashionable dress, and their unmistakable accents. While the Argentine embassy says they only number twelve thousand, other estimates are as high as one hundred thousand. (The majority are employed off the books with expired tourist visas.) Apart from the highly visible executive class, they also tend to work as waitresses or bartenders in trendy restaurants, where it is almost obligatory to have at least one pet Argentine on staff.

They are also the most reviled of the city's new denizens. Argentines are widely despised in Latin America, for what is perceived as their superciliousness, their snobbery, and their superiority complexes. Dozens of jokes about them circulate here, the most emblematic of which goes:

Q: What is good business?

A: Buy an Argentine for what he's worth and sell him for what he *thinks* he's worth.

Many Mexicans also believe that the Argentines are "taking jobs away" from them. However, Mexicans, ignoring evidence of their *malinchismo,* rarely address why their own countrymen employ Argentines in jobs that Mexicans could just as easily fill.

As much as one would like to avoid stereotypes, it is easy to find Argentines who spend their days and nights in Mexico complaining about life here. Many maintain friendships exclusively with other Argentines, noting, like Analía, a belief that it is difficult to befriend Mexicans.

Two years after I talked to Analía, she was sharing an apartment with two roommates. She'd lost her job at *Playboy* but was getting by with a combination of teaching and freelance journalism. She has no imminent plans to leave. The last time she consulted the *I Ching,* the book advised her that it wasn't a propitious moment to cross oceans.

By the age of twenty-five, Jaspar Eyears had already burnt out and risen from the ashes. From a family of English restaurateurs, at seventeen he decided against going to university, seduced by a glamorous bar scene in London. "I have huge regrets about this," he says, as if he were already an old man and not a twenty-eight-year-old with a movie-star haircut and intense doe eyes. "I lost myself in the nightlife. I wanted to study engineering."

In the mid-1990s, under the wing of Dick Bradsell, London's most celebrated barman, Jaspar worked at the hottest of the city's hot spots: the Atlantic, the Flamingo, the Detroit, the Groucho Club. He quickly ascended from bartender to manager to general manager.

Some out-of-town customers, dazzled by the London nightlife, decided that they wanted carbon copies of the glamorous bars back home. Jaspar rented himself out around the world, to repeat the success of the places where he'd worked. He stayed at each locale for two or three months, working toward opening night. Among his duties were hiring a staff, teaching the owners a crash course in bar economics, and helping them find sponsorship from liquor companies.

He came to Mexico City in 1998 to help a friend, Crispin Somerville, open El Colmillo, a dance club with electronic music. In the months he was here, he explored myriad bars in the city, from the dingiest cantinas to the most exclusive clubs.

Not long after, he experienced his burnout. He'd opened 120 bars and clubs. "I spent a year and a half living in hotels," he says. After a minor breakdown, his family forced him to stop working for five months. He gave up drinking; to this day he won't even try a new brand of liquor he is marketing or a cocktail he has concocted.

Looking for a place to settle, he decided on Mexico City. Finding his function was easy. "There were absolutely no high-end cocktail bars here," he says. "They didn't even have Cosmopolitans. So I started blowing people's minds making drinks."

It wasn't easy to get off the ground. "I tend to sell a product that is two years ahead of its time. I'm always interested in discovering the gaps in cities, in the market, and in general expertise. But few people want to put their necks on the line in Mexico City. Everyone wants to be number three."

Among his first jobs was to help the Absolut vodka marketeers

launch the brand's mandarin flavor—he mixed drinks atop a platform connected to a truck, as it moved through the city streets. Then
he designed an extensive menu of cocktails at a restaurant called
Prima.

He was working against a culture where most people's idea of a
cocktail is to mix a slug of vodka or tequila with Squirt, a grapefruit-
flavored soda. There are other complications. "It's difficult to com-
municate my passion here," he says. "There is a basic distrust between
restaurant owners and their staffs. They don't look after their people.
If a bartender or a waiter fucks up, he gets fired, instead of trying to
sort it out." Hence, the locals don't normally share Jaspar's enthusiasm when he tells the story of a bartender who made five hundred
martinis a night, dispensed at seventeen pounds a pop, at a London
hotel bar.

In Mexico City, restaurant owners above all value employees who
know their place. "It's a subservient workforce. There are no stars. In
London, a star bartender earns as much as the general manager of a
group of restaurants. There is a community of bars and bartenders;
the word spreads, there's competition. Here, you get trained, and it
stops there."

With a Mexican partner, Jaspar opened a public relations and
marketing agency, and promotes not only liquor, but also fashion
and tourism. He has opened three sneaker boutiques in Mexico City
and plans to open two more in other parts of the country. He also
opened his first bar, the Tiki, with a kitsch Polynesian island motif. It
took about a year longer than he anticipated, and various palms
needed to be greased to gather the necessary licenses and permissions.
However, after a year or so in business, the authorities closed down
the Tiki. More palms were greased and the bar was reopened, but
Jasper had lost heart. "We finally sold it," he says. "I think I'm out
of the bar business. At least I hope so."

Netucia Pires, from Minas Gerais, Brazil, just shy of six feet in her high heels, has honey-colored skin and an improbably long waist that she displays with pride, at least during an appointment in the offices of a modeling agency, which hires her out. However, on the streets of Mexico City she covers up almost as completely as if she were a nun; she finds the catcalls and gestures that men make jarring and offensive.

Between television shows where they often appear as eye candy; shoots for magazines, print, and outdoor advertisements; trade and fashion shows, and catalog work for department stores, there is more work for a model in Mexico City than anywhere else in Latin America, except perhaps São Paulo. Without a doubt, the pay is much better here. Netucia would only have earned about five hundred dollars a month if she'd stayed in Brazil, while in the D.F. she can earn that much—and more—in a day. For instance, she earns six hundred dollars when she films a game show called *Vas o no vas* as one of the *bamboletas* (who wear provocative outfits while assisting the contestants). In trade and fashion shows, her daily rate fluctuates between two hundred and three hundred dollars. Her worst job was an extra in a movie, for which she only earned fifty dollars.

The competition among models is intense. Both men and women are principally South American, although there is also a smattering of Europeans working in the city. The surfeit of models is bringing down everyone's price. An advertising photo, for which she used to earn one thousand dollars, now only fetches about half as much. "There's always someone who will work more cheaply," Neticia says.

There are other land mines in the business. Agencies are full of swindlers eager to exploit the lack of experience of their young charges. Netucia first arrived here with a three-month contract and says the agency that hired her, despite extravagant promises, only gave her a share of her earnings equivalent to what she had been paid in Brazil. For leverage, they held on to her passport and airline ticket. She worked for two months illegally while raising the money to buy her own ticket, and returned to Brazil without the agency's support. She came back to Mexico wiser and began to work on more favorable terms.

Freelancers the world over complain about how long it takes to be paid for work already accomplished. Still, in Mexico City employers are especially passive-aggressive about payment. "There are a lot of bad people," says Netucia. "You call them ten thousand times but they don't pay. It's exhausting."

Cities all over the world—even those with no discernible fashion industries—have Fashion Weeks, and the D.F. is no exception. During the event there are daily fashion shows from youth-oriented Mexican sportswear companies, as well as the few designers trying to eke out a living here. I covered it for a magazine in 2004. During the previous two years, the employment of hordes of Argentines as models had caused great discord here, and was interpreted by many as an insult to national pride and an affront to Mexican beauty. Yet in 2004, the sore point backstage was among the Argentines, who complained about the invasion of Brazilians taking away their work.

Among the entire pack, I only found two Mexican models. One had a curvaceous body type and cinnamon skin; I'd guessed she was either South American or from the Spanish-speaking Caribbean. The other model, although from León, Guanajuato, had white skin, auburn hair, and a Dutch surname.

Mexicans in the advertising business say flatly that they hire foreign models because their countrywomen are ugly. Could there be a clearer instance of *malinchismo*? Yes and no. On the one hand it is true that the majority of Mexican women have an indigenous body type—short, round, and brown-skinned—that doesn't correspond to the ideals of beauty proposed by women's and men's magazines in the United States and Europe. On the other hand, there are some who fit those standards, and I wonder if they are overlooked by the advertising agencies.

Netucia has an explanation for why Mexicans don't find work in her profession. "Mexican models say we're stealing their work, but it's not true. Like anywhere, if you get with it, you can compete. We're always on time, but they come an hour late and without makeup. They don't take care of themselves. They don't go to the gym and they eat too much."

When I spoke with her in 2006, Netucia felt she had already gone as far as she could here. "There are no top models in Mexico," she says. "You're just another one in the line. In Brazil, if I had appeared on the same kind of magazine covers as I have here, I'd be a star."

As we spoke, she was planning her retreat from Mexico within a year, hoping to try her luck in Miami or Paris. In fact, at twenty-five, she already had a diagram for her retirement. "I'm in this for two more years. In the future I'd like to study advertising and be on the other side."

On the cusp of her fortieth birthday, soon after giving birth to a child, caterer Sonia El-Nawal broke up with the baby's father. She'd lived in New York for eleven years, and her stints as a pastry chef in trendy restaurants such as Jean Georges, Jo Jo, and Nobu had earned her favorable notices in the *New York Times, Time Out,* and *New York* magazine. Still, the economics of that city are harrowing to many residents who, despite professional success, barely make ends meet.

A zaftig redhead with ice-blue eyes, Sonia decided that what she really wanted was to leave town. Given her background, finding a new abode was less daunting than it might have been for others. Born in Tripoli, she was raised in Beirut until she was twelve, when her mother moved the family to San Francisco. Apart from New York, she has also worked in restaurants and catering in Paris, Brussels, and Miami.

She was flown to Kuwait and offered work running several franchises of a bakery called Le Pain Quotidien. Certain signals made her reticent. The planes back and forth were filled with soldiers, which brought back the panic of her early adolescence, when a civil war broke out in Lebanon. At the job interview, her prospective employer asked if her son, Amani, used her surname or that of his father. "I decided it wasn't a country I wanted to live in," she says.

A call from food-and-beverage entrepreneur Jonathan Morr, with whom she had worked both in Miami and New York, came as a relief. He was designing the "concepts" for two restaurants, a bar, and a nightclub at what would become the Hotel Condesa DF, the first hostelry in Mexico City's trendiest neighborhood. She was offered a job as pastry chef, at six thousand dollars a month, with a rent-free, two-bedroom furnished apartment in Polanco and benefits that included medical insurance for herself and her son.

Rafael Micha, one of the owners of the hotel, doesn't consider himself a *malinchista* for hiring Sonia rather than a Mexican. He explains that the first hotel he opened, the Hábita in Polanco, had drawn enormous attention in the international press. Because of the Hábita's success, the stakes for the second hotel were even higher. The employment of a foreign chef was a virtual guarantee of greater press attention than would have been garnered by a Mexican (perhaps evidence of *malinchismo* in the press's food columns).

Due to delays in the hotel's opening, Sonia and the executive chef (also recruited by Morr out of New York) spent six months at full salary, traveling to different parts of the country researching food and testing recipes. Her Mexico City—between Polanco and Condesa, the city's two most cosmopolitan areas—strikes her as "a cross between Cairo, Europe, and Beirut." The architecture reminds her of the Old World, and the manners of the neighborhood merchants bring back memories of the Middle East.

After a little more than a year she was promoted to executive chef at the hotel, but left that job two years later to open her own gourmet shop. Much of Sonia's delight in Mexico City has to do with economics. For instance, in New York, she could never afford an apartment the size of the one she lives in here, in as upscale a neighborhood. Her son's private-school tuition costs her four hundred dollars a month, and the nanny who helps her daily only charges three hundred dollars monthly.

She has visited the United States several times during the four years she has been in Mexico, sometimes mulling over the prospect of moving back. Each time she returns she seems more resolute to stay here. "New York is transient, and it's great for people in their twenties. But I got older. I no longer have the same tolerance or patience for certain things, like the extreme cold. I don't want to schlep in the subway during a snowstorm. Also, I'm a single parent now, and New York is hostile to children.

"The lady who cares for Amani treats him like he was her grandson. She takes him to play with her nieces or they come here to play, and he calls her *abuela*. They feel deeply about families here, and that's important to me now."

There are many more stories like theirs—the Japanese who take photos of the Friday night wrestling matches for magazines in the land of the rising sun; the Frenchman who fell in love with a Mexican at the

Petit Palais Museum and followed her back here (only to be dumped and then try his luck as a *telenovela* actor); the Venezuelan beauty who not only sings, but also plays the trombone in nightclubs.

Foreigners with a few extra dollars in their pockets can hire an immigration lawyer to legalize their status here, while the rest can survive indefinitely in the underground economy. No significant authorities cast looming shadows. Among the city's twenty million residents, there are fewer than ten immigration investigators. They're not patrolling the street looking for wetbacks; instead, they respond to complaints, which are only intermittently made by the odd citizen with a grudge.

In a globalized economy, such anecdotes inform but are less likely to surprise. Today, in any large city, and even many small ones, enterprising people from any number of countries have traveled a long distance to change their luck. What differentiates Mexico City from many other places is the relative ease with which a foreigner finds his place, and how privileged that place most frequently is. History at least gives a clue as to why.

La Malinche—also known as Malintzín, and later Doña Marina after being converted to Catholicism by the Spaniards—is among the two or three most controversial figures in Mexican history. What little is known about her life reads like a fairy tale. In an essay, author Margo Glantz compares La Malinche to Ion in Greek mythology, Joseph in the Bible, and Dickens's Oliver Twist.

Born to an aristocratic Aztec family in 1496, when La Malinche was still a girl her father died. After her mother remarried and had a son, La Malinche was sold into slavery. Her buyers were the Potonchanes, a powerful Mayan tribe. When Cortés and his band of conquerors marched through the region on their way to Tenochtitlán, they demanded a tribute from the Potonchanes. Among the gifts granted were jewelry, gold, corn, hens, and twenty women, one of whom was La Malinche.

When it was discovered that she could speak not only Mayan, but also Náhuatl, the language of the Aztecs, Cortés tapped her to be his interpreter and adviser. She learned Spanish quickly, making her even more valuable to the conquerors.

Apart from being an integral part of Cortés's court, she was his consort, after which she bore him a child, Martín, who was legitimized by Pope Clement VI in 1529. At that point the conqueror turned her over to Juan Jaramillo, one of his comrades in arms—just as the Potonchanes had "given" her to him, and her mother to slave traders.

Despite her role in the conquest, for much of Mexican history La Malinche was a highly revered figure, nearly as exalted as the Virgin of Guadalupe. In the codices drawn by the indigenous, and the written accounts of the Spaniards, she is a key figure in the negotiations between the conquerors and the Aztecs. In his account of the conquest, Bernal Díaz de Castillo praises Malinche as well-bred, noble, and above all "manly," meaning brave.

Perceptions about La Malinche began to change in the nineteenth century. At that point, as anthropologist Roger Bartra writes, a duality emerged between her and the Virgin. Nationalists began to exalt the sanctified Guadalupe while destroying La Malinche's reputation. She evolved from the brilliant, enterprising, blue-blooded heroine of lore into an "Indian" prostitute who betrayed and sold out her people.

It is worth mentioning that the stories of the Virgin and La Malinche are complementary. They are both legends—La Malinche's true, the Virgin's unlikely if not downright preposterous—that chronicle the origins of the Mexican race, the *mestizaje* of Spanish and indigenous blood. With the supremacy of Catholic iconography, the

Virgin of Guadalupe became the sanitized and acceptable account of the story, while La Malinche's was turned into the sordid and intolerable rendering. At least implicit in both versions is the notion of the Spaniards as a civilizing influence of the barbarous natives. The Virgin offers a Catholic chasteness to counter their supposed savagery and hedonism.

Since the 1970s, there has been a literal avalanche of scholarly and creative texts about La Malinche, principally from Mexico but also from United States and European sources. However, by far the most influential material is a chapter from Octavio Paz's 1950 book-length essay on the Mexican character *The Labyrinth of Solitude*.

In his chapter "The Sons of the Malinche," Paz shocked and provoked his countrymen by referring to them as the historical offspring of a rape. We don't really know if La Malinche gave herself willingly to Cortés, but the Spaniard subsequently abandoned her, leaving her vanquished. Thousands of other nameless, faceless indigenous women were simply taken against their will. With knowledge of this history, according to Paz, the Mexicans suffer from chronic mistrustfulness, an inferiority complex, and an outward servility and submission that disguise cunning, resentment, and a lust for revenge.

An inkling of the vastness of writing about La Malinche can be found in the anthology *La Malinche, sus padres y sus hijos (Malinche, Her Parents and Children)*, edited by Margo Glantz. The book offers a glimpse of how she has been claimed, declaimed, and reclaimed by feminists, structuralists, and psychologists, marginal academics and best-selling hacks, novelists, playwrights, and poets. The sheer preponderance of these writings highlights Paz's thesis—now close to sixty years old—that Cortés and La Malinche are not mere historical figures. Rather, he writes, "They are symbols of a secret conflict which we haven't yet resolved."

A clue to this lack of resolution—or at least one symptom of it—might be found in the preferential treatment that foreigners have nearly always gotten, and still get, on Mexican soil. At various moments in its history, Mexican presidents have officially welcomed foreigners here. In the nineteenth and early twentieth centuries, Europeans helped establish or expand banking, mining, oil exploration, breweries, and light and heavy manufacturing, among many industries in Mexico.

Some political exiles have also been admitted, such as the Spaniards who came during and after the Civil War, the Jews who immigrated here to escape Russian and Polish pogroms in the 1920s, and the Syrians and Lebanese who escaped persecution in their own countries. In the 1970s, South Americans from various countries were allowed to emigrate here, escaping military dictatorships. Still, even the political exiles were most often seen as valuable for their ability to offer knowledge and infrastructure that would help modernize Mexico. This perception has secured our advantageous position.

Thus today's immigrants also play a part of the unresolved "secret conflict" of *malinchismo*. It is tiresomely common to listen to *chilangos* refer to each other as lazy, irresponsible, scheming, dishonest, or on the lookout for any possible scam. If this perception is even partially true it is at least to some extent due to centuries of subjugation and decades under a paternalistic government that rewarded cronyism rather than individual initiative. Since social mobility is practically nonexistent in Mexico City, many Mexicans with enterprise seek work in the United States, where in most cases they have better chances than they do here of accumulating money to get ahead.

In another of the essays in *La Malinche, Her Parents and Children,* Carlos Monsiváis writes that the story of La Malinche "no longer corresponds to relevant historical or social conflict." Referring to the globalized world, he adds, "the new conquerors don't need interpreters, they need partners." His viewpoint strikes me as naïve, if not disingenuous. In a globalized world, the new conquerors need a few partners, but mostly they need a serf class of workers willing to put in long hours for low wages. In the space where the circles of globalization and *malinchismo* are concentric—Starbucks, Wal-Mart, McDonald's, factories that produce goods sold by multinationals—they'll find limitless numbers of those people. Hence, the social conflict remains especially pertinent.

However, even this situation won't last forever. One of the hallmarks of a globalized economy is that the multinationals are always on the lookout to get the job done more cheaply. If Mexicans are small change in the world economy, there are even tinier coins in other parts of the globe.

The Other Side

Ciudad Satélite, in the north side of Mexico City, began to be developed in the late 1950s after the model of a middle-class U.S. suburb. Through most of the 1970s, it was sufficiently isolated from the center to offer the bucolic charms of a commuter hamlet, but by the end of the 1980s it became engulfed by the massive expansion of the city. Today, Satélite offers all of the inconveniences of the suburbs (isolation from the engaging parts of urban life, malls as a substitute for downtown, cultural poverty) and none of the benefits (expansive greenery, tranquillity).

Still, Satélite is not without its surprises. Every Tuesday and Thursday night the parking lot of the Chedraui supermarket in the Mundo E shopping center has become the studio and headquarters of a revolving group of B-boys that rehearses break dancing routines on the slippery tile floors. Consumers, on their way to empty their shopping carts in the trunks of their cars, often stop and watch as the boys, mostly in their teens, pirouette, contort, and twist themselves into pretzels. They balance their bodies on one hand and jump, stand on their heads and extend their legs, whirl around on their shoulders, and sometimes fall with such shuddering thuds that it hurts to merely watch. It is an almost exclusively male world. Some of the boys' girl-friends come to hang out, but Mexico City has no corresponding set of B-girls.

Although most of the parking lot B-boys are from Satélite itself, others from the surrounding areas—notably less prosperous—some-times come to show off their moves. While there are great shows of mutual respect and no visible tension, it is unmistakable that the Satélite B-boys are white and dressed in new and clean outfits, while their counterparts from elsewhere are browner and scrappier.

That was certainly the case with the Other Side, a crew that hung out at Mundo E one Tuesday night. The Other Side is from Ecatepec, a section of the north that is largely industrial slum. Rogelio, with thick black helmet hair, a flat stomach, and a strong upper body, is their ipso facto leader. This is because he is thoughtful, well-spoken and, at twenty-two, the elder statesman of the group. Not to mention that he's the only one with a car.

There are few green areas in Ecatepec, and as such, its youth has almost nowhere to hang out. Many notoriously succumb to drugs and crime. Rogelio said that some years ago, break-dancers were de-rided and often mistaken for drug addicts or gang members. But at this point it is has become popular among Ecatepec's teenage boys, and an accepted hobby.

Mexico City B-boys dance *por amor al arte*—for love of the art. Every so often there are contests here or in other cities, in gyms or soggy spaces rented out for parties, but rarely is the top prize more than two or three hundred dollars, to be divided among the entire crew of five or six guys. It is highly unlikely that Madonna will pass through Ciudad Satélite to cast her next video. Rogelio told me that a group of B-boys had approached Nike representatives here to spon-sor them (as it and other sporting-goods enterprises do in other coun-tries) but were treated with contempt.

The following Saturday there was to be a contest in Atizapán, another neighborhood in the north of the city. In its center, Atizapán is a pleasant, middle-class neighborhood, but is surrounded by the one- and two-story brick and concrete boxes of the struggling. Rogelio agreed to take me with the rest of the crew to watch the contest.

There were six of us in the car. One of the boys gave me his space in the backseat, which I shared with two others. Rogelio drove and Juan Jesús, the boy whose place I took, sat on the lap of Vicente, who occupied the passenger seat. During the entire ride, Juan Jesús, who has a pretty face with heavy-lidded eyes, rested his hand on the back of Vicente's neck. While I didn't assume that they were gay, it would be basically unfathomable for two heterosexual Mexicans to be so intimate in such an open and casual manner.

It isn't unusual that the crew's name is in English—most Mexican crews are called Little Flex, Explode Element, Rhythm Invade, Spin Masters, and so on. But "the other side" (*el otro lado*) usually has one of two connotations. It either refers to the United States on the other side of the border, or to the metaphysical space that homosexuals occupy. However, I didn't feel that I knew the boys long enough, or had built enough trust with them, to ask which other side they were on.

We finally arrived at Aries, a party space, at about one o'clock in the afternoon. It was a high-ceilinged, suffocating concrete barracks with no windows and no ventilation. The B-boys, their posses, and girlfriends sat on the floor on all sides of the hall, while those who were dancing performed in the middle of the room. Ramen instant soups and bags of chips were sold, as were sodas and bottled water. Nothing alcoholic was consumed on the premises.

Although the contest was supposed to start at noon, it would be three o'clock before it got off the ground. In the intervening hours, various crews arrived and warmed up, to assorted mixes that included everything from Spanish-language hip-hop to James Brown to electronic music from the United States. In Spanish laced with English-language terms, Rogelio explained what the dancers were doing: *toprock,* moves that involve graceful footwork; *power moves,* which show off acrobatic abilities; *freeze,* where motion is suspended during a contortion. He's a tough critic, although when he commented on his colleagues' weaknesses he showed no aggression, sounding more like a professor lamenting a slow class than a competitor.

B-boys in Mexico City, he explained, are stronger on heart than on talent or consistency. He bemoaned that few crews concentrate on footwork any longer. Most try to impress with their power moves. "But see, that guy just fell. You shouldn't do a power move until you're really ready. And most of these guys doing freezes are half-assed. Look at that one, he fell out of it in half a second. That's not a real freeze." Little Flex, which won second place in 2006 in Battle Sonic, the most important Mexican break dancing championship, while extremely athletic, is not particularly graceful. Rogelio grieved that few groups excelled at both. "Look, that guy is good, but he has his head down the whole time. The whole point is to have your head held high and look the other guy in the eye, defying him."

I never mustered the courage to ask whether or not their name was used in its homosexual context. But I did notice that they were treated with great respect by the other crews, something that would be un-likely in most Mexico City environments if they were openly gay.

Many crews had two or three members who seemed to know what they were doing, but the other two or three would be dead weight. Other groups would be inspired for half of their routines but then run out of gas. During the competition, I thought the Other Side was the best group, but perhaps I wasn't objective because they had let me into their circle. They were more subtle and less ostenta-tious than most of the others, concentrating on dancing rather than acrobatics. Unlike most of the crews, who with varying success appeared to imitate moves they had seen in videos, the Other Side had some inventive routines, including one in which they simulated a bullfight. (There were also a couple of moves I considered unfortunate, such as Rogelio's contortion with a sneakered foot in his mouth.)

However, the judges—local B-boys, including one who was treated as a man of respect because he had spent some years in the United States—didn't let them past the semifinals. Rogelio and his crew accepted the judgment with a stoic satisfaction.

Piedra

If you see passengers safely exit from a street taxi, then you can assume that its driver is legitimate and not a criminal. One night I left a bar a couple of blocks from the Plaza Garibaldi, a risky area, and hailed a beat-up Volkswagen Beetle after I saw a couple leave. The driver was a lean, hawk-faced man with a tilted baseball cap and bulging eyes. After he drove off, I asked if he was going to use the meter. He went into a song and dance about how he would have to charge a little more than the normal rate. With the meter running, the ride would have cost thirty or thirty-five pesos.

"Don't worry, it's late, I'll get you there, it'll just cost you a little more."

"Okay, but how much is a little more?"

"I've got a list of rates here somewhere. . . . Where is that list of rates? It's got be around here somewhere." He looked over what appeared to be a pamphlet from a furniture store.

"Just give me an idea, more or less."

"I'll take you there for ninety pesos."

"I'll give you fifty."

"Come on, *compadre,* lighten up. How about sixty?"

At that point, he exchanged words with another taxi driver who had pulled up alongside him. As far as I made out they were going to meet at a café later. Suddenly he tore down the street at a dangerous pace. I asked him if he was angry that I had negotiated the price with him.

"No, I don't care about that," he said. "I just cut off my *compadre* there. If I didn't do it first, he would have cut me off. He always does that."

The driver—who introduced himself as Raúl—began to tell me the story of his life. He had been a cabdriver for more than thirty years. As a kid, he hated to study, and at seventeen mustered the courage to tell his father that he was quitting high school.

"My dad had one answer to everything: He hit us. Where you come from, if a father hits his kid, the kid sues him. But my dad would smack me across the face three or four times a day. When I told him I was quitting school, he really went after me."

His father told Raúl that if he would no longer study, he'd have to earn his own living. The owner of a fleet of twenty-odd cabs, he sent his son out to work his first shift at four in the morning. Raúl liked the job immediately: an hour later, around five, he picked up a dancer getting off work from a cabaret and took her home.

Soon, among his regular customers were a dozen beauties from the same club. Shyness prevented him from making a pass at any, but one, a woman of thirty-five called Marisol, seduced him. He fell in love with her, but soon she ended the affair. "In no time, you'll want a younger woman, and I wouldn't be able to bear that," she told him. But she counseled that he should go after Gladys, one of the youngest of the girls, who didn't drink or do drugs, and despite long nights was still in school.

Raúl drove very quickly, dodging in and out of traffic. On Avenida Chapultepec, a six-lane boulevard, he sped around and past a police van as he continued his story.

Gladys and he were an item for six years. At the halfway point, she finished school and became a *licenciada*—a university graduate with a bureaucratic job. At that point she began to annoy him, repeatedly wondering why he was still a cabdriver. If she could do it, so could he—why didn't he go to medical school?

"I was afraid of my father. And if I didn't stay in school for him, why was I going to stay in school for Gladys? And to tell you the truth, I was in love with Gladys the *puta*. I really didn't like Gladys the *licenciada* very much."

I asked if he had ever married.

"Three times," Raúl said, bumping along the street. "With the first two, I had one child each. But I didn't have any with the third. Look, I'm fifty years old. And I like to have fun. It wouldn't make sense for me to have another kid. To be truthful, I like drugs."

"What's your drug of choice?"

"*Piedra,*" he said. "What's it called where you come from?"

"Crack," I said.

"Right, crack." He showed me his cylindrical pipe and the paper packet in which the drug was folded. "I do one or two of these a night. I've got it under control. Fifty or a hundred pesos a day and that's all she wrote. If I get tired, I smoke a little and *bang,* I'm whizzing along. At one point it controlled me, but now I control it." He was zigzagging down the street. I imagined various scenarios: crashing into a lamppost; running over pedestrians; the cops stopping him and taking us both downtown on drug charges.

"*Piedra* is strong, but it doesn't have hands or feet or a brain, like I do. I'm in charge, not the drug." Finally we arrived. It felt like a near miracle. I gave him one hundred pesos—for the entertaining stories, for getting me where I was going in one piece, and somehow, because I felt he had earned it.

The Politics of Obstruction

The Legislative Assembly of the Federal District, where sixty-six deputies make law in Mexico City, is located in a nineteenth-century building with a Beaux Arts façade on the corner of Donceles and Allende in the *centro histórico*. On the afternoon of a December visit, it was a challenge to get inside the building. Protesters affiliated with the Movimiento Urbano Popular had set up brightly colored plastic tents and hand-lettered signs not only on the steps of the entryway and the sidewalk in front, but also on both streets. Blocking pedestrian and vehicular traffic, they were calling for the city to build low-income housing.

Once past the protesters, I wasn't sure I'd be allowed in the building. A few days earlier, the demonstrators had barred the front door to the Assembly, effectively shutting it down for the entire day's session. If I were to get in, I was particularly interested in a piece of legislation that was supposed to be on the table during that period. The Assembly was set to discuss whether or not obstruction of the streets could be considered a crime.

The Mexican Constitution includes the right to protest publicly. Yet it also includes the right to freedom of transit in public. In Mexico City, the former liberty trumps the latter. Public protests that interfere with the streets are an everyday occurrence.

Demonstrations can be small affairs, with a couple of dozen marchers around a traffic circle—sometimes rallying stark naked—who've come in on a bus from some *pueblo* a few hundred miles away, trying to settle a land dispute in their home state. They can also be huge. After the 2006 presidential elections, thousands of supporters of candidate Andrés Manuel López Obrador, claiming fraud, blocked nine miles of Paseo de la Reforma, one of Mexico City's principal boulevards, for a month and a half.

Some deputies at least pay lip service to the idea that blocking the streets ought to be a genuine offense with the possibility of jail time. The problem is that the great majority of the protesters are affiliated with the left-wing Partido de la Revolución Democrática (the Democratic Revolution Party), which has governed Mexico City since 1997. Two-thirds of the deputies in the Assembly are with the party (known as the PRD, for its Spanish initials) and thus would be loath to pass legislation that could make waves among their supporters.

Clearing the streets of demonstrators was one of the many campaign promises of Marcelo Ebrard when he ran for mayor of the D. F. on the PRD ticket in 2006. Unlike López Obrador, he won with a clear margin and his election was not contested. After López Obrador and the *perredistas* (as the party faithful are known) occupied Reforma, a reporter asked Ebrard what he thought of their inconvenient, not to say illegal, barricade. Despite his pledge, the politician's response was *ni modo*—the Mexico City equivalent of "tough titty."

The day I arrived, the protesters were apparently in a benevolent mood; they allowed people to enter and leave the building. The main hall of the Assembly is similar in design to the U.S. Senate. It is circular, with tiered seating. Facing the president and vice president of the deputies, who sit on a raised dais, the deputies sit up front. Their aides are in the stalls above them, while the balcony is reserved for groups of guests who sometimes are called upon to speechify to the Assembly.

Before the session started, many of the deputies and their aides stood or milled about in small groups. Some were busy scanning laptops, while others passed around photocopies of press clippings. A half-dozen photographers walked around the room snapping pictures of the various politicians. I asked a deputy's aide if the cameramen were with the newspapers. "No," he said, "these photos are for the *egoteca*"—a word which translates as "the library of the ego."

Everyone was talking, either with each other or into cell phones, and the resulting din was enormous. Once the president of the Assembly called the session to begin, I was surprised to see that everyone spoke even louder, so they could hear each other above the official business. The extreme decibel level went on unabated throughout the afternoon session.

The first item to be called for a vote had to do with criminals who try to extort money via cell phones. Most frequently, these are bogus calls made from jail. The callers tell their victims that a family member has been kidnapped and they will not let him go until a quantity of money has been deposited into a bank account. (On one day in the fall of 2007 twenty such calls were made to different people inside the Federal Chamber of Deputies.) Strangely, according to Mexico City law, this endeavor qualified as little worse than a misdemeanor. The proposition before the Assembly was to turn it into *un delito grave*—a serious crime.

I would have thought that no one could possibly have objections. And indeed, all forty-three of the sixty-six legislators present that day voted in favor of the law. Electronic voting has not yet come to the Assembly. So the measure was not decided until the slow and tedious process of calling each deputy's name aloud, and waiting for his or her voiced response, was finished.

The proposals that followed were even less controversial. Should eleven police be given citations for their bravery in the line of duty? Again, forty-three deputies voted in favor, one by one. Should the route of a *pesero* be changed to divert from a dangerous intersection notorious for traffic accidents? The forty-three well-considered *políticos* all said *aye*. Should the thirtieth of November be established as El Día del Artista Intérprete (Vocalist's Day) in Mexico City? Should the Assembly urge the mayor to establish a school and museum for mariachis?

Around the time that the deputies were mulling over that last one, word buzzed through the hall that the protesters had closed the entrance to the Assembly once again. No one else could come in, and all of us inside were trapped until the demonstrators decided we could go.

Chilangos talk incessantly about the politicians who represent them, but nearly always with cynicism, scorn, or outright disgust. Generally, citizens believe that elected officials are liars and thieves who only have their own interests at heart.

Although a lot more than politics goes on in Mexico City, it is an all-important factor that keeps the urban wheels spinning. Apart from the sixty-six members of the ALDF—and their aides—most of the federal government is centralized in Mexico City. There are five hundred federal deputies here, as well as 128 senators, each with his or her staff. All the government ministries have their headquarters here, even the Natural Resources and Fisheries Ministry (although Mexico City is four hours from the closest sea) as well as the Agriculture and Rural Development Ministry (we're also very far from anything with a semblance of the bucolic).

The Supreme Court is here, and the Central Bank, and the national and local offices of all the political parties. So are Transportation and Communications, the Social Security Institute, the Federal Electricity Commission, the Office of the Indigenous People, the Postal Service, the National Petroleum Institute, the Mexican Trade Commission, the Industrial Development Bank, the National Institute of Public Health, Defense and Military, the Institute of Geography and Statistics, ad infinitum—they're all here, and they all employ hundreds of people. Some employ thousands.

The Federal District is divided into sixteen delegations, and each has its own government. Each delegation has offices of administration, of development, of public works, of law, urban services, social communication, accounting, crime prevention and civic protection, social development and citizen participation, etc.

There are seventy-seven foreign embassies in Mexico City, and countless nongovernmental organizations, from the United Nations, to the Front for Economic Rights, from the National Council of Manufacturers of Balanced Foods, to the Youth Network of Sexual and Reproductive Rights. Each has its own staff, adding platoons to the bureaucratic class.

Close to 180,000 people work for the city government. If you include the federal government and the NGOs there are probably a million bureaucrats in the D.F. The bureaucrat is a Mexico City social stereotype. Although this is not a particularly formal metropolis, thousands of men (and some women) are seen on the sidewalks every day, and in the restaurants and cantinas long past lunch hour, wearing gray, black, or blue suits in a synthetic fabric, with an every-strand-in-place hairstyle (thanks to gel or spray) and a stiff, formal, ambiguous manner of speaking that marks them unmistakably as civil servants. They are only the most traditional. Thousands of younger, less orthodox bureaucrats fit into the more stylish and less clichéd social molds.

Politics is one of the few realms in Mexico City where there is the possibility of earning real money. For instance, each of the deputies of the Assembly earns about sixty-nine thousand dollars a year. Not only do Mexican officials earn far more than the great majority of the people they are ostensibly serving, they are doing much better than many of their counterparts in more prosperous countries.

George W. Grayson, professor of government at the College of William and Mary, published a background paper in 2006 that included some salient details. Mexican federal deputies earn $148,000 a year as opposed to the French, who make $78,000, or the Germans, who earn $105,000. When they show up for work, they only participate in two legislative sessions a year, which collectively last six and a half months (less weekends and holidays). State legislators earn $60,632 a year, more than double that of their counterparts in the United States, who make $28,261.

Even more money is made through the traffic of influence and corruption. Using the power of one's office to make business deals is common in the city. The most famous, and oft-quoted, comment by a Mexico City politician is from former mayor Carlos Hank González: "Show me a politician who is poor and I will show you a poor politician." His story is exemplary.

Hank began his professional life as a schoolteacher who sold candy to supplement his income. He would go on to become not only mayor of Mexico City, but also governor of Mexico State, and minister of both agriculture and tourism. In 2001 he would die a billionaire through his interests in banking, construction, and transportation (he owned an airline), among other industries. In the late 1990s, Hank and his two sons became the object of an investigation by various U.S. government agencies, under suspicion of political corruption, tax evasion, money laundering, racketeering, and links to Mexico's most important drug cartels. The only charges that stuck were for violating bank regulations, and in 2001 the Federal Reserve fined Hank's son Carlos Hank Rhon some $40 million.

Hank's is an extreme case. While today it would be difficult for a politician to get away with becoming that wealthy while occupying public office, corruption is still the norm. In 2007, a friend pitched a freelance job to one of the government ministries. After several meetings, the bureaucrats decided they liked his idea, and asked him for a budget.

He'd figured the amount to the penny—what work he could do himself, what he would need to outsource, and how much he could charge, to assure himself a reasonable profit without bidding so highly that he would lose the job. He mentioned a number.

The finance guy nodded his head. Apparently it was within the ministry's budget—well within it, for he flatly informed my friend that he would charge a figure between 35 percent and 40 percent higher. This meant that the bureaucrat expected a kickback of the difference between the two estimates.

There has been a great show in Mexico City in the past few years about "transparency" in government. The era of corruption is supposedly over. The wild old ways—in which fortunes were made by even petty officials with access to a budget, the ability to grant contracts, or even the slightest possibility of gathering money under the table—are gone.

People who today deal with the government assure me that my friend's experience at the ministry is the way that corrupt officials operate today. You name your price, they name a higher one. Their piece of the action is calculated into the established amount for which they are contracting a job, and is later delivered in cash, hence remaining hidden in the contracted party's receipts. So much for transparency.

Making money through connections is also par for the course. In 2006, a special committee in the Federal Chamber of Deputies investigated the stepsons of former president Vicente Fox. They came up with what they considered sufficient evidence to warrant a criminal investigation, alleging that they had trafficked influences to seal illegal real estate deals worth about $30 million. It is up to the attorney general's office to bring up corruption or fraud charges, but it is unlikely they ever will.

Mexico City didn't have an elected government until 1997. Mayors were appointed by the president and expected to follow the boss's orders. Some had their own initiatives, but only carried them out inasmuch as they fit whatever plans and policies the president had for the capital. The system worked fairly well throughout the twentieth century, the last seventy years of which were dominated by the Institutional Revolutionary Party (known as the PRI for its initials in Spanish). When times were flush, the PRI was a good provider. The most important politicians may have robbed a lot of money, but they made sure to leave enough crumbs to keep the populace satisfied.

On a national level the majority of Mexicans lived off the largesse of the PRI system, at least to some extent. Government employees, subsidized farmers, unionized workers (they represented 75 percent of the workforce until the 1970s, but today make up less than a third), student, professional, and business groups, and community organizations in both cities and rural areas were all given concessions and handouts of some kind or another. Party bureaucrats had the power to give jobs to their friends, their children, or their friends' children. Few of them had to work very hard, and some didn't have to show up at all.

But with the incessant peso devaluations at the end of the twentieth century, the PRI became a less openhanded benefactor. Although there was a smaller pie to split, politicians of the era of Carlos Hank González became greedier, leaving fewer scraps for their constituents. At least in part as a result of the perceived betrayal, when *chilangos* were given the opportunity to elect a mayor for the first time in 1997, they voted against the PRI and chose the PRD. They have voted the same way ever since.

The PRD has been most significant in Mexico City for its social programs, particularly under Andrés Manuel López Obrador, who was mayor between 2000 and 2005 before declaring himself a presidential candidate. During his tenure as Mexico City mayor, there was an expansion of medical and education services for the poor, and the establishment of cash benefits of about seventy dollars a month for single mothers, senior citizens, and the handicapped.

Many of the recipients of these programs, among the city's struggling class, perceived López Obrador as distinct from the rest of the politicians. Some even saw him as their savior or, as Professor Grayson dubbed him, "the Mexican messiah." At the same time, critics see the political machinations of the PRD as identical to the traditions of the PRI. (Indeed, most of the party's important politicians—including López Obrador—were formerly with the PRI.) The allowances for the poor were seen as a way to buy their votes and keep them beholden, rather than a means to improve their lot in life in any significant way. Moreover, while the poor in Mexico City may have access to better services under the PRD, compared to a decade ago, when the party took office, their salaries buy them less and they have to commute ever greater distances to and from their jobs.

The PRD has many interest groups. Apart from one hundred thousand licensed taxi drivers, Mexico City had an additional fleet of thirty thousand gypsy-cab drivers that operated for more than a decade without paying any official taxes. As a passenger, I asked a variety of gypsy-cab drivers how they were allowed to operate. They told me that for years they had been giving ten or fifteen dollars a week to PRD slush funds, in exchange for which they were "tolerated" as they roamed the streets. In December 2007, with Marcelo Ebrard installed as mayor, close to twenty-five thousand of them were granted official taxi licenses. The move was seen by political commentators as payback for their service to the party.

Many of Mexico City's street vendors were also said to give kickbacks to the PRD, although it remains to be seen whether they will be content with being banished from the streets of the *centro* and placed in inconvenient shopping plazas.

PRD rallies are often well attended because gypsy-cab drivers and street vendors are obligated to show up. Others who come to rallies are fed and given souvenirs, such as T-shirts, gimme caps, or plastic drinking cups. Regardless of one's employment status, being an active member of any political party can bring additional and more important favors, such as jumping a very long line for state-sponsored housing.

It is important to point out that in countries where the great majority of the population is cash-strapped, politics have nothing to do with ideology (except in the rarefied spheres of academics, intellectuals, and a few of the politicians themselves). Most *chilangos* negotiate their loyalty on a rational basis, measuring where they perceive their greatest interests lie. In Mexico City, no one votes at the point of a pistol. You may show up at a rally because someone will give you a sandwich, but that is not a guarantee of your vote if someone else will give you two.

If Mexico City citizens aren't getting a sufficient number of sandwiches, they can always take to the streets. Groups of them do it so frequently that the rest of us rarely notice them until they are blocking our paths.

No one in the city would argue that ex-mayor López Obrador's occupation of the Paseo de la Reforma in August and September 2006 was the mother of all obstructions. According to the official vote tallies, he lost the presidential election by a tiny margin—about half of one percentage point, or 243,000 votes. Although he called it fraud, and presented supporting evidence, the Supreme Court didn't rule it substantive and declared his opponent, Felipe Calderón of the right-wing National Action Party, the winner. There is no doubt—even the court acknowledged this—that López Obrador's loss was largely due to a smear campaign against him in the alarmist, sensational TV commercials of the PAN.

While the avenue was held hostage, President Vicente Fox, only months before the end of his term, had no desire to play the bad guy and send in military police to break up the protest. So López Obrador and a couple of thousand of his most faithful acolytes made themselves at home under huge tents. The forty-seven-day standoff was a scenario with no winners. Fox was seen as weak and ineffectual for doing nothing, and most *chilangos* were outraged by López Obrador's appropriation of public space.

The greatest losers were the people who were supposedly the candidate's most important constituents—the poor. Instead of having to travel two or three hours to and from work, with Reforma closed to traffic, they needed four or five. Some, particularly those who worked in hotels and restaurants on the avenue, lost their jobs. Business organizations claimed the occupation represented losses of $35 million per day. By the time his group evacuated, many of López Obrador's followers—even a swath of those who had seen him as their redeemer—had given up on him.

López Obrador's successor, Marcelo Ebrard, is a lifelong politician. Literally. As children, he, his six brothers, and his sister would play candidates, parties, and elections the way other kids play hide-and-seek.

Ebrard joined the PRI in 1976 when he was seventeen years old, and at thirty-three became secretary-general of the city government, a remarkably young age for such an important post. He left the PRI in 1995, and in 2000 tried running for mayor with a newly formed party. After failing to make even the slightest noise, he threw in the towel and offered his support to López Obrador, who two years later named him chief of police and then minister of social development.

Ebrard is extremely intelligent, in both the analytical and shrewd senses. He plays his cards extremely close to the vest, tending not to announce any of his plans until they are faits accomplis. This is a smart strategy in Mexico, as opposition politicians will always put down, and often try to obstruct, declared intentions.

As of this writing, Ebrard had just completed a year in office. It hasn't been easy to separate the bread-and-circus aspects of his actions from the substantial ones. In the summer he installed free "beaches"—sandpits with swimming pools—in poor sections of the city. Detractors claimed they were poorly set up, and indeed during their first few days photos appeared in the newspapers of children covered in filthy water. When Ebrard set up free skating rinks in the Christmas season, critics said the money would have been put to better use building a school or a hospital. If they were populist strategies guaranteed to elevate the mayor's approval rating, it was also affecting to see how grateful the attendees were, many of whom had never been to a beach or a skating rink in their lives.

His expenditure on public works is also ambiguous. Ebrard has added one line of public transportation and extended another, but these are only patches to a system that is clearly dysfunctional. His ten-week program to service the city's drainage system was a good opportunity for him to be photographed in a tunnel wearing a hard hat, but was considered by engineers to be completely inadequate.

Mayor Ebrard also traveled a great deal in his first year in office, including trips to New York, Los Angeles, Berlin, London, and even two visits to China. He is always ostensibly promoting something, usually investment, but few in Mexico City doubt that he is mostly trying to promote his international profile and fuel presidential aspirations for the next elections in 2012.

When the protesters blocked the entry to the Assembly during my visit, my worst paranoiac fears were fueled. Would I be stuck there for days, or weeks? In fact, in less than an hour they gave in, and allowed people to come and go again.

The discussion over whether to regulate protests so that obstruction of the streets would no longer be tolerated was delayed until after the Christmas recess. Given that it is the impulse of a PRI deputy, it is doubtful that it will be passed by a PRD Assembly. But there was a unanimous vote in favor of opening a school and museum for mariachis.

In Mexico City, people survive despite the politicians, rather than as a result of anything they are doing. Like the protesters, when the politicians get in the way, *chilangos* just take the long way around.

Transa

The fish stinks from the head.

—Yiddish proverb

In Latin America, the verb *transar* indicates the concession of one party to another, or the exchange of buying and selling. Yet in Mexico City, the word has another meaning—to cheat, trick, or con. A *transa* is a way of obtaining money that you've done nothing to earn. It happens at all levels. For instance, when I arrived in Mexico City *chilangos* warned me that I should always check the arithmetic on a restaurant or bar bill before paying it. *Chingar al prójimo*—to fuck over your fellow man—is considered by cynics to be a way of life here.

A few nights after my friend told me about the deal he had made with the government ministry—which involved a huge kickback that would come out of his elevated bid for the job—we went for drinks at a cantina. My friend left his car on the sidewalk with a parking attendant. A couple of hours later, as we left, I handed the ticket to the attendant to recover the car, which was parked a couple of yards away. I gave him the twenty-five-peso fee printed on the ticket.

"That'll be forty pesos," he said.

"The ticket says twenty-five."

"No, it's forty."

"But the ticket says twenty-five."

He had a mustache, a brown impassive face, and spoke patiently. "That's for the customers of the restaurant over there. For the cantina, it's forty."

"Why should the cantina's customers pay more than the restaurant's?"

"Those are the rules, *jefe*."

"I'm not going to pay you forty pesos. I'm going to give you what the ticket says."

"Okay, just give me thirty-five."

Many scenarios went through my brain, now softened from the tequila I'd just drank. Could there really be a higher charge for the cantina's patrons? Was I being irrational and taking bread out of a parking attendant's mouth?

"It's okay," he said. "Just give me thirty." His eyes were pleading. Didn't he deserve a piece of the action, too?

Epilogue: *China Libre*

I n the heart of Mexico City, as I mentioned, the Barrio de Tepito is
a seemingly endless labyrinth of alleys encrusted with merchandise:
clothing, electronics, CDs and DVDs; contraband, pirated, even some
legitimate. Its hidden patios, once residential, now tend to be warehouses that secrete huge caches of goods, drugs, and guns. Walking
through its complex of streets, I got the sense that it was unknow-
able, at least for someone who didn't have a few years to spare.

For anyone attempting to comprehend Tepito, even in a super-
ficial manner, an encounter with Alfonso Hernández H. is obligatory.
For the past twenty years, Hernández has chronicled the neighborhood as the director of the Centro de Estudios Tepiteños (the Tepito
Study Center). Students researching any number of disciplines arrive
like clockwork at Hernández's door, to find out, as he wryly suggests,
"if it is true that Mexico City is still the Tepito of the world, and if
Tepito is the synthesis of Mexico City."

Hernández, bearded and bespectacled, is the sort of man who
wears a necktie even to a hole-in-the-wall where a friend of his has
been serving tripe tacos for more then forty years. There, I asked him

how he would define the neighborhood. *"Es China libre,"* he said. Literally translated, that means "It's free China."

I understood the reference, which harks back to a shameful moment in Mexican history. In the early twentieth century, Mexico invited thousands of Chinese workers to help build its railroads and highways, particularly in the north. Yet for a brief period during the revolution and into the 1920s, due to racist motives, some of these Chinese were killed, while others were jailed. After the incarcerated were released they became *chinos libres*—"free Chinamen."

Today, *soy chino libre*—"I'm a free Chinaman"—is still used as a slang expression in Mexico City, principally to evoke one's independence or liberty of choice. For example, if one night a man asks a friend if he is able to go to a cantina or a brothel, despite his familial and matrimonial responsibilities, the friend might answer, *"Soy chino libre."*

Still, I didn't quite understand what Hernández meant by *China libre* in the context of Tepito. After I asked, he took a deep breath and looked at me as if it were a very simple notion and I a slow student.

Various urbanists and futurists have made two predictions about the twenty-first century. They suggest that it is shaping into the century of emerging markets, and that it will also be the century of supercities.

Today, more than half of the world's population lives in cities, and an enormous number of them are concentrated in very few places. Some of those futurists see the world as a network of parallel and complementary cities rather than countries—Paris, London, New York, Moscow; Mexico City, Buenos Aires, São Paulo; Delhi, Mumbai, Karachi; Beijing, Tokyo, Seoul. However, the European and U.S. models of cities are resisting change, and some are even ossifying.

The cities in the developing world are the true representatives of the future.

With these trends, Mexico City is poised to be part of the vanguard of this century. Culturally, economically, and politically, it can be seen as the capital of the Spanish-speaking world. It is without a doubt among the most important Latin American hubs, along with São Paulo and, regardless of their geographical locations, Miami and Los Angeles. As the United States becomes more Latino—the census estimated that by 2020, the Hispanic population will reach 60 million, or almost 18 percent of the total U.S. population—it is increasingly relevant for Americans to have some inkling of how Mexico City works.

But what will the future of Mexico City look like? Predictions often sound like something that Philip K. Dick dreamed up after swallowing a fistful of amphetamines. There is a prevalent, nearly apocalyptic scenario, painting the transformation of a megalopolis into a monster that doesn't yet have a name. In this version, by 2050 the city will expand some forty miles to the west to envelop the city of Toluca, about sixty miles due south to swallow Cuernavaca, and another sixty miles to the north to absorb Pachuca, resulting in a gargantuan entity of some forty-five million inhabitants. Commuter trains will supposedly help people go back and forth between homes and workplaces of increasingly long distances.

The Disney version, purported by some architects who are perhaps whistling in the dark, suggests that intelligent urban planning will suddenly kick in from somewhere. Rather than sustain an endless and unremitting horizontal growth, instead the four central delegations of the city will increase their populations vertically, with apartment buildings of ten, twenty, and thirty stories sprouting on principal avenues like Insurgentes and Paseo de la Reforma, and around public parks and squares.

The two scenarios are not exclusive. Indeed, they are both in the works. The city's largest office tower was completed just a few years ago at Reforma and the Periférico (an inner-city throughway). On the corner of Reforma and Insurgentes, in another tower that is part of the St. Regis group, they are pre-selling apartments at the unheard-of price—here anyway—of four thousand dollars per square meter.

Since the early 2000s, there has been a construction boom of apartment buildings of between five and ten stories in the central area, with condominiums generally selling for between $150,000 and $400,000, depending on the neighborhood. As these developments suggest, the growth of the center will depend on the will of the limited number of people with money, and the expanding sector of individuals with access to credit.

However, the central area will likely be increasingly less available to the poor, who will need to continue to populate the ever-extending outskirts in the only housing they can afford—one- or two-story brick bunkers.

In the short term, obvious vulnerabilities for Mexico City's future include the lack of tangible steps to improve public transportation. Plans are frequently announced to add more lines to the metro, to update the polluting and inefficient system of *peseros*, and to increase the number of routes of the Metrobús, the inner-city trolley. So far there is only one line, on Insurgentes, with another in the works.

Apart from the establishment of the Metrobús, the only completed transportation project in recent years has been the assembly of a second story in the Periférico. Expansion of the inner-city throughway only benefits people with cars, as does the increasingly easy access to loans for new cars that banks and credit agencies are making available to Mexico City's residents. Political will here seems to favor the automobile industry rather than the citizenry or the environment.

Nearly everyone points to water as the greatest danger area of the city's future. According to newspaper articles in 2006, 72,000 liters of water were consumed per second in Mexico City, 25 percent of which was pumped eighty miles uphill from forests to the west. Seventy percent of the city's water is extracted from the subsoil through 3,500 wells, nearly twice as quickly as it takes to replenish them.

Yet each year rain reliably falls on a daily basis for five or six months. Instead of recycling rainwater, drains are clogged and streets flooded regularly, particularly in the city's most impoverished neighborhoods. Sewers in many areas haven't been cleaned in years; each year during rainy season the tabloids run photos of people in their homes, up to their belly buttons in wastewater. Serious flooding in the low-lying areas, along the lines of what happened when the levees broke in New Orleans after Hurricane Katrina, is predicted by urbanists here.

Another serious problem is garbage collection. In the beginning of 2008, it was reported that the Federal District generates 12,000 tons of trash per day, but only 6 percent of it is recycled.

Giving minimal handouts to the impoverished and the aged was the only palliative to the problem of inequality implemented by politicians in recent years. The private sector has not created any significant job programs that reward bright students; most employment with a future here is obtained through family or social connections.

On the other hand, there are some positive signals. In December of 2006, the D.F. established a science and technology institute to encourage study in those areas, and for 2008 it was funded to the tune of $64 million. In January of 2008, Mayor Marcelo Ebrard committed to build 186 miles of bicycle paths around town by 2012 (although convincing residents to use them might prove harder than setting them up).

There is some evidence that, despite the rampant inequality in Mexico City, the dynamic of the economy is trickling down. As the rich grow richer, it is becoming easier for people who struggle to maintain themselves at the margins of the middle class to obtain credit for cars and housing.

While this is generally good news, the fate of Mexico City is more than ever tied to the global economy. Should world markets continue to suffer, Mexican banks could become titleholders to hordes of apartments and houses whose owners can no longer pay the mortgages.

Gloomy scenarios in Mexico City should also be taken with skepticism. Doomsday has been predicted not only for as long as I have been here but as far as memory serves. One Mexican suggested that if I had been a Spanish journalist who came with the conquerors, I would probably have written off Mexico City for dead at the time. "Who are these idiots who built a city in the middle of a lake, with no room to expand, frequent floods, and no hope for a practical future?" he said I'd have surmised.

Indeed, throughout the history of the city, no matter what the benefits of living here, obstacles often seemed insurmountable. In the colonial period, 90 percent of the indigenous population was wiped out, mostly by imported diseases, such as smallpox, typhus, measles, and flu. Between the mid-sixteenth century and the beginning of the seventeenth, there were five major floods in Mexico City (including that of 1629, when the city was submerged under six feet of water, from which it didn't emerge until five years later).

Accounts from the eighteenth through the twentieth centuries name rampant crime, illness due to more flooding and poor sanitation, and inequality as among the problems from which the city suffered.

Yet Mexico City is still here. Despite its foibles, it's still going to grow, it's still going to be important, and most significantly, it's still going to be driven by ingenuity and improvisation. What gives the city its dynamism today is the resilience, ingenuity, and talent for improvisation of its residents. There is a spark of tough cleverness and a spirit of entrepreneurship, however basic, that you can see on any central street corner. It would be wonderful if there were a sudden consciousness and will on the part of the powerful, both in politics and industry, to solve or even alleviate the city's worst problems. Unfortunately there is little evidence of that determination, so for the moment, the *chilangos* will continue to exercise their own, a day at a time.

When I asked Alfonso Hernández what he meant by defining Tepito as *"China libre,"* he said, "Anything goes here." Referring to the sale of clothes turned into designer merchandise with the use of homemade labels made with scanners, to the fake Rolexes that had been manufactured in sweatshops on boats floating in international waters, to the correspondence between the economic crisis and the rise of the informal economy, he said, "In Tepito, you'll find the new Marco Polos, creating new routes of production and commerce.

"There are no standards that regulate this commercial niche, no norms for this way of working. *Chilangos* are ingenious. They know how to impose their own invention. Tepito is the epicenter of a chaotic city. We're immersed in this. We don't even know where the chaos began. It's disorder, complete bedlam. But you know what? That's us. We're not formal."

I had that conversation with Hernández four or five years ago, and the more I think about his argument the more I'm convinced. Here in Mexico City, we're twenty million *chinos libres,* making up the rules as we go along.

A NOTE TO THE READER

Mexico City is such a complex place that, while writing *First Stop in the New World*, it occurred to me that each chapter could have been the basis for an entire book. Luckily, some of those other books have already been written. For those interested in reading more about the city, here is a partial list of books that inspired me while at work on this one. When multiple editions have been printed I have tried to list the most recent (and hence most likely to be available) rather than the original.

No one has ever chronicled the history of Mexico City more thoroughly or lovingly than Jonathan Kandell, whose *La Capital* (Henry Holt, 1990) can even make prehistory, when there was nothing but geological formation in the D.F., seem fascinating. Bernal Díaz de Castillo's *The Discovery and Conquest of Mexico* (De Capo, 2004) outlines the point of view of the Spaniards when they arrived in Tenochtitlán, and *Life in Mexico* (BiblioBazaar, 2006), first published in 1840, is the diary of Frances Calderón de la Barca, the Scottish-born wife of the Spanish ambassador to Mexico. It offers a detailed view of the social mores of the city when Mexico was newly independent from Spain.

Countless insights into contemporary life in Mexico City are found in *The Mexico City Reader* (University of Wisconsin, 2004). Edited by Rubén Gallo, it includes essays and chronicles by some of Mexico City's best writers, many of whom have barely, or never, been translated into English. The Mexico City chapters in Alma Guillermoprieto's *The Heart That Bleeds* (Vintage, 1995) are essential, particularly the one about garbage. Also absorbing are the chapters about the capital in Sam Quinones's *True Tales from Another Mexico* (University of New Mexico, 2001) and Alan Riding's *Distant Neighbors* (Vintage, 1989). Rubén Gallo's *New Tendencies in Mexican Art* (Palgrave Macmillan, 2004) provides a lucid outline of Mexico City's art movement of the 1990s.

More personal accounts, amusing and of historical curiosity, are offered in the paranoid hipster Mexico City sections of William Burroughs's novels *Junky* (Penguin, 2003) and *Queer* (Penguin, Open Market Edition, 1987), both written in the 1950s. Although he lived in Mexico City for about twenty years, there is only one chapter about it in Luis Buñuel's *My Last Sigh* (University of Minnesota, 2003). But what a chapter.

The travel book *Mexico, Places and Pleasures* by Kate Simon (Harper Collins, 1988) may be out of print and out of date, but it is perennially charming. Some chapters of Octavio Paz's reflection on the Mexican character, *The Labyrinth of Solitude* (Grove, 1994), remain sharply relevant nearly sixty years after it was first published.

For those who read Spanish, the offerings are even greater. Mexican novelist and playwright Jorge Ibargüengoitia wrote newspaper columns for many years, and a lot of them were hilarious reflections about the foibles and complications of living in Mexico City. His journalism has been collected in various volumes by the publisher Joaquín Mortiz, among them *Instrucciones para vivir en México* (1990) and *La casa de usted y otros viajes* (1991).

Contemporary novels that are set in, or have anything to do with, Mexico City are scarce, with a couple of notable exceptions. The prolific Guillermo Fadanelli has written some cynically funny novels and short story collections set here, among them *Comparé un rifle* (Anagrama, 2004), *La otra cara de Rock Hudson* (Anagrama, 2004) and *¿Te veré en el desayuno?* (Plaza y Janés, 1999). J. M. Servin's apocalyptic novel *Al final del vacío* (Grijalbo Mondadori, 2007) and *Cuartos para gente sola* (Joaquín Mortiz, 2004) ambitiously take on the most violent aspects of the city.

In the panorama of Mexican letters, essayist and cultural critic Carlos Monsiváis is more or less our Susan Sontag. Several of his essay collections include material about Mexico City or Mexico City figures, including *Amor perdido* (Era, 1976) and *Escenas de pudor y liviandad* (Debolsillo, 2007). Sergio González Rodríguez's *Los bajos fondos* (Cal y Arena, 1988) is a chronicle of the culture of bars, cafés, and cantinas in Mexico City in the nineteenth and early twentieth centuries, while Armando Jiménez's *Sitios de rompe y rasga en la Ciudad de México* (Oceano, 1998) covers similar ground but of more recent vintage. Jose Joaquín Blanco's *Función de medianoche* (Era, 1981) and *Un chavo bien helado* (Era, 1991) also offer insights into the city, albeit with an insistently Marxist point of view.

Citámbulos (Oceano, 2007), by Ana Álvarez, Valentina Rojas Loa, and Christian von Wissel, takes a reader through some of the city's odder phenomena through photographs and brief texts. While not specifically about Mexico City, the following essay collections offer great insight into the Mexican character and psyche: *La Malinche, sus padres y sus hijos* (Ed. Margo Glantz, Taurus, 2001) and *Anatomía del mexicano* (Ed. Roger Bartra, Debolsillo, 2005). Two books of sociology, one first published in the 1970s and the other in the 1930s, while dated, are also valuable for anyone interested in Mexico: *El mexicano, psicología de sus motivaciones*, by Santiago Ramírez (Grijalbo, 2002) and *El perfil del hombre y la cultura en México*, by Samuel Romas (Colección Austral, 2006).

ACKNOWLEDGMENTS

Although there were some years in which I divided my time between here and New York, I have called Mexico City my home since 1990. That is enough time to build up an enormous cache of contacts and informants, partners in crime and secret sharers, advisers and amanuenses, *cuates, carnales, compadres, compinches,* and *cómplices.* A list of their names would be nearly as long as this book, but in one way or another they are all in here. It couldn't have been done without them.

Before and during the process of writing *First Stop in the New World,* magazine and newspaper editors on both sides of the border gave me assignments in which the research was sometimes parallel. They are also numerous, but each knows how grateful I am. Key to the progression was Sergio González Rodríguez, who in the pages of the newspaper *Reforma* was the first editor to foist me on an unwitting Mexican public. Subsequently, he took me to the most sinister and depressing dives of the city. For those and many other reasons he remains *mi hermano mexicano.* I am also beholden to Guillermo Osorno: when he offered me a job on the magazine *D.F.,* he handed me the keys to the city.

The photos on the title-page spread are by Federico Gama. He is the best photojournalist in Mexico City, and it is always flattering when his work is alongside my text.

Pete Fornatale and Ethan Nosowsky made concise suggestions when I put together the proposal. Scott Baldinger, Philip Herter, Yehudit Mam, and Eric Martin gave happily merciless opinions after reading an earlier draft. Sean McDonald, my editor, worked miracles. Anything wrong with this book is my fault, but much of what is right about it is due to his sage intervention. I am immensely thankful to him, Emily Bell, Matthew Venzon, Meighan Cavanaugh, Diane Hodges, Marie Finamore, and the rest of the Riverhead team.

It is with a continual sense of gratitude that I observe how diligently literary agent Jennifer Carlson has worked on my behalf through—at least in economic terms—thin and thin.

One night in a cantina early in 2005, Francisco Goldman suggested I write a nonfiction book about Mexico City. Employing his customary hyperbole, he said I was the only person capable of doing the job in the English language. Furthermore, he said that if I actually did it, it would be a huge success and as a result I would be able to sell anything I wrote, even my grocery lists. If you liked this book, rest assured I will never try to publish what I buy in the *tianguis*. If you didn't like it, blame Francisco. In either case, it is dedicated to him.

For the first year or so that I worked on it, I didn't mention the book to my Mexican friends. I was afraid that they would ask a question I still can't possibly answer—why a gringo took on the project to begin with. The one exception was Aura Estrada. That she—beautiful, a brilliant writer, and a *chilanga* to the marrow—offered support and encouragement, never expressing the slightest doubt that I was the right author for the undertaking, meant the world to me. Her death in 2007, at the untimely age of thirty, is the source of a universe of regret, only a tiny part of which is that she never got to hold this book in her hands. It's for you, Aura.